READINGS IN AFRICAN HUMANITIES:
African Cultural Development

READINGS IN AFRICAN HUMANITIES

African Cultural Development

Edited by
Ogbu U. Kalu

Fourth Dimension Publishing Co., Ltd.

First Published 1978 by
FOURTH DIMENSION PUBLISHING CO., LTD
16 Fifth Avenue, City Layout. PMB. 01164, Enugu, Nigeria.
Tel+234-42-459969. Fax+234-42-456904.
email: fdpbooks@aol.com, fdpbooks@yahoo.com
Web site: http://www.fdpbooks.com.

Reprinted 2002

ISBN 978-156-028-2

Photoset and printed in Nigeria by
Fourth Dimension Publishers, Enugu.

Table of Contents

Foreword

The University of Nigeria was a pioneer in General Studies in this country. No one today can seriously question the validity of the idea behind this aspect of university curriculum. For it daily becomes more apparent that the danger of the two mutually unintelligible cultures which C. P. Snow spoke about in his famous Rede Lectures is rather more imminent than science fiction.

General Studies is thus one bridge which the university must erect to safeguard the essential unity and purpose of human knowledge. Without this unity the university itself will disintegrate into a multiversity; emerging, as it were, from the ivory only to retreat into a Tower of Babel.

But sensing a need is one thing, and being able to serve it effectively can be quite another. Universities, both here and abroad, are generally agreed on the need for some kind of General Studies, but none has as yet found a totally satisfactory way of achieving the basic purpose of bringing scientific and humanistic disciplines into a continuing and meaningful dialogue. What is offered in this book is a progress report from the University of Nigeria borne out of our experience of wrestling with the problem in an African setting.

I hope that our community of students and teachers will find the book handy and valuable, and that it may also appeal to the general educated reader outside our walls.

I want to congratulate the editor of this anthology, its many contributors and the Division of General Studies for the thought behind this effort and its fine execution. I know the book will develop in years to come to keep pace with our continuing questioning and endeavours in this important but difficult area.

J. O. C. Ezeilo

Office of the Vice Chancellor
University of Nigeria,
Nsukka

18 July, 1978

Preface: Culture as an Anchor

It is obvious that Africa has witnessed a shell-burst from foreign cultures. Much of her history is so imprisoned within European histories that some historians, like H. R. Trevor-Roper, surmised that Africa has no history. African scholars of various hues have pounced on Trevor-Roper's remarks and took to the battlements in defence of Africa's glorious cultural heritage. Poets like Mabel Segun cursed the:

Benevolent despots to an unwilling race
Straining at the yoke,
Bull-dozers trampling on virgin ground
In blatant violation.
They trampled down all that was strange
And filled the void
With half-digested alien thoughts;
They left a trail of red
Wherever their feet had passed. ("A Second Olympus")

The Regius Professor was using the word, "history," in a technical sense but more important, he drew attention to the waves of assaults which have eroded the African past and threatened the ability of rulers in modern Africa to stabilize the volatile political, social, moral and economic structures of the continent. Africa has been the dumping ground of rotten goods as well as multifarious ideologies, diagnoses and prescriptions from Europe. The rulers are virtually rootless (though hardly detribalized) men struggling to move their so-called independent nations into a technological age.

It is argued here that in this struggle, culture could provide a vital anchor, preventing a changing society from drifting. We shall later define culture more extensively, detailing its characteristics and the problems related to the study of African cultures. Suffice it to say that culture provides society with the inherited transmissible code of conduct as both part and function of the total system of ideas, values, knowledge, philosophy, law, moral and belief systems which constitute the content of life of a society. Culture provides order and guidance for social behaviour and stability amidst rapid change.

But culture is not a static concept. It changes as man evolves new ways of existence and as man's physical environment is transformed by natural forces. This book, therefore, is based on both the recognition of the crucial role of culture in the development of Africa and a historical consciousness of the evolution of African cultures.

After intoducing the concepts, problems and role of archaeology in the reconstruction of African cultures, the second section moves on to analyse various themes or aspects of African cultures in the pre-colonial times: world-view, music, dance, festival, oral and written literature, art, modes of communication and socialization process. It is underscored that African cultures must be studied in time perspective. Descriptions of the world we have lost should teach us core values, especially salient ones which are capable of signalling change. But then, there was the enigmatic colonial fact which brought much good as well as extensive dehumanization. Perhaps the most devastating instrument of colonialism was education, the deliberate effort to condition the minds of individuals. The chapters on the colonial period not only examine the contributions of education and urbanization in creating social change but also the reaction of Africans who perceived the cultural effects of colonialism.

The studies on the modern or post-colonial period achieve three goals: tracing the development of certain cultural forms such as music and philosophy to the modern period; critically examining how artists, dramatists, writers and the mass-media can contribute to an intense awareness of being Africans and the contribution of culture in creating new African societies posing the fundamental and uncomfortable question about the ability of Africans to invent.

Scientific innovation has been crucial to the development of European cultures. Africans can take the cynical option of shouting.

> Hurray for those who never invented anything
> Hurray for those who never explored anything
> Hurray for those who never conquered anything

Admittedly, Aime Caesaire did not set out to deny the realities and achievements in Africa's heritage. On the contrary, like many members of the Negritude movement, he wished to carve out a niche for Africa's contribution to world civilization and made the unfortunate choice of myth-making:

> But who, in awe, give themselves up to the
> essence of things,
> Ignorant of the shell, but seized by the rhythm
> of things,
> Not intent on conquest but playing the play
> of things.

Surely, this is not enough and the dose of romanticism is much. The conquest of Africans by Europeans was a case of the conquest of one material culture by another. Therefore, the question is raised whether there is an element in African language or thought-pattern which poses a hinderance to scientific innovation.

Finally, in the quest for cultural renaissance or African cultural development, world-wide festivals of black peoples have been organized. The most gigantic of them all took place in Lagos, Nigeria in 1977. So much money was spent that doubts emerged. Admittedly, serious doubts already existed about cultural revivalism and festivals. Ezekiel Mphalele, the South African novelist, once asked:

> What would be the point of moaning about "our traditional culture" much of which has been knocked about as a result of military conquest, economic and industrial activity, the migrant labour system — which destroys communal and family life, the removal of whole communities from place to place by government decree, the conscious efforts of old-fashioned missionaries, etc? To fight a rear-guard action by trying to revive pure traditional culture among five million urbanized non-whites, three million detribalized labour tenants on white people's farms, or to arrest the situation among the remaining three million unsettled Africans in the rural reserves, would be unrealistic — and even fatal — for our efforts to break down the present political structures.[1]

A certain ideological consciousness challenges the festival idea. We shall not rush to reply but rather pass the buck to a Nigerian literary critic in our closing chapter.

O. U. K.

[1] Ezekiel Mphalele, "The Cult of Negritude," *Commonwealth Challenge* X/1 (3 October, 1961), 22.

PART I:

Introduction

CHAPTER ONE

The Study of African Culture

Dr. H. N. Nwosu and Dr. O. U. Kalu
Faculty of Social Sciences,
University of Nigeria, Nsukka

The Concept of Culture

As this term is used commonly in the social sciences, it refers to a totality of people's ways of life. It is the "distinctive way of life of a people, their complete design for living".[1] In another sense, culture refers to the gamut of the knowledge, beliefs, customs, traditions and skills that are available to the members of a society. Cultures are man-made rather than God-given. They are designs, prescriptions and responses, which are deliberately fashioned to guide all aspects of a people's life. Consequently, as a distinctive group of people endeavours to tame and subordinate a given physical environment, as it attempts to provide for its economic and security needs, as it devices norms, values and principles that govern patterns of its social relations and interactions, as it finds solutions to the problems of order and authority relations, as it rationalizes on the "why" of its existence and problems of life and death, and as it institutionalizes the notions of good and bad, right and wrong, beauty and ugliness, truth and falsehood, and patterns of stable and shared expectations, it brings a new culture into being.

Culture is, therefore, a distinctive and transmissible network of symbols which characterizes a designated aggregate of people. Obviously, this term embraces a great deal: man-made artifacts, activities that people perform, and ideas and feelings. Some of a culture's traits may be universally shared and others restricted to one's age or sex. Some traits emanated from other cultures, arriving perhaps in trade to become elements of the culture in question. Every culture is a unique constellation of traits even though some of the traits are very widespread in human society.

[1] For an elaboration of this idea, see Clyde Kluckholm, "The study of Culture" in Daniel Lerner and Harold Lasswell (eds.), *The policy Sciences* (Stanford: Stanford University Press, 1951), p. 86.

Culture is not synonymous with civilization, let alone western civilization.[2] There is no universally accepted criteria for evaluating the different kinds of world cultures. The utility of prescriptions of a given culture is assessed within the circumstances of the culture. According to Ruth Benedict, each ingredient of a culture makes sense only within the total context of that culture.[3] This analysis implies that one culture is as good as another. The culture of pre-colonial Lozi in Zambia served the same purpose as the Athenian culture served the people of ancient Athens. Beals and Hoiler emphasized the same point by stating that:

> Culture is not restricted to certain special fields of knowledge; it includes ways of behaving derived from the whole range of human activity. The designs for living evident in the behaviour of the Eskimos, the natives of Australia or the Navahos are as much a part of culture as those cultivated Europeans and Americans. Culture includes not only the techniques and methods of art, music and literature but also those used to make pottery, sew clothing or build houses.[4]

Culture, therefore, covers all aspects of life: technological, economic, social system and structure, political education, language and religion.

In the study of a culture it is germane to analyze the symbols, customs and conventions, values and norms which distinguish a particular culture from another. First and perhaps the most common symbol that is found in all cultures is *language*. Language is a major instrument through which people express their ideas, thoughts, feelings and sentiments and through which they communicate with each other. The different spoken languages of the world are more than mere codes of recording messages and labelling names; they are systematic means of conceiving and underscoring social realities.[5]

[2] Nineteenth-century anthropologists often used "culture" and "civilization" interchangeably and they also held the view that a "lower" culture evolves in successive stage to a "higher" culture. Edward B. Tylor (1832—1917) was a leading evolutionist. He held the idea of unilineal development of culture. He believed that a given culture develops from sewagery through barbarism to civilization. See, Edward B. Tylor *Primitive Culture* (London, Murray, 1891).

[3] Ruth Benedict, *Patterns of Culture* (New York: Mentor Books, 1959, Original 1934).

[4] Ralph Beals and Harry Hoijer, *An Introduction to Anthropology* (New York, Macmillan, 1953), p. 207.

[5] Edward Sapir emphasizes this point. He argues that "language is a guide to 'social reality'. Though language is not ordinarily thought of as of essential interest to the students of social science, it powerfully conditions all of our thinking about social problems and processes. No two languages are ever sufficiently similar to be considered as representing

In essence, every linguistic group constitutes a cultural group. It is within the framework of a language that a people conceives its own realities and gives expression to these realities.

Secondly, *customs and traditions* constitute an integral part of any culture. They are based on shared and stable expectations of a people. Traditional custom has been defined as "a mass of detailed behaviour more astonishing than what any one person can ever evolve in individual actions, no matter how aberrant".[6]

It is, therefore, through the intermediary of customs and traditions that individuals conceive their notions of the world, their experiences, and beliefs. No matter the level of education and sophistication of a people, their behaviours with regard to the daily routines of life are guided mainly by the standards and principles traditionally transmitted to them by their ancestors. Customs and traditions are not static; they are modified or changed entirely as a result of deliberate actions or as a result of interactions with other customs and traditions.

Thirdly, every culture has a set of *values and norms* that govern the behaviour of its adherents. A cultural value refers to "a widely held belief or sentiment that some activities, relationships, feelings, or goals are important to the community's well being".[7] Cultural values can be held unconsciously or may be expressed as themes to guide the various components of life. For instance, one culture may hold a world view which is open while another holds a closed world-view; one culture may propogate a value which advocates passive adherence to political authority, another may allow legitimate opposition against incumbents of authority roles.

Cultural norms, on the other hand, stem from cultural values. They are more specific than cultural values. Cultural norms are normally couched in rules, blue-prints, procedures, prescriptions and standards which guide conduct on specific situations. Consequently, in every cultural group, there are norms governing the roles of a farmer, a labourer, a teacher, a politician and the head of a household. In most human organizations, there are specific norms governing the members. A given cultural group enjoys a high degree of stability to the extent that the members of the group allow their actions to be governed by the dominant values and norms.

the same social reality." See Edward Sapir, "The status linguistics as a science" in David G. Mandelbaum ed., *Selected Writings* of Edward Sapir (Barkeley and Los Angeles, University of California Press, 1958), p. 62.

[6] Ruth Benedict, p. 1.

[7] Leonard Broom and Philip Selzmele, *op. cit.*, p. 54.

African Cultures

Having defined the concept of culture as the totality of a people's way of life which includes their modes of tackling physical, technological, political and socio-economic problems, the next problem is whether we can speak of an African culture, whether we can identify broad values which define us as Africans. The huge size and varieties of ways of life in the continent are obvious.

Anthropoligists have devised a shorthand way of describing the way of life of thousands of peoples in a whole continent and still emphasize the element of unity. This is the concept of *Culture Area.*

A culture area is a geographical area occupied by peoples whose culture exhibit a significant degree of similarity with each other as well as a significant degree of dissimilarity with the cultures of others. Culture areas are delineated by categorizing cultures according to standard classifications such as techniques, physical environment, religion and language. Naturally, some regions within a culture have a higher incidence of such configurations of cultural traits than others. Often, there is no sharp break between culture areas especially as border regions tend to merge culturally.

In Africa there are ten broad culture areas among the myriads of ethnic groups, namely: Hottentot, Bushman, East African Cattle, Western Cattle, the Congo, the Guinea Coast, the East Horn, East Sudan, West Sudan, and Egyptian and Mediterranean.[8] Each of these may be subdivided into subculture areas for in-depth study.

The criticism against the culture area concept is that it tends to atomize a culture and to obscure the common denominators. African scholars are particularly aware of this possibility out of dominant nationalist ideology. It is often asserted that Africans, in spite of their various cultures, share some dominant traits which identify them as Africans. These traits are their perception of the world (world-view) which will be described in greater detail later (in Chapter 2), the social system especially the kinship marriage and affinity, social sanctions, economic and property relations, the system and their field of ritual (religion and magic), political organization, arts and crafts. One hastens to add that the pursuit of common denominators does not imply that African cultures are static; rather, it is argued that a crucial task

[8] John Middleton, *Black Africa: Its peoples and their Customs Today* (London: Macmillan Co., 1970), p. 3 identifies four culture areas but see M. Angulu Onwuejeogwu, *The Social Anthropology of Africa* (London: Heinemann, 1975), p. 9.

for scholars is to reconstruct the past from which we emerged. According to one proverb, a man who does not know where he came from can hardly know where he is going.

We can now examine some of these common features. Throughout Africa, there is a wide-spread emphasis on kinship ties. In fact, in pre-colonial Africa, the basis of intimate social organizations and formations was kinship ties. An African attaches great importance to his line of descent, which may be either patrilineal or materilineal. Those cultures that adopt the patrilineal principle attach more importance to the masculine role in conception and those who adopt matrilineal principle attach more importance to the feminine role in conception.[9] Maquet points out that:

> the patrilineal principle is very often followed by the cultivators of the Equatorial forest, who belong to what we have called the civilization of clearings, whereas descent through women is particularly found in what is known as the "matrilineal belt" in the savanna region which extends south of Equatorial forest at the 4th parallel South, West to east, crossing the whole continent, and approximately corresponds to the civilization of the granaries[10]

The kinship ties in Africa find most intimate expression in the joint and extended family systems. The extended family is a large domestic cluster, consisting of several persons: fathers, mothers, brothers, sisters, uncles, aunts, nephews and cousins. Usually the eldest member of the cluster serves as the head of the extended family. Assisting him are other senior male members. The relationship that exists between the elder members of the extended family and the other subordinates could be likened to those of patron and clients. As patrons, the elders provide protection, supply economic values, prestige and esteem. On the other hand, the subordinate members provide loyalty, obedience, free labour, and support in the community.[11]

The African extended families provide social security against sudden death, crop failures, natural disasters and group feuds and incursions. It also serves as a useful instrument of socialization. The feeling that each individual must be another's keeper is well entrenched in the extended family system. In some African communities, land ownership and inheritance, occupational differentiations and communal labour are organized under the

[9] Jacques Maguet, *Power and Society In Africa* (New York: McGraw Hill Book Company, 1971), p. 40.

[10] *Ibid.*, p. 41.

[11] Ronald Cohen and John Middleton, eds., *From Tribe to Nation In Africa* (Scranton, Chandler Publishing Company, 1970), p. 22.

fabric of the extended family. While the process of acculturation has not yet destroyed the African extended family system it has certainly modified it. The close-knit cohesion that marked patterns of relationships among the members has been undermined by urbanization, changes in economic relationships, the patterns of division of labour between men and women, as well as by the emphasis that the African educated elite place on the primary of nuclear families.[12]

The core issue is not merely to describe the social organization built around the extended family system but to delineate the signs and directions of the breakdown of the old order. It must be realized that before the Europeans became technically industrialized, they were first socially decommunalized. Individuality aided inventiveness and creativity.

There are also a variety of political forms and processes in Africa. In pre-colonial Africa the political formations and practices can be divided into four main groups:

1. Large centralized states: such as the Emirate system of the Northern Nigeria. The elaborate political organizations of the Baganda, Mende, Temne and Wolof. These political organizations have centralized political structures and large bureaucratic organs.
2. Centralized chiefdom: other political organizations which are found in several parts of Africa are centralized chiefdoms. These systems consist of an influential chief or king at the head of the kingdom with provincial chiefs exercising varied powers and influences in the provinces. The Ashantis, the Yorubas and the Bantus have this kind of political organization.
3. Segmented societies: this kind of political organization is typified by Igbo, Kikuyu, Tiv and Nuer societies. They are marked by segmented political structures and an absence of elaborate bureacracies. Decision making is usually collectively done by various social formations such as the family heads, elders and age grades.
4. Autonomous communities: this system consists of a plethora of small groups of people often not living far from each other, but have destructive political and social organizations. They are found in the Cross River basin of Nigeria, Cameroon and in several parts of East and Southern Africa.

With the rapid political changes in the wave of independence, this analysis looks like so much anthropological jargon. Africa is now strewn with various

[12] For greater elaboration of changes on African extended families see Elizabeth Colson, "Family Change in Contemporary Africa" in John Middleton, pp. 152–153.

political systems designed to organize new political units: military, socialist one-party, legislative and barefaced dictatorship.

The traditional economies of pre-colonial Africa is based on subsistence agriculture. The technology was based on simple tools such as the matchet, hoe and plough. Farming was the main occupation of the people of East and West Africa. The Khoisan people of Southwest Africa were mainly hunters and food gatherers. All the Africans living in the coastal and riverine areas invariably engaged in fishing. Here and there were carvers and sculptors but the Edos of Benin and Yorubas of Ife distinguished themselves in the excellence of their sculpture while the Ibibios were noted for their carvings. The imposition of colonial rule and the introduction of a cash economy have left permanent marks on African occupational patterns.

Pre-colonial African countries were small-scale producing units. Mercantile and industrial colonialism (from Saharan gold trade to the modern and euphemistic "transfer of technology") transformed them into industrial consuming units. The major problem for Africa is that she has not evolved a satisfactory economic system to meet her needs and give her a measure of independence.

Influences on African Culture

Our earlier discussions have pointed out that no culture is static; every culture is susceptible to change. Historically, man has improved his ability to cope with the problems and constraints of his environment through the exchange of techniques and knowledge among cultures. The degree of cultural exchange varies from one culture to another. However, the rate of acceptance or rejection of elements of one culture by another culture is influenced by three factors:

1. *Transaction flow*: the level and intensity of communication and cooperation between two or more cultures. The amount and the nature of interactions between African cultures can be therefore measured in terms of the flow of mail, telephone calls, labour mobility, and the volume of economic and political relations.

2. *Functional interdependency*: the degree of functional cooperation that exist between two or more cultures. Functional interdependence may be induced for the mutual benefit of the cooperating cultures or it may be induced by the use of force or threat of it. Most African peoples were coerced by threat of force to assimulate aspects of European culture as a result of imposition of colonial rule.

3. *Congruency of values*: two or more cultures can trade off some cultural values and norms as a sense of common purpose develops between them. It has been pointed out that common value orientations bring people together to produce new ideas and adjustments that must be made by the various groups.[13]

The imposition of colonial rule on a number of culturally distinctive groups and the meshing together to form territorial states has brought many changes to African life patterns. For instance, colonial rule has affected the political structures and processes of the African peoples. Invariably every former colonial state has evolved or adopted political structures and processes of its former metropolis. At independence, the former British territories of Nigeria, Sierra Leone, Gambia, Kenya and Uganda adopted various forms of parliamentary democracies with such "liberal" structures as parliament, cabinet, independent judiciary, competitive political parties, elections and pressure groups. In the same vein, the former French territories have adopted governmental systems modelled on that of France. As a result of an increased rate of transaction flows between the metropolis and the former colonies, the metropolis exported such ideological orientations as capitalism and socialism to the latter.

Another area in which cultural contact with Europe has left a permanent imprint on African cultures is the area of religion and socialization. Missionaries often accompanied the colonial adventurers not only to christianize but to bring "civilization" to the primitive peoples of Africa. Consequently, the establishment of various Christian denominations saw a steady erosion of the various African cultural values, especially those that govern marriage, ritual, worship and burial ceremonies, title taking, membership of secret societies and festivals. In most cases, the acceptance of Christian faith meant the rejection of indigenous practices. The churches also established formal education institutions. This, in turn, has affected patterns of socialization, the rate of urbanization and the level of occupational differentiation. Ironically, adoption of western values by the colonized led to revolts which not only resulted in the establishment of African churches but the winning of political independence.[14]

In spite of such vast and fundamental effects of foreign cultures on Africa's traditional systems, many of the traditional traits have persisted.

[13] Ronald Cohen and John Middleton, p. 6.

[14] See Chapters 7, 8, and 9 for fuller treatment.

At the family level, the old kinship ties still bind. Social relations especially sex and age differentiations still govern the patterns of interactions and social deference. The village political and administrative units are still important in spite of changing administrative policies and boundaries. A number of social clubs, especially the secret societies, still constitute power groups though they have lost their former pre-eminent role. Perhaps, the strongest cultural trait which has survived relate to religion. At moments of life crises, even Christians resort to the traditional modes of controlling time—space events. The rise and rapid spread of indigenous churches have often been explained by the congruence of their practices to African spirituality and rituals.

Many reasons have been given for so much persistence of traditional cultures. Historians of the colonial era argue that the colonial government wished to use the indigenous political structures as a mode of domesticating their new systems. Thus, the village administrative units were allowed to operate under a superimposed, extra-ethnic and national adminstrative structures. They also argue that the colonial governments were in fact more conciliatory towards indigenous cultures than the missions. Limited resources, shortage of manpower and diversions of the two World Wars forced the colonial powers to seek the most inexpensive means of running their new colonies.[15] The French went to the extent of assimilating the colonies into the French nation and using the retrained intelligent members to govern under the watchful eyes of the army.

Years ago, the American sociologist, W. F. Ogburn, built on the organic conception of society enunciated by the classical sociologists to explain the persistence of old traits amidst change. He drew a distinction between *material* (objective artifacts) and *non-material* (ideas, beliefs, behaviour) parts of culture. The *culture lag theory* proposed that material culture changes more rapidly than non-material culture, so that a lag is created between the two realms. Eventually, Ogburn contends, a more harmonious adjustment of the invention and its related cultural parts will occur.[16] Now we can begin to understand the deposition in a military tribunal in 1976 that Ghanaian

[15] For a summary of such evidence and new ones, see O. U. Kalu, "Missionaries, Colonial Government and Secret Societies in South-Eastern Igboland, 1900—1950 forthcoming in *Journal of the Historical Society of Nigeria*, 9 (1978).

[16] William F. Ogburn, *Social Change* (Chicago, 1922): For fuller treatment of this and other theories, see. O. U. Kalu, "Gods in Retreat: Models of Religious Change in Africa," *Nigerian Journal of the Humanities*, I/1 (September, 1977), 42—53.

soldiers who were planning a coup invite native doctors to "fortify" them against the bullets of loyal forces! However, other variables explain cultural persistence.

The Trend in the Study of African Cultures

Since the 1960's when the "wind of change" or wave of political independence hit Africa, there has been a rising interest in African studies. It would appear that the membership of these small nations in large international organizations with possible diplomatic and political repercussions and their potential as new markets made Europe realize that little useful information existed on Africa. Various arms of European governments have sponsored studies on Africa. They have also financed associations which co-ordinate such studies in both Africa and the rest of the world. New interest in China and Japan might be supplanting African studies but huge strides have been taken.

A basic problem with these foreign sponsored studies is one of ideology. He who pays the piper calls the tune. The pay officers would like to influence the trend of development in Africa by the type of analysis which they produce. For instance, if one employed western theories, especially the functionalist theory of social change, the tendency would be to urge that change in Africa could only occur by gradual transformation. Thus, one of the greatest problems which confront the study of African culture is the enunciation of a creative methodology. A survey of past methodologies indicates that whites have fashioned Africa according to their own image and to suit their own interests. Fair enough, the pursuit of self-interest is a basic characteristic of the human species. Africans are, therefore, challenged to identify their own true interest through the study of their cultures.

The first attempt at the study of the various cultures of Africa was made by Christian missionaries and colonial officers who concentrated their efforts on the identification of the various ethnic and sub-ethnic groups which inhabited a given colonial territory. They gathered information designed to facilitate subversive "civilizing missions".

The efforts of the missionaries and colonial officials were supplemented by social and cultural anthropologists such as Kuper, Fortes, Daryll Fordes, Victor Turner, Nadel, Harris, Evan-Pritchards and Lucy Mair. Social anthropology was defined simply as the study of primitive peoples. Initially their primary concern was the "small-scale" or "primitive" societies who had not been affected by impact of western civilization. As the "primitive societies" disappeared as a result of their incorporation into the larger territorial states, the social anthropologists changed their techniques. They then became interested in the patterns of social interactions among the various destructive cultural groups as well as the patterns of "incorporation" or "integration" with other members of the larger state. Today's social anthropologists are not interested on change as an item of behaviour but on change in the entire social structure.[17]

There are three main approaches to the study of Africa in these studies and other studies. First, there is the *Evolutionist approach*. This is based on the assumption that existing cultures evolve gradually from a "lower" to a "higher" one. There is an embedded idea of unilineal development from a backward to a more progressive or modern culture. An evolutionist theorist sees progress as an attribute of a cultural system. He further assumes that there is a correlation between technical advance with "higher" culture. In this sense "civilization" becomes synonymous with culture. However, a civilized society may have sophisticated technology, but its culture may or may not be of a "higher quality". In fact, a technological society may be premised on "mass culture" which is less than ideal. Among the leading evolutionist theorists are Edward Tylor, Max Muller and Maclennam.

1. *Diffusionist approach*: The diffusionists attack the evolutionists on the ground that evolution alone cannot explain the plethora of differences which are visible in "primitive" societies. Diffusionist approach maintains that there is no universal standard by which an outside observer can use to evaluate other cultures. Consequently, each culture and its various aspects must be studied and evaluated on its own terms. The contribution of various aspects of a given culture must be seen in terms of the contributions it makes to the culture of which it is a part. The diffusionists are sometimes criticized for delineating cultures into various components. A leading diffusionist is F. F. Liraebner.

2. *Sociological approach*: This approach emphasizes the society and sees culture as an aspect of societal life. The type and nature of the society will determine its cultural traits; hence the mechanical and organic societies with varied cultural heritages. The leading proponent is Emile Durkheim.

Other problems in studying African cultures include:

(a) Cultural variety. This is reflected in the existence of several distinctive cultural groups with diverse cultural heritages such as languages,

[17] Lucy Mair, *New Nations* (London: Weiden Feld and Nicolson, 1969), pp. 16–17.

cultural values, and norms, cosmologies, and religious practices and rituals.

(b) The impact of colonial rule. This has led to the imposition of foreign structures and the disintegration of social cohesion that had existed among the various groups. It has also created problems of relevance – what should be studied and what should be preserved.

(c) Ethnocentrism. The concern to restore relevance, the need to extol the African cultural heritage could blindfold African scholars to the cultural enrichment which results from acculturation.

Finally, a third group of people who are studying African culture are the African black scholars. In their own way they search for relevance to remove the slurs and misconceptions created by foreign scholars. Early African scholars tended to be defensive and even romantic about the African past. The Negritude movement was suffused by the same type of romanticism as one finds in Camera Laye's *The African Child*. Modern scholarship has moved away from this. Still, modern black scholars can be subdivided into two broad categories: those having black skins with white masks having utilized European theories uncritically and producing what could be characterized as "literature of tutelage," and, the ineffectual minority who are seeking to evolve new creative approaches and more "critical literature". The task is formidable because of years of acculturation in western culture and the current system of education in Africa. But this is the challenge in the African's quest to understand his cultural heritage.

CHAPTER TWO

Archaeology and the Reconstruction of African Cultural Heritage

Prof. Donald D. Hartle
Department of History/Archaeology,
University of Nigeria, Nsukka

The Background to Man's Evolution

More than five million years ago, just prior to the emergence of the Pleistocene epoch,[1] some form of Hominid[2] evolved from a generalized primate[3] structure. The basic biological evolution of this hominid or proto-man consisted in an anatomical shift towards bipedalism, or the ability to walk upright on two feet. As a consequence of this physical change to an erect, upright posture man evolved both biologically and culturally (or bioculturally) on the African continent.

It is not possible to view man's biological (physical) evolution as a separate entity, that is, apart from man's cultural evolution. Culture and biology have been intimately interwoven, each influencing and affecting the other since the time of man's emergence. Biologically, the erect posture does not make man significantly different from other animal forms. Rather, the specific quality that differentiates man from all other animals is culture. But it was as a result of biological changes in his anatomy that man's culture emerged, and as this culture emerged, particularly in the use of tools, man's biological structure changed. The entire process of man's evolution throughout time has been a series of adjustments and readjustments, of adaptations and readaptations, to ever changing physical and cultural environments.

The word "culture" was first introduced into the social sciences as a specific, scientific term by E. B. Tylor in 1871. He defined culture as "that

[1] A geological term denoting the last epoch of the Cenozoic Era. It corresponds to the Age of Man. In Africa it begins with the Pluvial Periods and in the Northern Hemisphere with the Ice Age.

[2] A general term comprising any form of man or protoman, living or extinct. By proto-man we mean modern man's immediate ancestors.

[3] An anatomical, taxonomic grouping which includes monkeys, apes, and man.

complex whole which includes belief, knowledge, art, morals, law, custom, and any other capabilities and habits acquired by man as a member of society".[4] To understand this definition the difference between material and non-material culture must be clarified because material culture is the basic concern of the pre-historian such as the archaeologist or paleoanthropologist. In general terms we can say that material culture refers to both movable objects (artifacts), such as tools, pottery, and iron, and to immovable objects, such as buildings, ditches and burial pits (these are grouped under the term "architecture"). Non-material culture refers to thought processes, social and political organization, religion, language, etc., that is symbolic behaviour.

Let us now return to the emergence of man. Some form of proto-man evolved a bipedal structure. This freed his hands from locomotion and made possible the manipulation of tools (material culture). This, in turn, stimulated the brain (biologically) which made possible further development of cultures. After the attainment of the erect posture, man biologically evolved a larger brain, the areas of the brain controlling the thumb were greatly advanced for better manipulation of tools in co-ordination with vision, and there were further structural changes in the foot, pelvis, vertebral column, skull and face. It is important to remember that biological evolution refers to the replacement of one organ by another. Cultural evolution is additive, and although a culture may introduce new traits and complexes, it still retains the traits of its predecessor.

The Law of the Acceleration of Culture Change states that the further forward man has come in time the greater the number of inventions, and the shorter the period between inventions. Thus, at the beginning of the Earlier Stone Age (more than three million years ago), man made crude, core tools, predominantly choppers, used for some three million years. He then learned to make tools on flakes, large and heavy at first, but later becoming smaller and more finely executed. This process continued for several hundred thousands of years until man learned to manufacture tools on blades which are thin, elongated flakes. After many thousands of years man discovered how to produce microliths, very small stone flakes, and these enabled him to make composite tools. During all this time other cultural traits were being discovered as well. It was only about ten thousand years ago that man began using ground and polished stone

[4] Tylor, E. B., *Primitive Culture* Vol. I (London, 1871), p. 1.

tools and this was replaced in a few places only by the knowledge of iron metallurgy as recently as 500 B.C.

The chronological[5] outline (terminological) adopted by the Third Pan-African Congress of Prehistory[6] was:

> The Earlier Stone Age (2 m. to 55,000 yrs. ago)
> 1st Intermediate (55,000 to 40,000 yrs. ago)
> The Middle Stone Age (40,000 to 12,550 yrs. ago)
> 2nd Intermediate (12,550 to 10,000 yrs. ago)
> The Later Stone Age (10,000 to present).

This classification is not adequate and needs revision. Therefore, I have omitted the Intermediate Periods and have added Food Production/Village Farming and Urbanization. In some African areas, as well as in the Near East, it probably will be discovered that Urbanization preceded a Food Production/Village Farming way of life.

The Earlier Stone Age

(3 million to 40,000 years ago)

Oldowan: 3 million to 750,000 years ago

By the beginning of Lower Pleistocene times some five million years ago, the ancestors of Home erectus[7] had evolved the erect, bipedal posture, but the foot had not as yet developed the fully-curved arch, so that this hominid could probably run better than he could walk. The hand had evolved so that the thumb had good opposibility,[8] with the fingers giving a precision grip. Superficially, the skull seems to have resembled that of other primates, but particular areas were well on the way toward more recognizable man; the skull was beginning to increase in size and complexity, particularly in the areas concerned with abstract or symbolic thought, sight, and manipulation of objects.

[5] Sequence in time.

[6] Clark, J. D. ed., *Proceeding of the Pan-African 3rd Congress of Prehistory Livingstone 1955* (London, 1957), p. xxxiii.

[7] Most authorities have believed this was *Australopithecus africanus* rather than *A. robustus*, but now it seems likely that it was a different form, perhaps *Homo habilis*, as earlier suggested by L. S. B. Leakey.

[8] A distinction must be made between the *opposibility* of the thumb to the fingers, and *prehensability* or grasping which is the human hand without a thumb.

Probably the most famous sites in the world, and those which yielded the original evidence of man's bio-cultural evolution were discovered in Olduvai Gorge, which is located in the Serengeti Plains in the Eastern Rift, Tanzania. Man began to occupy the sites in the Gorge sometime in the Lower Pleistocene, about two million years ago, and continued there through the Middle Pleistocene (and Acheulian culture, cf. p. 6). The geology of the Gorge indicates that the environment some two million years ago was much as it is at the present time: plains, savannah, grassland, with shallow lakes and streams, and large community trees. It would appear that hominids lived here in small groups. Their temporary camps or home bases were located on mud flats, and from here they made forages into the plains and grasslands in search of animals.

These hominids had developed a taste for raw meat, which is not a primate characteristic (primates are vegetarians). There are a number of theories suggesting why man acquired a taste for meat, but they are not important here. What is important is that the acquired trait of meat-eating determined, to a great extent, the entire course of man's biocultural evolution. Thus, man's ancestors became hunters as well as scavengers and gatherers of plants and animals. To kill or scavenge animals was not a major problem, the real problem was to devise a way to cut up the carcas as it is nearly impossible to chew through the skin of most animals. The inventory of cultural traits of Olduvai, which includes all of the artifacts and architecture, indicate the foregoing course of man's life-way.

The hominids of the Oldowan Industrial Complex constructed crude floors in their temporary campsites. On these floors was an accumulation of stone and bone. This was artificial because many of the stones were not natural to the area; they had been carried in. Further, many of the stones and bones were artificially broken, and this has led a number of archaeologists to refer to the culture as a "bashing" culture. Apparently, the hominids were breaking open the long bones[9] to get at the marrow inside. These bones indicate the type of animals hunted or scavenged: mostly immature antelope and pig, since it would appear that the hominid had not yet developed his tools well enough to hunt large or mature animals. Oldowan man also ate tortoise, snake and catfish. It must not be assumed that these hominids lived on meat alone simply because no plant remains have survived. Vegetal foods probably provided some 75 per cent of the diet of these and later hunting and gathering groups.

[9] Bones of the arms and legs.

Prior to the Lower Pleistocene Era primates had probably been tool-users for several million years, but with the Oldowan culture appeared the manufacture of tools with a cutting edge, and the standardization of tool types. Thus, four major components define the Oldowan: tools, utilized materials, debitage and manuports. The most characteristic or diagnostic tools of the Oldowan are a wide variety of choppers made by two directional, percussion flaking[10] in order to produce a wide-angle cutting edge. Earlier some of these tools had been made by one-directional flaking, and later they were manufactured by multi-directional trimming. Because many of these choppers were made on river pebbles the Oldowan is frequently referred to as a "pebble" culture. However much of the raw material utilized was angular lumps of lava and granite. These choppers were undoubtedly used to cut through the animal skin and for bashing the bong bones for marrow. Other tools included polyhedrons for bashing, discoids and crude proto-bifaces for cutting, spheroids for hunting, heavy and light scrappers for removing bits of meat from skins, and other sundry tools.

Utilized material refers to any object which was used rather than manufactured. This included various types of anvils and hammerstones. Debitage means all the waste materials resulting from tool manufacture, and manuports are those things which were carried into an area from another place, "hand carry".

Other sites such as those in the Lake Rudolf area of Northwest Kenya and the Omo Valley of Ethiopia has produced even earlier Oldowan materials than those found at Olduvai, while those in North Africa, including Cassablanca, Morrocco and Ain Hanech, Algeria, seem to be later in that the Oldowan tools are better made.

More than a million years ago, just prior to the termination of the Lower Pleistocene, a new form of man evolved, *Homo erectus.*[11] This form, compared to the *Australopithecines*, was structurally larger, a bit massive and definitely more closely similar to modern man, *Homo sapiens*. The skull had doubled in size and the convolutions[12] of the brain indicate a complexity of this organ not far removed from modern man. It was *Homo erectus* who was responsible for the diffusion and dispersal of man and his culture, not only throughout Africa, but the Near East, Europe, India and the Far East as well.

[10] To strike one stone against another.

[11] All forms of animal (and plant) life are classified according to genus and species, and for finer divisions to race, variety, etc. (cf. p. 8).

[12] The "folds" or wrinkles of the brain providing a greater surface area.

So, the dawn of Africa's and the world's cultural heritage was in the Lower Pleistocene marked by the appearance in East Africa of the earliest known culture or proto-culture, the Oldowan, and the carrier of that culture, man or protoman.

Acheulian: 750,000–55,000 years ago

The physical and intellectual advance of *Homo erectus* beyond that of his earlier progenitors made possible the production of new sets of tools and, thus, different cultures. Two cultures developed from the Oldowan: Evolved Oldowan and Acheulean.[13] Evolved Oldowan, as the name implies, was a growth or progression from the Oldowan but still retained most of the basic traits found in the earlier culture complex. It soon died out in Africa but before that time it had diffused in two directions from the African continent. One route of diffusion was eastward through India, Southeast Asia and north into China. This eastern area continued developing along the chopper-chopping tool tradition for hundred of thousands of years. The other route was northward into what is now eastern Europe and there it does not seem to have persisted very long.

The Acheulean culture of the Middle Pleistocene apparently evolved in East or Northeast Africa more than a half a million years ago. Since man was now a predator, he moved away from the fringes of the forests to waterside sites in the savannahs, plains and grassland, and even off the African continent. Man's advance in tool-making permitted him to enter nearly every environment except the deserts and heavily forested areas.

At the beginning of this period man had developed organization, and soon thereafter the social organization became quite complex. In the initial stages he was a hunter of medium-sized animals such as deer, duiker and horse, and later he hunted large game animals including the elephant, rhinoceros, giraffe and hippopotamus. Man's hunting techniques were so well developed that when the animals were approaching the water holes they were driven into the mud where, being helplessly bogged down, they could be killed. It has been suggested that perhaps language and religion as ritual may have evolved about this time.

There were two major stages of development of the Acheulean which have been identified at Olduvai Gorge. Toward the end of the Acheulean, only 60,000 years ago, African man discovered the use of fire. This was another of man's major contributions to culture. Fire was used as a tool in a large

[13] First identified at St. Acheul, France.

variety of ways: for burning large areas to drive animals into the swamp mud, for clearing animals out of caves and thereby making them habitable and warm, for shaping and hardening pointed sticks, and for cooking food, a process which converts undigestable food into edible items.

Although the earliest developments of the Acheulean were not present in the Sahara because it was too dry, that area was occupied later during wetter conditions. The latest stages of the Acheulean were also not present in the Sahara because of another dry period, and by 100,000 years ago the Sahara became an impenetrable barrier between North and sub-Saharan Africa. This dry phase lasted until about 40,000 years ago, well into the Middle Stone Age. Thus, long before the end of Acheulean times sub-Saharan Africa began evolving culturally in ways entirely different from those in North Africa and Europe. From that time to the present, North Africa, Egypt and the rest of the Mediterranean world evolved in more or less a similar fashion.

During the Acheulean period *Homo erectus* had discovered or refined a variety of tool-making techniques. The most important of these was the use of secondary flaking and trimming, which gave fine precision to toolmaking. Essentially, only percussion flaking had been used in the Oldowan. A type of flaking called "levallois" was not introduced, which is a prepared platform technique of flaking. In this technique the tool was actually prepared on the core of a stone, and with one blow the tool was removed. This required foresight because the tool could not really be identified while still on the core. A third major innovation of tool making is called the cylindrical hammer technique. In this flaking process the flake was removed by using a cylindrical hammer, usually of bone, but perhaps of wood as well. This produced thinner and flatter flakes.

Most of the tools of the Acheulean culture were made on large flakes, as opposed to the Oldowan core tools. One should keep in mind the "persistence of tool types"; the Acheulean tools did not wholly replace, but were added to the cultural inventory of the Oldowan culture. The hallmark of the Acheulean is the handaxe and, not infrequently, because of this tool the Acheulean has been called the "handaxe culture". This bifacial tool varied from some 10 to 30 cm. in length, had a rounded end for holding in the hand, two cutting edges, and a point.[14] Actually it was anything but an axe, and would better be referred to as an over-all utility tool for piercing, cutting, and general butchering. It

[14] This tool had evolved from the crude biface of the Oldowan toward the end of Acheulean times. Because of better and more advanced techniques, beautiful handaxes were produced.

was used primarily for skinning and cutting up the carcasses of large game animals. Another major tool was the "U"-shaped cleaver. This tool was shaped as a "U" and instead of the point of the handaxe the top of the "U" was used primarily for skinning and cutting up the carcasses of large game also a major tool for cutting up the game killed in the hunt. Other tools included picks and scrappers, smaller scrapping tools, etc. Although we haven't any evidence for it we can safely presume that early man also made tools of wood and bone.

Terminal Earlier Stone Age: 55,000 to 40,000 years ago

The Acheulean gave rise to three cultures, the Sangoan[15] and Fauresmith[16] which evolved in sub-Saharan Africa, and the Mousterian[17] which evolved in central and southeastern Europe and later diffused westward into Egypt and across North Africa.

Some broad generalizations may be made about the similarities of the three cultures, but each only represents a major cultural configuration of a wide variety of sub-cultures within which they evolved. These three cultures adapted to three different environments and thus their inventory of cultural traits differs in that each was a response to a particular ecological nitch. Furthermore, it must be remembered that from this period to the present the bracketing of time for the beginning and ending of different cultural periods is, at best, only a mere approximation. Cultures did not evolve in parallel fashion. Each culture evolved differently because each one selected specific non-similar cultural traits which took precedence over others. In time their differentiating traits changed the fabric of every societal group.

In general, then, it can be stated that the ancestors of modern man had evolved: *Homo sapiens neanderthalensis* in North Africa, and Europe, and *Homo sapiens rhodesiensis* in sub-Saharan Africa. These forms were much further advanced than *Homo erectus* physically but, in fact, only a physical anthropologist can identify the differences in bone structure. Additionally, the size and convolutions of the brains are nearly equal to that of modern man, *Homo sapiens sapiens*. For all three cultures the use of fire had become common, and, in general, the peoples were inhabiting caves and rock shelters. Man's move into forests, plateaus, and elsewhere marked the beginning of the secondary dispersal of mankind, not only in Africa but also throughout

[15] First identified at Sango Bay on the eastern shore of Lake Victoria, Uganda.

[16] First identified from a site near the town of Fauresmith, South Africa.

[17] First identified at Le Moustier, France.

the entire world. It could well be that this was the real beginning of sub-Saharan cultural developments which distinguish its cultural heritage today from that of the rest of the world.

Fauresmith

In south and east Africa the Fauresmith culture occupied nearly every environment except the forests and deserts. In caves adjacent to water this culture existed in the high veld, acacia grasslands, sandy and stony sclerophytic parklands,[18] plateaus, mountains and open country. The culture could well be called "evolved Acheulean" since the inventory of artifacts indicates that this was a direct continuation of the Acheulean. The major difference is that the tools of the Fauresmith were much finer made; man had, by this time, developed far better techniques for manufacturing tools. The hallmark of the Acheulean, the handaxe, became smaller, and the most frequent type was almond-shaped. The cleaver also became smaller, but cruder, indicating that this tool was not as important as it had been previously. Other tools included side and end scrappers, trimmed projectile points and flakes, blades, polyhedrals, burins, stone balls and discoids. Most of these tools were produced on prepared cores by the levallois technique (as in the Mousterian culture), and were further refined by step-flaking.

Sangoan

In the forested areas of East and Central Africa the Sangoan culture evolved from the Acheulean, and from there it spread southward to Natal, eastward to the Great Lakes and westward throughout West Africa. This was a root-grubbing, riverine culture found along rivers and around lakes in the forests, not actually "in" the forests. These peoples were probably exploiting the wild yams and other tubers as well as a variety of plants and animals indigenous to this type of environment.

The tools of this culture represent, in many ways, a degeneration from the Acheulean tool types, for they seem to be crudely manufactured. The major tool characteristic of the Sangoan period was a large, heavy, crude pick, presumably used to dig or grub tubers. Evidence of handaxes continued but were not nearly as well made as previously. But, the Sangoan peoples had a wide variety of scrappers, the most characteristic of which is called a "push plan" 3 type, and towards the end of the period lanceolate blades and tranchets appeared. In addition to grubbing tools the Sangoan peoples developed

[18] Characterized by very hardy, strong plants.

a tool kit to include all sorts of artifacts for woodworking and most of these smaller tools were, as in the Fauresmith, produced by the step-flaking technique.

Mousterian

Some 150,000 years ago the Mousterian culture evolved on the European continent in the area which is now France and northern Spain. These people were big game hunters and lived primarily at the mouths of caves although some sites have been found in open areas. The dead were carefully buried with offerings, and the presence of altars with offerings indicate a belief in an after-life. In the dim, dark recesses of the uninhabitable parts of caves were created beautiful drawings and paintings. Almost all the pictures were those of animals hunted, particularly pregnant females. Does this indicate some sort of sympathetic magic, both for success in the hunt and for the continuation of the species? Most authorities believe so.

Towards the terminal part of the Earlier Stone Age Neanderthal man, carrying the Mousterian culture, had entered Africa via the Near East. Apparently he had followed the Euro-Asiatic migrating animals such as the bear, rhinoceros, and deer. Later, three regional forms of the Mousterian evolved in northern Africa: Nubian, Cyrenaican, and Maghrebian. After this culture became extinct in Europe, the Near East, Nubia and Cyrenaica, it continued to flourish until it became almost fossilized in the Maghreb.

The tools of this culture evolved for both hot and cold climates and included skin clothing and the extensive use of fire. Tools consisted of a wide variety of those necessary for an existence dependent on hunting: handaxes, scrappers, knives, points, blades, etc. Most of these were produced by the levallois technique. With the Mousterian in Africa this technique reached its highest peak of development in the world. Famous tool types produced by this technique are called "tortoise cores". Thus, levallois technique gradually evolved into the discoid or Mousterian method which produced a "discoid core". This core was prepared to produce many blades; it could be carried as a single, small stone and when blades were needed they were removed with one blow. Each of these blades or flakes was usable.

The Middle Stone Age

(40,000–10,000 years ago)

During the Middle Stone Age *Homo sapiens neanderthalensis* evolved into fully modern man, *Homo sapiens sapiens* in North Africa. South of the

Sahara from the site of Broken Hill, Rhodesia, a skeleton of *Homo sapiens rhodesiansis* was found along with Middle Stone Age materials. Further south in the Transvaal a proto-Bushman skull was found at Boskop. Throughout Africa fully modern man evolved during the Middle Stone Age.

The Middle Stone Age is generally characterized by many regional industrial complexes, each of which exhibited more localization and specialization of tool types, depending upon the nature of the culture and environment. There was a decline in heavy core and flake tools and an increase of smaller flake tools produced by better bifacial flaking. Perhaps one could say that the blades were the major innovative product, particularly those produced by the levallois technique, but there were many variants and the end products were different. Additional evidence of religion exists in the careful burial of the dead, the aesthetic value placed on the adornment of the body with paint and in the use of ornamentation.

From about 38,000 to 31,000 B.C. there was an intrusive Upper Paleolithic blade and burin culture from the Near East, which inhabited the Mediterranean coastal area and extended south-ward into the East African Rift. However, three of the best known Middle Stone Age cultures were the Aterian[19] of North Africa, the Lupemban[20] of West Africa and the Congo, and the Stillbay[21] of South and East Africa.

Aterian

Long after the Mousterian culture had become extinct in Europe and most of North Africa, it continued to persist in the Maghreb until about 30,000 years ago when it gave rise to the Aterian culture.

The major contribution the Aterians gave to African cultural heritage was that they invented or discovered the "tanged" point. This was a bifacial projectile point and because of the shape of its base it could be hafted, that is tied, to a shaft, leading in time to the invention of the bow and arrow. They also produced discoid and triangular flakes, blades and scrappers. Most of their tools were a development based on the survival of the prepared core tradition of their progenitors.

At the end of this period the Aterians, because of the invention of the bow and arrow, swarmed into the Sahara, then a grassland, to hunt the ungulates[22] there, as had been done from time to time by earlier peoples when

[19] First identified from a site in eastern Algeria.

[20] First identified from the southern Congo area.

[21] First identified at Bambata Cave in the Matopos Hills, Southern Rhodesia.

[22] All hoofed animals.

the environment permitted it. The migration of the Aterians was so successful they soon diffused throughout the Sahara from the Atlantic Ocean to the Nile Valley, and southward to the Sudan. This rapid spread ended almost as quickly as it began, and by 8,000 B.C. the Aterians were confined to a few mountain massifs in the Sahara. However by this time the bow and arrow had diffused throughout most of Africa, Europe and eastwards as well.

Lupemban

In the forested areas of West Africa and the Congo the major culture to evolve from the Sangoan was the Lupemban which is actually a general name for a wide variety of cultures. As expected, the Lupemban is found in approximately the same environments as the Sangoan, but with finer and better tools the Lupemban peoples expanded their area of living. From the crude, heavy Sangoan tools there evolved smaller and better made tools, including chisels, bifaced axes, boat-shaped side scrappers, core axes, picks, and tranchets, most of which were associated with wood-working. Throughout this time there was an increasing use of blades, elongated flakes, some of which were "backed". Still later, tanged points appeared, undoubtedly diffused from the Aterians to the north, and lance heads, laurel-leaf points, and blades gained increasing importance. These were probably for hunting. By the end of the period the levallois technique of tool production was common.

Stillbay

In a wide variety of environments, high veld, mountains, open country, etc., especially the same ones occupied by the Fauresmith peoples, there evolved a number of different cultures, each having devised cultural equipment for their own particular mode of living. One of the best known of these was the Stillbay and its many variants. Proto-Stillbay did not differ much from its antecendent and the tools were mainly unspecialized and lacked any careful retouching. These included large core choppers and handaxes, missel stones, thick biface points, some trimmed uniface points and scrappers, some of which were notched. At Broken Hill, *Homo sapiens rhodesiensis* was discovered along with bone and ivory tools and simple stone gouges and points. By the end of Middle Stone Age the tools were more carefully made by pressure flaking, fully bi- and uniface leaf-shaped points were present, and lanceolate or willow-shaped points, probably hafted, were characteristic.

The Later Stone Age
(10,000–5500 B.C.)

Around 10,000 years B.C. a maximum pluvial or wet period began to recede and an extreme period of dryness occured about 7,000 B.C. The desiccation and expansion of the Sahara desert forced man into extreme conditions around the edges of lakes, along the rivers and sea coasts. Because of aridity, plant and animal life diminished in the greater part of these areas, and man then became an intensive forager and collector of all sorts of plant and animal life. All around the coasts of North and West Africa, along the rivers that continued to flow and the lakesides, is evidence that man exploited water animals and plants. These are primarily in the form of shell middlens or heaps where man discarded the shell after removing the animal from inside. In many of these places he tended to become more sedentary than he had been previously. Fishing became the major subsistence activity for many groups, and where possible some groups exploited and hunted animals.

In addition to camping around water sites, man lived in rock shelters and in the mouths of caves. This was modern man, and throughout most of Africa the major inhabitant was the Bushman, who is at present confined to South Africa. By 8,000 B.C. the ethnic map of Africa was fairly well set, and it remained so until the spread of the Bantu several thousands of years later. It is interesting to note that the earliest recognizable Negroid skeleton comes from Khartoum and was associated with Later Stone Age materials. Although it has not been dated, it has been suggested that it is some 10,000 years old.

The most important addition to the over-all accumulation of tools was the utilization of microliths. They had been present before, but now their use became commonplace in most cultures. These were very small pieces of stone, most of them in the shape of crescents, trapezoids, or semi-squares, many of which were used to make a composite tool such as arrow points, barbed hooks and harpoons, knives, sickless, etc. It is significant to note that in order to inset these microliths into a shaft or any other form, man must have acquired the knowledge to use some kind of gum, adhesive, or resin. Thus, many scholars have suggested that, because of the adverse environmental conditions, this was the greatest period of adaptative specialization in the history of mankind and produced many distinctive cultures.

Food Production/Village Farming

(5,500 B.C. – present)

The change from a hunting and gathering way of life to that of producing one's own food was perhaps the greatest, and most important transition in the cultural history of mankind. The domestication of plants and animals covered a long period of time. It was not a "revolution", but built upon the foundations of the intensive foraging of the preceding period, sometimes referred to as the Nesolithic in Northern Africa, Egypt and the Near East, and the Later Stone Age in Sub-Saharan Africa.

The origin and diffusion of domesticated plants and animals in Africa is one of the most complex, obscure, and confused issues in the cultural history of Africa. However, in spite of differing opinions, a few generalities can be suggested. Some authorities believe that food production first appeared in Africa about 5,000 B.C. in two widely separated areas, and each contained entirely different cultural traits. One was in the delta area of Egypt and consisted in domesticates[23] which had originated and diffused from the Near East. The most important food products were wheat, barley, oats and rye, grains which actually prefer a cooler climate than most of the sub-Saharan area, and cattle, sheep, goats and pigs, which have now diffused throughout most of Africa except in the desert and tse-tse fly areas. The assimilation and adaptation of these elements by the various African cultures completely revitalized and changed their ways of life.

The second major area where food production appeared in Africa although there were other centres of domestication as well, is at the headwaters of the Niger River among the nuclear Mande, which have been credited with the indigenous domestication of such crops as millet and sorghum in the savannah, grasslands area. To the south, in the forested areas of West Africa, many species of yam, rice, and the kola were domesticated and in East Africa and on the southern fringes of the Sudan the ensete or false banana, sorghum, and other crops were first produced.

Somewhat later other species of yam and rice, the coconut, banana, and plantain diffused into Africa from south-eastern Asia and much, much later, about A.D. 1,500, maize (corn), cassava (manioc or gari), and potato were transported from the Americas, first into West Africa and later throughout the continent. Different indigenous crops became the staple for different groups. Diffused crops became the staple for some groups, and still other groups

[23] Any domesticated plant or animal.

combined both indigenous and diffused crops. Once domestication appeared the inventory of both material and non-material cultural traits was so drastically altered that little evidence remained of the old hunting and gathering way of life. However, most peoples even today supplement their food production with some hunting and gathering. In a few instances, as with the Bushmen of the Kalihari Desert in Southwestern Africa, groups continue to exist today by hunting and gathering, probably due to environmental factors. It is most important to remember that these Bushmen can give us great insight into the culture of early man prior to the discovery of food production.

The major cultural innovations which occurred at this time made possible three major ways of life based on domestication: the cultivation of plants, the herding of animals, or a combination of the two (which most people have done since the beginning of food production).

Because of the time required for the reaping or harvesting of food crops, people were required to become more sedentary. This encouraged and made possible the construction of rather permanent living quarters, that is, houses. The quality of thrift or saving appeared in the form of surplus production which economists refer to as "social surplus". Every farmer had to produce enough food to feed his family until the next harvest, he had to save enough for the next planting, and even more than that in case he should have a crop failure. He also had to produce enough for purposes of trading for other commodities.

So, in addition to pottery, a number of other storage items either made their initial appearance or increased in number. Pits were dug in the ground and some containers were constructed above ground for the conservation of grains. For tubers such as yams, man learned how to construct barns, so that the air could circulate around the crops. There is also evidence to indicate that there was a tremendous increase in population, really a population explosion, as a sedentary existence such as this provides an assurance of food supply and life is not nearly as precarious as that for a wandering hunter and gatherer. Older people and children were much easier to care for and more people could produce more food.

Because of the relationship of soil fertility to food production, land became much more important, a thing to fight over, and it has been suggested that this was the beginning of real warfare.

Little equipment, if any, has been preserved to indicate animal domestication, but that associated with crop production is much more in evidence. The permanence of habitation encouraged the development of a large variety of pottery types, which were now of tremendous utilitarian value and some items of aesthetic qualities were present as well. Pottery is the earliest known of the plastic arts. Stone tools, now polished, appear in abundance indicating agricultural practices. Grains must be ground and for this purpose a variety of querns were manufactured. They had appeared in the intensive foraging stage, but had not become common. Probably, the first agricultural tool was a wooden digging stick called a dibble. This was simply an elongated stick with a sharpened end used to break the soil. The pre-historic evidence for this is a ground, perforated stone disc, *kwe*, which was used as a weight for the dibble. In some parts of Africa we find stone hoes, particularly in the forested areas, and in other parts shovels are found.

The socio-political structure of the food producing economy underwent a drastic change although it still continued to operate along kinship lines. The prehistorian does not have evidence for this, but based upon the village settlement pattern, one can infer with validity, that the social and political organizations were at this time directed toward a sedentary, larger village group, whereas previously group control was only concerned with a nomadic, small band. The problems of living in large groups is one of the major focal areas of research for sociologists and anthropologists today. It is not easy for large social groups to organize themselves when they are well beyond a small, consanguineal unit. Moreover, a labour force must be conscripted to carry out communal activities of benefit to the overall village. With such changes, it can be inferred that there was a change in the religious structure as all groups have a major religious focus directed toward their basic subsistence pattern. The concern of the farmer is obviously toward food production and fertility of the soil and that of the herder toward the fertility or reproduction of cattle, sheep and goats.

The rise of the artisan, the craftsman, also occurred during this stage of development, although these roots, again, extended much further back in time, and a much higher degree of specialization appears in the next stage of development.

By 6,000 B.C., the Sahara began to enter another wet period and between 5,500–2,500 B.C., it experienced the Makalian pluvial. Mediterranean vegetation, aleppo pine, cypress, and juniper moved southwards, and, in the mountains, cedars, oaks, and walnut trees grew in abundance. Fauna[24] followed these plants into the Sahara, and Mediterranean peoples from the north and Negroid peoples from the south moved into the area. Waterside habitats became important in the Sahara not only at its fringes but also

[24] Animals.

in the interior sections as well, because, with the advanced technology learned in the intensive foraging period, peoples began exploiting water animals to the utmost. Many fishing villages arose indicated by equipment such as bone harpoons and gouges. These "water traits" appeared all over Africa.

In addition to the foregoing, the peoples brought herding and agriculture with them. Of the two, it would appear that pastoralism was probably most important. Near Eastern grains were not well suited to the environment but the African millet and sorghum were adaptable. Most food producing sites in the Sahara belong to this period and the rock paintings and engravings have been suggested to date from about 3,500 B.C. It is certain that Egypt was in a food producing/village farming stage of development at least as early as 5,000 B.C. and it is probable that West Africa also was progressing toward this at the same time. The two complexes met in the Sahara much later.

By 2,500 B.C. desiccation again decimated the Sahara and once more peoples moved toward its fringes. Acacia replaced Mediterranean vegetation, and the Sahara began to take on the aspect it has today. But the peoples who migrated out of the Sahara carried many new and renovated traits with them, and, in time, these set the stage for another of man's greatest innovations, and the beginning of the disintegration of millions of years of kinship ties: urbanization.

Urbanization (3,200 B.C. – present)

Urbanization, the artificial grouping of peoples into large cities or towns, occurred in a few places only. Although village farming was a prerequisite to urbanization, most people throughout the world remained, and continue to remain, in a village farming way of life. The origin of urbanization is speculative but it is possible that this developed in Africa from trading centres sometime prior to 3,200 B.C. The process of urbanization seems to have been greatly accelerated with the coming of iron metallurgy which occurred in two widely separated areas, Nok and Meroe, about 500 B.C.

Once again the configuration of African culture underwent a dramatic change as the social and political structures of urban areas are based upon an entirely different set of principles than those which obtain in the villages where all such elements are based upon the kinship structure. These cities are parasitically attached to the village farmers although they are in complete control of them and, indeed, are thoroughly dependent upon the farmer for their very existence. It is the village farmer who provides the raw material for cities. He provides the food, the raw materials to be converted by the factories, and even the individuals, since no city has ever been able to reproduce its population density. The village farmer is frequently quite ignorant of urban life and looks upon it with hostility.[25]

The beginning of the dynastic periods in Egypt when Menes unified the north and south in 3,200 B.C. marks the emergence of urbanization in Africa. Egypt became one of the greatest civilizations in the world with a distinctly unique cultural configuration which differentiated it from others. It possessed all the traits of urbanization, particularly control in the hands of a few, and tremendous accumulation of wealth for a very small minority. In addition, Egypt had a mathematical system, a method of writing (pictographical), a calendar, and tools and weapons of bronze. The glory that was Egypt lasted for nearly 3,000 years, but it was a Bronze Age civilization and readily succumbed to the invading Assyrians in the 7th century B.C., because the latter possessed superior iron weapons. Urbanization in the rest of Africa did not appear until thousands of years after it did in Egypt, but eventually large empires and kingdoms arose throughout the continent.

The knowledge of iron metallurgy was discovered by the Hittites of Anatolia[26] about 1,500 B.C. This remained a closely guarded secret for some time, but since such a monumental discovery could not remain in the hands of a few indefinitely, the knowledge of iron metallurgy diffused throughout the Near East a few hundred years later, and along the coast of North Africa and Egypt by the 7th century B.C. In sub-Saharan Africa two centres vie for the earliest centre of iron metallurgy, Meroe in Sudan and Nok in Nigeria; in neither place is it considered to be indigenous. Most scholars now have discarded the idea that Meroe was the diffusion centre of iron metallurgy throughout central and southern Africa in favour of Nok, where this knowledge probably had diffused over the Sahara trade routes from North Africa. The earliest date for iron metallurgy in sub-Saharan Africa is known from the site of Taruga, a Nok culture site, in north-central Nigeria.[27] From here it diffused throughout the general area, and about A.D. 1 with the knowledge of agriculture, diffused throughout central and eastern Africa with the spread of the Bantu. It reached the most southern parts of Africa in relatively recent times.

Except for a few grinding stones such as querns, stone tools practically disappear from the cultural inventory of all groups with the introduction of

[25] For example, note the attitude of the rural peoples toward the tax collectors who are sent on orders from the cities.

[26] Modern Turkey.

[27] 440 ± 140 B.C.

iron metallurgy, a cultural complex that supplied superior tools and weapons and permitted man to conquer the remaining uninhabited environments such as the forest.

Summary Statement

In summary: What has the archaeologist or prehistorian contributed to the reconstruction of African cultural heritage?

In the first instance we have revealed that man evolved on the African continent, probably in East Africa, some 4 million years ago. It has been discovered that the earliest known culture in the world, the Oldowan, evolved in the same place, and it was then that man began his biocultural evolutionary development. Since the physical structure of man permits a limited range of functions, man's cultural equipment evolved within that range of functions as he progressively became capable of utilizing an ever increasing variety of tools. Later man's culture became more dominant than his biology, and now man is dominated by his culture.

This progression is best seen in the early stages of bio-cultural evolution in the physical changes of early man and the gradual advance of making finer and better stone tools. The first tools were core tools, crudely flaked to make a cutting edge; they hardly looked like tools at all. After a couple million years man discovered how to make tools on flakes, again crude and heavy at first, but later culminating in beautiful workmanship producing the well-known handaxe, scrappers, etc., tools for big game hunting. Then blades for knives and projectile points were produced, and still later man discovered how to make composite tools of microliths and to grind and polish stone. With the introduction of iron metallurgy most of the stone tools disappeared from the prehistoric record.

As with all gregarious animals, from the time man first evolved, he has had some sort of social organization. How the social and political organizations, language, and religion evolved we do not know, but we are sure the non-material cultural equipment was evolving along with the material traits with which the archaeologist works. We begin to have evidence of this when early man cooperated to drive large herd animals into swamps for killing and butchering; much later there is more concrete evidence in the food producing stage of evolution and by the time urbanization was achieved, the warp and weft of African culture was set.

And finally, the archaeologist has uncovered the foundations, the very building blocks, upon which all of Africa's cultural heritage has been constructed.

PART II:

Pre-Colonial Society

CHAPTER THREE

Precarious Vision: The African's Perception of His World

Dr. O. U. Kalu
Senior Lecturer, Department of Religion,
University of Nigeria, Nsukka

Very often after arriving at a new place, the dominant feeling is one of being hemmed in. This is quickly followed by attempts to establish familiarity with the new location and, in common parlance, "get to know the place". As soon as familiarity is established, a sense of security is ensured as the mind automatically arranges the new reality in an orderly fashion. One gets to know the survival modes (political and cultural) in the new environment. It is, therefore, a very natural approach to the study of any culture to describe the way people perceive their word.

In fact, communities very assiduously preserve their myths of origin as an explanation of why things are the way they are. There is nothing perculiarly African about this trait. The Jewish version is amply illustrated in the Genesis saga. Old Testament scholars agree that the story of Creation in the Book of Genesis is not the beginning of the history of Israel; that history started when the Jews were already settled in Palestine. Naturally, they wanted to establish who they were and how they came to be there. The story was that their founding ancestor was an Aramean, named Abraham. The saga moves through the sorjourn in Egypt, a miraculous rescue, untold years of wandering in the wilderness (symbolically expressed as forty years) and the settlement in Palestine. The climax of the story, of course, is the miraculous way in which they conquered and settled the land. The explanation was a *covenant* made with Yahweh who supplanted other gods (both Jewish and Palestinian) and became the ONE and TRUE GOD, the source of Jewish uniqueness. The story did not end there. One step backwards, the origin was stretched to the foundation of the whole inhabited earth and the cosmos by the powerful word of mouth of that ONE and TRUE GOD.

The evidence that the story was developed and perpetuated is clear in Deuteronomy 26:5ff. which gives a record of a response to be made in a festival liturgy:

> And you shall make response before the Lord Your God, "A wandering Aramean was my father; and he went into Egypt and sorjourned there, few in number; and there he became a nation, great, mighty, and populous".

And so the myth of origin ran to conclusions which were drawn from it. The basic conclusion was a perception of the world in which God was Supreme and in which the relationships between man and nature and between man to man were governed by the sovereignty of God and His Covenant with men. The conclusions are spelled out in Joshua 24.

If we move nearer home, we find similar accounts. For the Yoruba, it was the enterprising god, Obatala, who first thought of creating a habitable world out of the watering domain of Olokun. Olodumare permitted it and Obatala sorjourned to earth by a chain, landed at Ile-Ife and succeeded in creating a world. However, while on a return trip to the abode of the gods to report his success, jealously enraged Olokun flooded the new earth. The destitute first men had to bargain with shrewd Eshu to carry their message to the Olodumare. Orumnila intervened and the earth was saved. There are variations on the story as details and twists are added as embellishments.

The Igbo tell it a little differently but in an identically incredible vein: the first man came down by a ladder to find a watery, marshy earth. Somehow an Awka smith was sent to use his fiery bellow to dry the earth. The problem was now how to feed the new human beings. Their leader, Eru, was asked to kill his eldest son and daughter and plant their heads. From the head of the son sprouted yam and from the head of the daughter sprouted coco-yam. Eru distributed the new products. Even today, yam is the prince of agricultural products and the yam-growing cycle dominates time reckoning and festivals. Just as an aside, the custom was established that the progeny of Eru, the Nri people, receive free food all over Igboland.

One could multiply the stories from the rest of Africa. The two variations range from myths when the earth and sky were clearly demarcated to those when the sky was once-upon-a-time near to the earth. It is said that a woman touched the sky with her dirty hands and the sky abashedly retreated upwards. Some less chauvinist accounts explain the separation by the evil doings of men which scandalized the sky — the abode of the gods.

It is palpable that as the myth spins out the outlines of a cosmology (which is the impressive term for world-view) emerges. Africa is vast in size, population and varieties of tribes. Myths of origin abound and the varieties in ecology make it possible for different peoples to perceive their worlds differently. It is essential to stress that world-views are the intellectual or rational explanations of the order which undergird human lives and environments. The pattern of this underlying order could be derived from the myths, taboos, customs and proverbs of a community. The functions of world-views are that first they assist man to explain reality. The insecure feeling of being lost in an inexplicable, uncontrollable cosmos is thus taken care of. Secondly, such intellectual ordering of reality makes it possible to predict space-time events and, finally, men can then exert control over these events. Thus, social order, various forms of divinations and the quest for survival and happiness are possible if men understand what makes the world tick and can control such forces. A world-view is the unified picture of the cosmos explained by a system of concepts which order the natural and social rhythms and the place of individuals and communities in them.

From the myriads of cosmologies a model can be constructed representing the basic and common features in Africa. If one must begin by reference to a white man, the German philosopher, Kant, observed that the two basic concepts which encapsules most other experiences are that of Time and Space.

The concept of Time among Africans is currently a subject of debate among scholars. The argument is over the perception of distant Future, or lack of it, in the African mind. Some would, out of nationalistic fervor, wish to argue that Africans conceive of time just as Europeans do in a chronological fashion, moving from the past through the present to the future. Others maintain that the African does not really pay attention to chronometric reckoning of time. Thus, we have developed what is called "African Time" which often means showing up at a function many hours after the appointed time. This last is a moot point. More seriously, it is recognized that Africans conceive Time differently from westerners. To westerners time moves in a continuum or linear fashion thus:

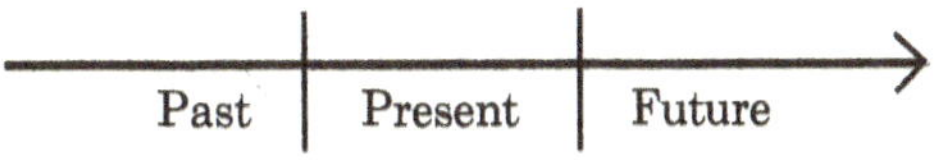

The Greek word for it is *kronos*, hence the English chronometric, chronology, chronometer which are all related to the linear measurement of Time.

Africans, on the contrary, reckon the movement of Time in a cyclical fashion. Perhaps this is derived from the cyclical agricultural seasons. Mircea Eliade has described a form of time-reckoning among non-complex societies as based on the myth of Eternal Return. This myth suffused Greek and Roman thought: the fiery chariot, the Sun, goes down under the sea at the end of a day's journey and rises again bright in the morning. The seasons of the year repeat in an eternal cycle. Non-complex societies perceive in the movements of these natural phenomena the eternal order which governs the universe.

Time is reckoned differently by Africans who measure it in non-abstract terms. It is never nine o'clock in the morning; rather, it is that time when the sun begins to climb to her seat. Time is measured by events. The Greek word is *kairos*. Time, is therefore, humanized and related to specific events. If an African went home to his village and some inquired as to when he returned, he would reply that he came home when the priests of Ifejioku first ate the new yam. The inquirer would recognize the time even though it is definitely non-specific, especially as the ceremony lasts for two native weeks. Time is peopled with events related to the movements of the sun, moon, important events in the lives of the family, clan and village-group and socio-economic events such as market days, etc. It is never abstract.

It is this fact which makes the conception of the future somewhat problematic precisely because events which form the point of reference have not occurred. The future is unreal because they do not contain events. Larger periods are counted by some in terms of successive age sets and are given the names of these age sets. Short-term future is obviously projected but the indefinite future is atrophied. There is a tendency to count backwards; hence the future is assimilated into the past. Christian scholars have explored the effect of this conception of Time on the important concept of Heaven. Scientists have wondered whether this materialistic conception of Time hinders development in theory and innovation in the physical sciences.

African conception of Space is just as problematic. In oral interviews the age preservers of native wisdom may end up pointing to the sky, earth and underground as the abode of the gods. The implications are that there are three dimensions of Space. The Sky is the abode of the Supreme Being and major divinities. The Earth is inhabited by the Earth-Goddess, nature spirits, patron spirits of human activities and ecology and, of course, human beings. In the World Beneath are the ancestors and the guardian spirits of human beings, for instance, *chi* the daemon spirit of the individual. The Earth is invested like a besieged city by evil spirits. These spirits are those of men and women who (a) lived bad lives during their sorjourn to Earth, (b) died "bad deaths" through smallpox, accidents, lightning or any others which are inexplicable, (c) did not receive proper burial rites. In obvious anger they would return to haunt their kin-groups for neglect. A fourth category refers to children who make pacts to visit the earth briefly. The Yoruba call them *abiku* and the Igbo, *ogbanje*. Worship and taboos are designed primarily to protect man from evil forces and to harness the good things of life.

The Supreme Being is the creator of all things, the protector of all beings, and the giver of all goodness. But he is, for the most part, not worshipped directly because other divinities and spirits perform this role. Confusion exists when the African God is a remote god, minding his own business and leaving the earth to ancestral spirits and others. The words in prayers (liturgy) definitely refer to his presence but in few parts of Africa are altars erected for his worship.

In spite of the remarkable awareness of spiritual forces, the African places man at the centre of the universe. He is a noble, rational creature. Yet there is the Job-like irony that his fate is determined by a personal god whom the Igbo call *chi* and the Tallensi, Yin. *Nuor yin* or BAD DESTINY spells failure in life. Man himself is made up of his body, personality, soul, the motivating breath of life or spirit soul, and that important element, blood. The Akan of Ghana with a more precise language structure distinguish between *sunsum* (personality soul) and *'kra* (spirit soul). One conjectures that it is the personality soul which reincarnates. The spirit-soul is the motivating force in life. The blood is like the distributor in a car. The blood also symbolizes the worth of the individual and his link to a kin group. Thus, pacts and expiatory rites are made with blood.

Reincarnation is crucial in understanding the African's perception of man and life. Life flows in a cycle from birth, naming ceremony through puberty rites, marriage, initiations into ascriptive societies, and non-ascriptive or achieved societies, adult roles to death. But death is not a terminus. The personality soul continues to live in the Spirit World until it reincarnates or acquires body again. A new life-sojourn begins. The Spirit World is a Mirror of the Human World with the same topography and similar social organization. Thus, the ancestors are often referred to as the living-dead. As an Aŋlɔ (Ghana) Prayer puts it:

> Grandfather, do you see this water?
> Please take it and give it to Toxla
> that he may pour libation to those
> who are asleep at Tagba.
> This will keep them in the know of all
> that we shall be doing,
> so that whatever we do,
> should bring us peace.

They still take active interest in the human kin-group.

Among the Yoruba, the ancestors come back seasonally during the Egungun Festival to warn human beings of the fate which awaits immorality in the Other World. More important, it is believed that the wealthy man on the Earth will retain his social status in the Spirit World; the same holds true for people of inferior social status. This explains certain bizarre funeral rites such as burying slaves alive with their masters or burying treasures with people of high status. There is none of the egalitarian hopes which Christianity offers all the sojourners to the Life Hereafter.

The ethical implications of such a world-view are immense. For one, the African world-view is predominantly religious; both human life and nature are held sacred, intricably intertwined and under the governance of the Supreme Being and His multifarious divinities. The predominant attitude is that human existence is precarious because of the machinations of evil spirits. In traditional African communities all forms of misfortunes — illness, death, failure — are explained by the activities of ubiquitous evil spirits, angry gods, revengeful ancestors and Destiny-Evil forces operating through man and nature. Thus, lightning, falling trees, animals and rivers could harm or kill the star-struck human. Witches are, in fact, unsuspecting and involuntary agents but sorcerers are more deliberate, voluntary, and ill-disposed.

In our traditional setting, men were faced with uncontrollable forces of nature; their reaction was to imbue these with spirits and to seek the aid of good gods, patron ancestors, magic, divination and elaborate propitiatory rituals as counters to the evil forces. Worship in such settings emphasized the wish of the client. A rotary would variously plead with patron gods, placate evil spirits and end by threatening the god that if he failed to perform, his grove would be overgrown with grass. Afterall, what use could there be in a god or a charm which failed to yield dividends on the amount of energy and money spent on it? The typical attitude is expressed in another Aŋlɔ (Ghana) prayer which asks the ancestors to:

> Please make us all very fruitful
> and give long life and prosperity to us all,
> If anyone wishes death to this lineage
> may he also suffer death.
> The wicked people are like fire
> which must be extinguished
> before the good people enjoy a perfect peace.

This perception of human existence meant that the moral order must be maintained so that men can live in peace and have abundant life.

Our forebears, therefore, constructed a number of controls. The first was to emphasize character. Character was neither beauty nor wealth. Admittedly, beauty and success in framing, hunting and trading were regarded as a favourable nod from the gods and were rewarded with titles.

Character however, referred to moral uprightness, peace with gods and peace with men. Purity was essential in blocking the anger of gods or the ruin of evil spirits. Hence, seasonal festivals included purification rites and the onslaught of epidemics, a bad harvest, or incessant disasters were countered with divination and special purification rites. Secondly, they devised elaborate taboos which spelt out the bounds of acceptable behaviour in the economic, political and social lives of the community. A host of ritual officials underwent formal and informal training to mediate on behalf of the community because purity and proper ritual techniques were considered essential for the efficacy. Careless ritual or immoral behaviour nullified the

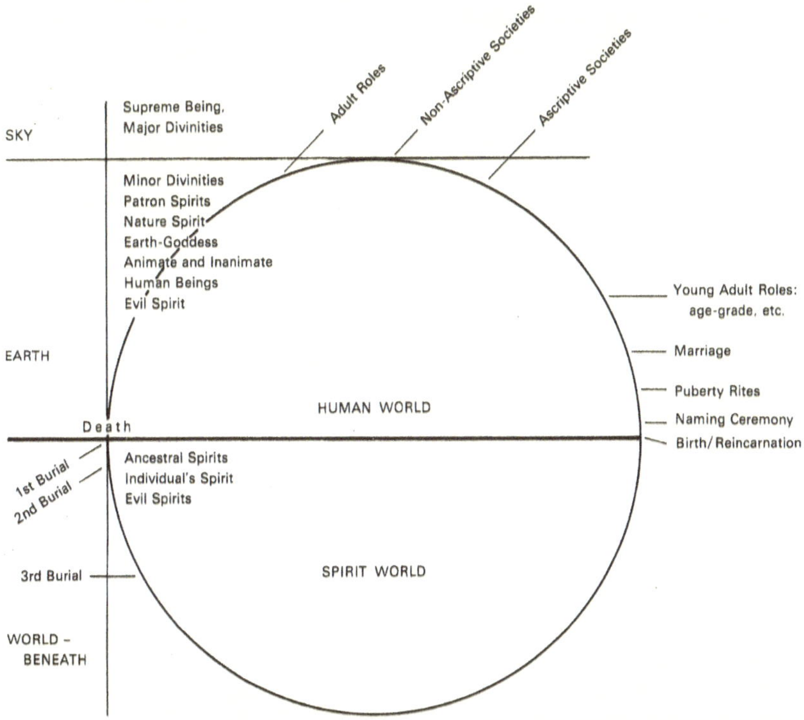

Diagrammatic representation of the African world-view.

action and endangered the life of the officiant. An inexplicable thunder could kill the offending priest.

In conclusion, the African perceived his world as a moral order, one in which his well-being or failure could be determined by the inscrutable will of the gods. He did not reject the gods by an assertion of humanity and thereby, as Prometheus, damning them. Rather, he evolved elaborate rituals and taboos with which he sought to manipulate the good gods for protection and abundant life. Human existence, in spite of occasional joys, was perceived as being precarious.

CHAPTER FOUR

Gods as Guests: Music and Festivals in African Traditional Societies

Dr. E. P. Modum
Department of Languages,
University of Nigeria, Nsukka

One of the things that first strike the ethnographer about African traditional societies is the sheer numerical importance of ritual festivals and ceremonies. Indeed it has been said that the earliest Europeans who came to Africa were so struck by the number and frequency of such ceremonies that they thought our people had nothing else to do. The truth is that every human society has its peculiar norms which not only characterize it but which determine the life of its members. In traditional African societies, this role is played by the festivals and ritual ceremonies.

Busia writes that among the people of Ghana

> Rituals surround important seasonal community activities as well as the critical periods of an individual's life. Planting, harvesting and fishing, birth, puberty, marriage – these are occasions for the community or kin group to come together, to join in song and dance or in ritual to give expression to the sense of dependence on the ancestors or on other supernatural powers.[1]

It will be seen in the course of this discussion that Busia's remark about Ghanaian societies can apply to most traditional black African societies. It is, of course, impossible to undertake in the context of this short study a complete morphological study of ritual festivals in all traditional African societies. Such a study would require volumes and would demand enquiries into a vast number of monographies dealing with the concept of the sacred in every society. Specific cases, however, do tell us much about the general characteristics and social functions of festivals. It is hoped that the sample presented here is broad enough to validate conclusions.

Whether it is the *Damba* festival widely performed in Northern Ghana[2]

[1] Cited by A. A. Opoku in *Festivals of Ghana* (Accra, Ghana Pub. Corporation, 1970).
[2] *Ibid*.

or the fishing festivals of the Kalabari of Nigeria[3] whether it is the *Ekurole, Obatala, Egungun, Ogun, Oranyan,* and *Ifa* rituals of the Ede people of Old Oyo[4] or the *Ekpe* festival among the Ngwa and the rest of Southeastern Igboland (Amankulor, *Ikenga,* 1972), whether it is the New Yam festival among the Igbos of Old Onitsha Province or the *Adae, Odwira* and *Apo* ceremonies of the Ashanti and Brong areas of Ghana, the social and moral life in African traditional societies should be seen to be organized around festive manifestations which fulfill the function of social and moral control as well as provide entertainment and diversion. These ceremonies are therefore important as indicators of group interests and values and various aspects of social life.

To understand the traditional African's psychological concept of life and the world we must differentiate between him and the so-called modern, "civilized" man. The present "space age" with its gigantic advances in science and technology and the ever dominant struggle for economic power in the world, have made of the modern man a non-believer and a materialist. For him, there are no more bounds to what science and technology can achieve. He considers science and technology capable of providing satisfactory answers to nearly all his problems. Dreams do not have much importance in his life because few things are now beyond his reach. The concept of a supernatural Being, the ultimate cause and explanation of the universal order, makes little sense to him. The only thing that really make sense to him is economic power and superiority which can be achieved by making fresh break-throughs in science and technology. The modern man's god is science and his religion is economics.

It is not so for the traditional African who remains basically a religious being. The traditional African believes strongly in the existence of a Being or beings whose wishes he must conform with and whose experiences he must emulate. In other words, he accepts that his existence in the world has a spiritual dimension, that there is some kind of Force which determines, as it were, the sense of his life and that he cannot afford to ignore this Force. While he lives, there are certainly some of his actions that involve only his superficial physical person, such as eating, conversing and quarrelling. But there are other actions of his which are more essential, metaphysical; there are situations in which he does not feel so free to act as he pleases, in which

[3] Horton, *Nigeria* Special Edition, Lagos, 1960 and O. Fubara, *Nigeria*, Lagos, 1974.

[4] U. Beier, "A Year of Sacred Festivals in One Yoruba Town," *Nigeria*, Special Edition, Lagos, 1959.

he feels an obligation to conform. This is the realm of taboos and moral restraints. Here he can very easily err and commit what the Igbo people call "alu" or "ememe". This sphere of his existence is associated with the sacred realm and the gods. It is this second sphere of existence that interests us here.

The traditional African visualizes life and the world as a whole in the context of his relationship with the sacred realm. More precisely, the essence and continuation of social life are guaranteed through well-determined and periodical contacts with the deities during which the society not only renews its faith in the gods but also reiterates the essential factors of life and death. We shall see in the later part of this paper what forms these periodic contacts take and the role they play in ensuring social and economic harmony in a traditional African community.

An important corollary to this perception of the sacred in a traditional African society, is the society's concept of life as a cosmic cycle or what Mircea Eliade calls the myth of eternal return. What is a myth? Put very simply, a myth is constituted by a set of human beliefs and behaviour, sometimes accompanied by rituals, which tend to emphasize the spiritual rather than the material aspect of man.

When we refer to myth, we are no longer on the superficial level of human existence but rather, we are grappling with its spiritual and essential significance. Myth embodies the strong beliefs of man that he is part of a spiritual unity, a cosmic entity. When a defenseless man charged by a ferocious tiger runs to save his life, we find it easy to understand this simple defence mechanism. When a man, or any living organism for that matter, is hungry, he eats. It is also easy for us to understand this natural law. But when a devout Christian has his personal sorrow mitigated during Christmas or Easter, when he feels emotional relief and sublime comfort upon hearing the priest pronounce the words "lift up your hearts", when the animist finds emotional bliss in communicating with his dead ancestors through sacrifice, the psychological bases of such activities are less obvious to us. Natural laws and pure logic no longer can be applied and this is so because we are now dealing with myths. Myths provide man with "something to hold to", they are fixed points of security in a world of bewildering changes and disappointments.

As Malinowski beautifully puts it: "Myth is an active force. Myth is a constant by-product of living faith which is in need of miracles; of sociological status which demands precedent; of moral rule which requires sanction".[5]

[5] Cited by C. Kluckholm in "Myths and Rituals: A General Theory" in J. B. Vickery, ed., *Myth and Literature* (Lincoln: Nebraska University Press, 1966), p. 39.

This is why eminent sociologists and historians of religions such as Eliade, Cassirer and Caillois, have insisted that "myths are primarily emotional in origin, and that their function is essentially practical and social, namely, to promote a feeling of unity or harmony between the members of a society as well as a sense of harmony with the whole of nature or life".[6] Mythical thought is principally concerned to deny and negate the fact of death and to affirm the unbroken unity and continuity of life.

This brings us to the explanation of Eliade's myth of eternal return or to the notion of a cosmic cycle. Eliade's thesis is developed along this line: in the beginning, there were supernatural beings who created the world and all that lives in it (cosmogony and anthropogony). Since this act of creation which took place at a primordial time, other significant events have taken place which have had extremely deterministic effects on the world and its creatures. For example, there were events which led to man becoming mortal as well as those which led to his adopting agriculture as a means of survival and livelihood. These events are therefore of vital importance to contemporary man. They too took place at a time that man could not recall — so they are mythical events. The result is that what man is today is a function not only of the initial act of creation "in the beginning", but also of the intervening mythical events that took place *in illo tempore.*

Therefore, man, as he is today, is a direct product of these conjugated mythical events. If he is mortal, it is because something happened at some unrecorded time in history to make that possible. If this event had not taken place, man would not be mortal today and could have been enjoying an indefinite existence just as the rocks for instance, or he could have had the power to renew himself periodically like the snakes, that is to say, he would have been able to begin again indefinitely. But the myth of the origin of death tells us what happened at that time and in relating the incident, it explains why man is mortal.

In the same way, if the people of a tribe live on fishing today, it is because at one mythical time in the course of history, a supernatural Being taught their ancestors how to catch and cook fish. The myth will tell the story of the first fishing expedition by the supernatural Being and how he taught human beings to perform this act. We are therefore provided with an explanation as to why the tribe should make their living in this way.

The same kind of mythical explanation can apply to farming in a predominantly agricultural society and palm wine tapping in a palm wine produc-

[6] D. Bidney, "Myth, Symbolism and Truth," in J. B. Vickery, ed., p. 9.

ing area. What all this means is that the traditional African feels that, in performing these essential activities that determine his existence such as farming, fishing, wine tapping, he is repeating acts performed by supernatural beings at different mythical times and, since these acts were all part of creation, he feels that by repeating them he is participating in creation. In other words, he sees in the performance of these acts a way of integrating himself in the cosmogonic pattern.

Further along this line, the world acquires for him a cosmic unity and he sees himself as a part of it. Each time he farms or fishes, it seems to him that he is performing a sacred act of re-creation. His existence is, therefore, marked by a series of such recreation. Also, if he is a farmer, he knows that each planting season is followed by a harvest season which, in turn, is followed by another planting season and this goes on indefinitely. If he is a fisherman, he knows that there are seasons when the tide favours his catches and others when it is less favourable and that these seasons succeed each other indefinitely. If he is a palm wine trapper, he does not ignore the fact that the quality of palm wine is better in some seasons than in others or that there are times when he will find his gourd full and times when it will remain dry. This means that seasons succeed each other indefinitely and each season comes and goes only to come back again. This is what the myth of eternal return means. The life of the traditional African is ordered around this cyclical view of the world; there are seasons for clearing the ground, for planting, for harvesting, for resting, for eating, for merry-making and the whole cycle begins again.

For the traditional African, the cyclical conception of life and the need for man to participate in the mythical acts of creation is symbolized by the agricultural or seasonal cycle. Among the majority of Igbos and Yorubas, for example, the New Yam festival is considered the most important event of the seasonal cycle. This is certainly because of the elaborate myth built around the origin of the yam crop among the Igbo and Yoruba people. Sociologically, this means that all other festivals of the agricultural cycle are seen as minor ceremonies of initiation or recreation which serve the important purpose of keeping the people busy while they wait for the yam harvest and the period of abundance. Among the Ogidi people and all the surrounding Igbo areas, for example, the seasonal year starts with the *Ifejioku* festival which is the beginning of the planting of yam and ends with the *Iwaji* which is the eating of New Yam. Between these there are such recreational and ritual festivals as the *Mgba Agbogho* (for women), *Nwafor* (for men), *Afa na Aguu* (for medicine men), *Alom chi* (for married women) and *Akaotite* (for all). These festivals, which are all conceived in function of the New Yam festival, are used to re-enact the process of re-creation and regeneration of the cosmos.

In the riverine areas of Nigeria, where fishing is the predominant occupation of the people, the same pattern of ceremony is performed not to the Yam gods but to the Water maids. What this means is that the concept of God in a traditional African society is functional; it is the needs, preoccupations and aspirations of the society that determine the gods it creates for itself. This functional concept also explains the proliferation of gods among traditional Africans.

It is important to say at this point that the notion of regeneration is by no means peculiar to traditional African societies or to the under-developed "Third World" as we deduce from Eliade. As a matter of fact, it is not difficult to see that such yearly Christian celebrations and seasons as Advent, Lent, Easter and Christmas are guided by the same strong belief in the process of regeneration among devout members of the Christian community.

It is a fact that Western European civilization owes a great deal to the Alchemists, and although Western Europe and America cannot now be said to live in an age of alchemy, much of their thinking is still permeated by the alchemists' principle of regeneration through the transformation of metals. What Eliade could have made us believe more easily is that, since Christianity and alchemy are not modern developments, the notion of cosmic recreation and regeneration should be associated with archaic societies of all races and disassociated from the modern areligious man. In other words, there are as many believers in regeneration in the "Third World" as there may be elsewhere, just as there can be as many modern men in the "Third World" as there are in the Western countries.

This point gives more relevance to the distinction we made in our introduction between the modern man and the traditional African. Thus we see that the same principle that characterizes the coronation of a new king in India guides the enthronment of a new Pharaoh in pre-Nasser Egypt and determines the consecration of a new king or queen in England. The idea is that the consecration of a new ruler represents the creation of a new epoch and ensures the continuation of harmony in the society; that is to say, it is a way of participation in the creation of the universe. This is why in each of these places, a king is considered a symbol, the centre around which the society turns; he is ontologically identical with the creater.[7]

In general, traditional African festivals are characterized by music and dances. Music is provided with such traditional instruments as the drum,

[7] M. Eliade, *Aspects du Mythe* (Paris: Gallimard, 1963), p. 54.

native flute, gong, balafon, kora and native guitar. Dancing is perfomed by men or women or in some cases by both sexes depending on the festival and the society. Cult priests and griots play a leading role with incantations and consultations of oracles. They serve as a link between man and the dieties. There is general euphoria and collective paroxysm as man invites the gods as his guests.[8] As Roheim beautifully explains, "the main actors in these mythic festivals are divine".[9] Humans form the crowd and, where they have to participate as actors, they must become superhumans.

In his article on the Kalabari of Nigeria, Horton describes how their social, religious and economic life is arranged around a number of festivals grouped at the end of the cyclical year. Though *Tamuno* and *So* are divine persons for the Kalabari, their divinity is conceived in the abstract sense. Therefore, while the people easily attribute the origin and course of the universe to *Tamuno* and *So*, they venerate in their festivals lesser but more relevant gods, the superior beings, who have a direct influence on man's immediate environment. These superior mythical beings are the *Oru*, the *Owu* and the *Duen*.

The *Oru* are considered to be examplary mythical beings who participated in one way or the other in founding the villages. Every *Oru* is deemed to have been at one mythical time or another, an expert in a particular human activity – dancing, drumming, singing, fishing, waging war, curative medicine – which he perfected and revealed to the rest of the community.

The *Owu*, on the other hand, are believed to be directly in control of those natural elements such as waves and water levels which are considered to be beyond the control of human skills. For example, each *Owu* is associated with a particular creek and all those who fish there must seek to be protected by this god if they are to succeed.

The *Duen* are departed but powerful spirits of dead ancestors who are supposed to have continued to exist but on the immaterial plane. They are believed to have kept their characters and the values they held in their lifetime and to participate actively in the life of the society. During the festivals, ritual dramatisations are performed to commemorate the *Oru*, *Owu* and *Duen*; the people thank them for all the good things they have done for them in the passing year, pray for more good things in the coming year, and demand protection from evil. Sacrifices are offered, praise songs are chanted in memory of the gods, human actors such as *Feni be So* Ojoye Adumu and Ekaki go through

[8] The title of this paper is taken from a monograph, "The Gods as Guests" by R. Horton, *Nigeria Magazine*, Special Edition (Lagos, 1960).

[9] G. Roheim, "Myth and Folktale," in J. B. Vickery, ed., p. 25.

sequences of behaviour which typify the characters and attitudes of the gods, thus reiterating the presence of the deities among them. These gods provide the meaningful explanation and control of every situation in the material world and, since the festivals are grouped at the end of every cyclical year, they are seen as symbols of the regeneration of society.

Ulli Beier describes the cycle of sacred festivals among the people of Ede in old Oyo. These festivals include Ekurole, Obatala, Egungun, Ogun, Oranyan and Ifa.

The Ekurole festival is reserved to the members of the secret Ogboni society. The ceremonies are in honour of Mother Earth as a deity and Beier tells us a myth built around this deity:

> The earth and the sky were once hunting together. They killed only a small rat. They began to fight with each other as to who should have the spoil. When they could not agree with each other, earth refused to bring forth any crops and there was famine. Then all the Orisa (gods) together went to heaven and persuaded him to submit.[10]

We are told that during the ceremonies, sacred chants are sung and incantations are pronounced by cult members led by the chief priest of Ogboni, the Oluwo.

The Obatala festival comes a few days after the Ekurole and is celebrated in honour of the sky god. Obatala is the father of all the other gods, the creator of mankind, and the giver of rain. His chief priest is Ajagemo. Obatala works by the process of possession and during the state of possession, the worshipper is ontologically transformed and becomes an embodiment of the spiritual ideals represented by the god. Goats are offered in sacrifice by the Ajagemo, drums are beaten, prayers are said for more rains and women sing ancient songs that recount the attributes of Obatala:

> He takes from the one who has and gives to him who
> has not. He takes one man and makes two hundred
> out of him.
> Everywhere, everybody is looking at him.
> He is the one who feeds us all . . .

All these activities are meant to create an atmosphere favourable for worshippers to come near their god.

The Egungun festival comes in June and is characterized by numerous masquerades each with its drummers and dancers. The spirits of dead ances-

[10] U. Beier, "A Year of Sacred Festivals in One Yoruba Town."

tors are worshipped here. The belief is that the spirit of a human being never dies and that it continues to influence the life of the community from another sphere after it has left the physical body. Each Egun represents the spirit of a particular ancestor and worshippers are expected to pay special tribute and desist from incurring the wrath of the ancestors by contravening the accepted moral principles of the society. There is no better example of gods taking up physical form in order to come down and participate in the activities of men.

The characteristic features of these festivals include a marked desire to associate by means of dances, musical performances, prayer, incantations and sacrifices with the persons of the gods and the spirits of the ancestors and with the life of the community. There is also a strong belief that in so doing, the community ensures the continuity of its existence through the process of periodical regeneration. The Egungun festival re-enacts the accepted fact that it is the gods who underwrite the moral bases of the human community; taboos and customs, moral codes and social ethics are not products of the capricious whims of rulers but are sanctioned by the gods. Obligations are, therefore, religious demands. The same thing can be said for the *Amarun Yanyan* performed by the members of the *Osanyin* cult to invite the god of medicine to dominate man's conduct and bestow his grave on society.

Among the Ngwa people and the rest of South-eastern Igboland, the Ekpe festival is a very important yearly event. It is the culmination of a series of seven religious festivals ranged along the agricultural cycle.[11] These festivals include the *Ikpa-Unwu* (April), the *Ira-Ugu* (June), the *Iwa-ji* (July), the *Igba-ogbom* (August-September), the *Itu-aka* (October and November), the *Ize-mmuo* (November) and, finally, the Ekpe (December). *Ikpa Unwu* festival comes after the planting season and is dedicated to the patron gods who protect the people from famine while the yams are in the soil.

Ira-Ugu (eating of both the pumpkin and the pumpkin leaves) is a ceremony of hope when women begin to harvest alternative foodstuff for succour while waiting for new yams. On a fixed day, each family cooks large quantities of pumpkin which is generously doled out to everybody. Soon comes *Iwa-ji*, the yam harvesting festival. The first yam is sliced by the chief priest of each compound who dedicates the new yam to *Njoku* or *Ifejioku*, the patron of yam-farmers. There is general merriment because people are now free from famine and hunger. The *Igba-Ogbom* is one of such merriments. Dancing is done to excellent music produced at the shrine, *Ogbom*, and the best artists

[11] J. N. Amankulor, "Ekpe festivals as Religious Ritual and Dance Drama," *Ikenga* I/2 (July, 1972), pp. 35—47.

compete for supremacy. This is folowed by *Itu-Aka*, a thanksgiving and prayer ceremony. Each family priest sacrifices he-goats and cocks to the ancestral gods to ask them for protection during the coming year and reprimands them for the misfortunes of the passing year.

Ize-Mmuo is of greater religious and ritualistic significance. During this ceremony, the chief priest of the village goddess, *Alumerechi*, must be chosen. If chosen, he must represent the entire village for the next year. The choice is made by consultation with the oracle of *Alumerechi*. To be chosen to serve *Alumerechi* means to be transformed ontologically, to shed one's physical body and assume enormous spiritual responsibility. This process is painful. Once chosen, the incumbent must die symbolically in the greater interest of larger community. The sense is clear and typically mythical: to die in order to be better born again. Through the physical mortification of one man, the community ensures its spiritual regeneration. It is significant that from Amankulor's report, the dialogue which takes place during the consultation with *Alumerechi* is done in the form of songs accompanied by the gong:

Eze Dibia:

Alumerechi, anyi abiala!
Onye nwe ala Umuode,
Futa gwa anyi ihe bu uche ghi.
Ura churu anyi l'anyasi,
Anya di anyi l'ama,
Biko, gwa anyi uche ghi.

Alumerechi:

Ekelee m unu umu m
Unu emee-la!
Ije unu abughi i je ọjọọ
Ama m ihe di unu l'obi, —
Onye yara Alumerechi gi-ibi.

Translation:

Nze Dibia:

Alumerechi we have come!
The owner of Umuode-land,
Come out and divine for us
Sleep forsook us last night
We are very expectant,
Please tell us your mind.

Alumerechi's voice:

Greetings my children!
I owe you thanks

Your visit is not a bad one,
I know the contents of your mind, –
A servant for Alumerechi.[12]

After this musical dialogue, *Alumerechi* emerges and names her elect who follows her into the shrine.

The Ekpe, the last of the religious ritual year is essentially a dance-drama. But it is also a ceremony of spiritual cleansing. The choir is led by the "epheboi" and he leads the people in praise songs and dances to *Alumerechi* and the village ancestors. For example, in the entry dance, the "epheboi" chants the following lines:

Alumerechi ndi Umuode . . .
Akwuwa nwa Wipi . . .
Chigbu nwa Enyia . . .
Ndi gbara ekpe la mbu
Anyi Afuwala ama . . .
Duru-nu anyi ga-wa . . .
Alili eleghi Umuode . . .

After each line the chorus comes in with the refrain:

Ehe – e n-ye
Ehe – e n-ye

Translation:

Alumerechi of Umuode people
Akwuwa the son of mpi
Chigbu the son of Enyia
Chief actors of Ekpe in the past
We are moving to the square
Lead us on to arrive
Shame shall never touch Umuode.

Apart from the entry dance movement, there are other dance movements during which different activities of the society are dramatized and prayers offered to the gods. Once again we find that all the festivals of the Ekpe cycle offer a typical example of the strong desire by a traditional African society to have the gods participate directly in the material, moral and spiritual life of the community. Quite significant in this connection is the role of the comic anti-masque. He satirizes the society in such a way people can laugh at

[12] *Ibid.*, pp. 35–47.

themselves. For instance, a recent performance by the anti-masque figure called *Ụdụ* (a description of his/her ragged looks) was a commentary on the increasing pursuit of wealth and the baneful erosion of communal values by the new Nigerian money naira and kobo. The *ụdụ* therefore, yelled questions and answers at the onlookers:

> nwanyi turu ime,
> o ga'mu gini -- e -- e?
> naira na kobo
> ma-a, ma-a, ma-a, ma-a!
>
> If a woman gets pregnant nowadays,
> what will she deliver?
> Naira and kobo
> ma-a, ma-a, ma-a, ma-a (which could be the bleeting of sheep indicating that the society has become quite sheepish in their sense of direction and scale of priorities).

To move briefly outside Nigeria for examples, the Akan people of Ghana have the *Adae* cycle comprised of nine festivals, each of which is in commemoration of a god or in respect of the spirit of a departed chief or an important ancestor. Some of these are the *Odwira*, the Yam festival and the deer-hunt festival.[13] Each reflects the dominant socio-economic concern of the communities.

In East and Central Africa, notes Brelsford,[14] traditional dances performed during ritualistic festivals are essentially an expression of man's participation in the cosmic control of the world. When such ritual dances are performed,

> the self can be lost and the urges of the subconcious acted in ecstatic movements; consciousness may go and the mind awaits spiritual possession from another world; unseen powers are propriated; and concord and harmony instilled in the community.[15]

We cannot agree more. Nor do we consider as far-fetched the sociological approach to historical interpretation which T. O. Ranger adopts in his book, *Dance and Society in Eastern Africa*. Ranger's method seeks to provide satisfactory explanation to the "colonial situation" in some East African

[13] A. A. Opoku, Festivals of Ghana.

[14] W. V. Brelsford, *African Dances of N. Rhodesia* (Salisbury: Livingstone Museum, 1948), p. 3.

[15] *Ibid.*, p. 3.

countries by studying the role and evolution of the Bini dance which is of great social importance among the people of the East Coast of Africa.

We can conclude that, in a society that had none of the modern recreational facilities such as television, cinema and tennis, festivals were bound to be an important element of diversion and relaxation as well as a means of social interaction. In terms of the moral values of society, they also played a regulatory role and constituted the best expression of the African's desire to communicate with his gods and ancestors, to take part in the process of cosmic regeneration and harmony. Festive life perpetuated certain values of the traditional society, even guaranteed its survival. During these festivals, the traditional African society truly celebrated itself, its cohesiveness, and affirmed its belief system.

Bibliography

Apart from essays, articles and monographs mentioned in the reference:

1. Rangers, T. O., *Dance and Society in Eastern Africa 1890—1970*. London: Heineinann, 1975.
2. Eliade, M., *Aspects du myths*. Paris: Gallimard, 1963.
3. Eliade, M., *Le mythe de l'eternel retour*, Paris: Les Essais, 1949.
4. Caillois, R., *L'homme et le sacre*. Paris: Gallimard, 1950.

CHAPTER FIVE

African Traditional Literature

Prof. D. I. Nwoga
Department of English,
University of Nigeria, Nsukka

In 1963, at an International conference on African Literature and the Universities, I mentioned in conversation with a newspaper editor of high standing that I was organizing a course on African traditional literature. His response to the suggestion was a scornful question as to whether there existed in African traditions anything of any interest beyond a few trickster stories of the tortoise or the spider.

His ignorance was excusable. What material had been published on the subject was hidden in erudite journals and in out-of-print books and exclusive archives.[1] At the present time, Africans who have grown up and been educated in Africa certainly do not qualify to be forgiven if they are ignorant of African traditions of literary excellence.

Literature in African Traditions

The question as to what is considered literature in African tradition arises because though most people would readily acknowledge folktales as literature, Africans do not have a corpus of verbal expressions which they conceptualize as literature. Moreover, for the people, the imagination was *a way of life* rather than an exclusive *area of life*. The aesthetic experience was democratic and pervasive, not a specific structure of experience for a leisure class. In

[1] To take the Igbo example, Northcote W. Thomas's *Anthropological Report on the Ibo-Speaking Peoples of Nigeria*. Published in 1973 had two volumes of its six devoted to Proverbs, Narratives and Grammar of Igbo. This book was out of print until 1969. G. T. Basden's *Among the Ibos of Nigeria* (1921) has its chapter XXVI reproducing "Fables – Folklore – Proberbs", and his *Niger Ibos* (1938) has Chapter XXX on "Fireside Stories". These were both out of print until 1966. Various journal publications by N. W. Thomas, J. M. W. Jeffries and M. M. Green in *Man, Africa*, etc. were even less available.

practical terms this means that creative verbal usage has part of the processes of religious and social communication (just as music was to be found in communal occasions and visual arts in religious and functional contexts). In modern technical terminology, this would be called "minor" as distinct from "major" art, that is, art as skill and craft rather than art as art. But then the fact of functionality did not deprive these creative verbal performances of formal artistic characteristics. Those who have achieved some distancing from the intrinsicality and homogeneity of aesthetic experience and moved into the formal awareness of the separation of literature from its contexts are in a position to appreciate where literature is to be found in African life.

A recent novel by the Kenyan Ngugi Thiongo, *Petals of Blood*[2] helps immensely in this context by presenting us with several examples of the imaginative life of traditional Africa. The novel is an intensely socialist oriented exposition of the painful transition of a rural pastoral community in Kenya into an urban centre. The simple village folk are progressively humiliated and dispossessed by big business and the new African middle class. One of the facets of the pastoral state which Ngugi presents with loving detail is the imaginative element.

A first example is that of children's play and song while looking after one another. A group of three children, "flies swarming around the sore eyes and mucus-blocked noses", becomes a handsome trio; one rocked a crying baby strapped on the back; the third would pat-pat the crying baby to the rhythm with a rocking lullaby:

> Do not cry, our little one.
> Whoever dares beat our little one,
> May he be cursed with thorns in his flesh,
> If you stop crying, child of our mother,
> She will soon come home from the fields
> And bring you gitete-calabash of milk. (p. 24).

In another example we have the spontaneous song of joy at moments of excitement, a combination of words, music and dance. An old woman Nyakinyua has her grand-daughter, Wanja, return in glory and beauty from town (where she had actually been a bar-maid and prostitute). The village is agog with excitement and Nyakinyua is full of happiness:

> Nyakinyua broke into Gitiro, for which she had once been famous in Ilmorog and beyond: she sang in a low voice in praise of Ndemi and his wives,

[2] Heinemann Educational Books Ltd., 1977.

> long long ago. The other women chimed in at intervals with ululations. Soon we were all singing and dancing, children chasing one another in the shadows, the old men and women occasionally miming scenes from Ilmorog's great past . . . (pp. 31–32)

The harvest failed in Ilmorog for two years in a row and the people were threatened with a famine. A decision was taken that the whole village should travel to the capital town to present their problem to their member of parliament who had never come to Ilmorog except to take their vote. This was a long, tedious, hazardous journey on foot over many miles and days. As they got ready to set out for the journey, Abdulla, "a sour-faced cripple" of a shopkeeper, was transformed and began to be cheerful and entertain the children:

> They surrounded him and he told them stories:
> Once upon a time Ant and Louse had an argument. Each boasted that he could beat the other in dancing Kibata . . . And so . . . Ant had no waist and Louse had no nose. He told them how Chameleon defeated Hare in a race; Why Hyena limped; how Death came to the world; of the woman who was lured into marrying a wicked ogre – and the children were insatiable in their cries for more. (p. 117)

Ngugi tells us how, during the journey to town, Nyakinyua talked to the villages "keeping up their spirits with stories of the past", and how, in that past, legends in song constituted a medium for the training of the young, especially during good harvest periods. During such seasons:

> the people would gather in groups, according to ages, and dance from village to village, spilling into Ilmorog plains, *hymning praises to their founders* . . . Sitting round the family tree in the front yard the aged would sip honey beer and tell the children, with voices taut with prideful authority, and nostalgia, about the founding patriarch. (p. 120)

During the journey there is also a remembering of the more recent past of Kenya, of the Mau Mau freedom fighters and here too we find another form of traditional literature, the song of war and protest. We see that when the freedom fighters met in the bush they rallied themselves by singing "in defiant tones and their one voice was like a roll of thunder":

> And you traitors to your people,
> Where will you run to
> When the brave of the lands gather?
> For Kenya is black people's country.

> Where will traitors run to
> When the clouds roll away
> And the brave return?
> For Kenya is an African people's country. (p. 142)

When the villagers finally reached the city, they found that their M. P. was only worried that this delegation must be an attempt by his political enemies to besmear his image. He had no solutions to their problems but offered them a lecture on democratic freedom and birth control. One of the leaders of the delegation, Abdulla talked to the M. P. in the parable of a folk-tale:

> Hare and Antelope once fell into a hole. Let me climb on your back first, then I shall pull you out, said Hare. So Hare climbed on Antelope's back and out he jumped onto dry sunny ground. He dusted himself up and started walking away. Hey, you are forgetting me, shouted Antelope. Hare lectured Antelope. Let me advise you, my friend. I fell into the same hole with you by mistake. The trouble with you, Mr. Antelope, is that you go jump-jumping leap-leaping in the air instead of firmly walking on the ground and looking to see where you are going. I am sorry but you have only yourself to blame. (p. 179)

The trip yielded strange results. The next year, the harvest was doubly excellent and there was a harvest festival which is described by Ngugi in terms which show an intensity of dramatic performance and involvement that can hardly be excelled in any modern theatre (pp. 207–210).

The novel contains more examples of literature, but I believe enough has been quoted already. All that has been illustrated from *Petals of Blood* could be duplicated from Achebe's *Arrow of God*[3] and Ngugi has publicly

[3] From the early sections alone of *Arrow of God* we have the following examples:
– the legend of Nwanyieke, the old woman deity. "Every Eke day before cockcrow she appears in the market place with a broom in the right hand and dances round the vast open space, beckoning with the broom in all directions of the earth and drawing folk from every land." This was to explain why Eke Okperi was such a big popular market and the story was told by Akukalia of Umuaro whose mother was from Okperi. (p. 23)
– The fairy tale about the man who thought himself such an excellent wrestler that he did not stop even when he had beaten spirits. He insisted on wrestling with the best of the best. So the spirits gave him his *Chi* "a little viry spirit who seized him with one hand and smashed him on the stony earth." This story was used by Ezeulu in explaining what happened to Akukalia in Okperi and in blaming the elders who had not been as good as the wrestler's flute player who had at least asked the wrestler to desist at some point.
– The Ogalanya masquerade at the Idemili festival. Ogalanya was the Man of Riches bedecked with mirrors and rich clothes of many colours. The boastful monologue of the masquerade is reproduced in the novel and related to events in the society that year with dramatic relevance. (p. 48)

acknowledged his debt to Achebe's inspiration. What I have tried to establish from the illustrations is that though the concept of literature started from an etymology of writing so that literature literally means written material,[4] there are, in traditional and rural Africa, certain oral performances which are imaginatively presented and which belong to literature in its modern meaning as an imaginative act of verbalisation. The examples also illustrate the various contexts and uses and qualities or oral traditional literature which I will now proceed to classify, expand, and illustrate.

At this point it is necessary to explain why there is this insistence on the oral when talking of traditional African literature. It is true that much African traditional literature is now collected and published.[5] But though this literature by this process becomes available to us in the written form it was oral in its conception and execution. There is also a growing body of literature written in the indigenous languages of Africa. But these are modern in their forms, contents, and characteristics rather than traditional. There did exist, however, some indigenous African scripts with which a tradition of African written literature could have been started. In other words, some African groups did have symbols which some people could write and thereby produce literature in the original sense. Two such scripts were developed in Liberia, the *Vai* script and the *Bassa* script.[6]

The *Vai* Script has an interesting story of origin and development. In 1816, Dualu Bukele, a messenger for a European, was deeply impressed by the mystery that a piece of paper could convey a message between people.

> He sat up night after night fasting and journeying, just to unravel the mystery. One night while Bukele was wrapped up in a dream a person draped in white appeared before him and said, "Dualu, I have brought you a Script with which you, too, can now write your language". (p. 378)

Dualu woke up with the script vigorously impressed in his consciousness and wrote down the items. He was aided by his friends to make up the characters for any sounds he could not remember. The people set up a

[4] It is in this sense that a student of, say geography, in writing up a project would be expected to start by reviewing the *literature* of the topic, i.e. the reports, essays and books already available on the subject.

[5] From Nigeria alone we have the following easily available texts: Umeasiegbu R. N. *The way we lived*. Heinemann, 1969.

[6] cf. Bai T. Moore, "Liberia's Contribution to the Science on Communication." New African *Literature and the Arts*, III, pp. 377–389.

school six months later "which was attended by almost every ambitious young man of the area". International interest in this script reached the point of the script and language being included in the University of Hamburg African Language Seminar in 1924. The Script is still in use.

The *Bassah Vah* script does not have the same elaborate origin and development. The *Bassah Vah* system originally consisted of "signs, codes and symbols used to convey ideas, thoughts, emotions as well as to give instructions. All forms of bodily movement winking, clearing of the throat, nodding and so on, were considered by the Bassah to mean "throwing Vah'". The next step was the use of leaves on which symbols had been bitten with the teeth. Later these symbols were scribbled on barks of trees and on animal skins. In 1910, a Bassah medical man, Dr. Thomas Lewis, transferred these symbols onto a more durable form. Through his instrumentality, a printing press was designed with which materials in the language could be printed.

Though some books have been written in these scripts, they have usually been transcriptions from the vernacular oral stories and proverbs.

Some other scripts have also been invented and discovered in Africa,[7] but one must come to Nigeria to the *Nsibidi* which is the Igbo contribution to this art. This was a secret society system of symbols — an extensive body of symbols examples of which are now being investigated and written down. It is practically established by scholars that the Script was originated for religious usage among the Ekoi of the Ogoja area but it has been extensively developed among the Igbo secret societies such as the Ekpe and Okonko. Though it was apparently capable of being used as a medium for other forms of communication and was actually used at some time intensively for symbolism between lovers, these other usages did not develop and what we have left are the *Nsibidi* signs used by secret societies.[8]

These African scripts were not phonetic. They were cumbersome and tended to be held in secret circulation. They therefore did not become vehicles for the production of popular and entertainment literature. We are,

[7] cf. Theodore Monod, "A new West African Alphabet used by the Toma, French Guinea and Liberia," *Man* 43 (1943), item 85; G. Maria, "An old PWO Karen Alphabet," *Man* 43 (1943), item 5; R. F. G. Adam. "Oberi Okaime: A New African Language and Script," *Africa* XVII/1 (January 1947), pp. 24–34.

[8] cf. J. K. Macgregor, "Some Notes on Nsibidi," *Journal of Royal Anthropological Institute*, 39 (1909), p. 210; Elphistore Daryell, "Further Notes on Nsibidi Signs with their Meanings from the Ikom District, Southern Nigeria," *JRAI* 41 (1911), p. 521; and "Some Nsibidi Signs" *Man*, X/8 (1910); an easily available presentation of Nsibidi is in Elizabeth Isichei's *The History of the Igbos*, Macmillan, 1975; cf. also Ogbu U. Kalu, Chapter VI.

therefore, back to the oral medium as that in which traditional African literature developed and is to be studied. Our literature is to be found in the folktales of animals and men and spirits, in the myths of supernatural origins and actions which underlie our rituals, in the legends of towns and heroes which are either dramatized in communal celebrations or told in the context of family discussion and drinking parties, in the heightened oratory of ceremonial occasions and oblique conversation of ordinary situations full as they are of proverbs and emotive words, and in the incantations, recitations and songs which accompany ritual, ceremonial, masquerade and dance.

Folktales

The African imagination has developed much expertize in the prose forms. If, for example, you go to Okija, you will see in two of the villages, tracks where there should have been water but there is no water. The reason is that when the river was passing through the town it went first to one of the villages and asked the people for male and female. They said they had too few people. The other village said it has not enough money for a he-goat and a female goat. The clever village had found out from the diviners that cola and pepper are male and female and paid easily so that till today the river can be seen flowing through the village. You might also be interested in knowing why the sun and the moon look the way they do, how the Lagos Lagoon and Abeokuta rock came about, and why the sky went so far up into the heavens, how death came into the world, how the tortoise got its shell and why its shell is all cracked, why the kite flies around where there is a fire and why the hawk carries away chickens; you may be more interested in why the ant has a large chest, the ram long pendulous testicles and the monkey a red bottom. There are explanations for all these. They are sometimes called etiological tales, or place legends, or myths of origin.

These stories raise the question of the extent to which they were believed in by the people. It is possible to talk glibly of the naive Africans who believe that lightening and thunder arise from the mischievous he-goat burning up other people's property in the sky and the mother goat shouting at her son. But we should realize that the genuine myths of the people, the ideas which they hold most sacred, are retained within the ritual situation and for the initiated.[9] These generally available stories have to be seen properly for what

[9] Jack Goody, *The Myth of the Bagre (Oxford: Clarenden Press, 1972); Marcel Griaule, Conversations with Ogotemmeli* (Oxford, 1965).

they are, the inventions of fertile imaginations using the natural phenomena as excuses for weaving delightful and quite often instructive tales.

The example of why the tortoise has a cracked shell will suffice. Various stories from various communities explain how it came about and in some localities more than one story is told on the same topic without any sense of contradiction being experienced. In one story Tortoise begged and wheedled the birds into lending him feathers so that he could fly with them to a festival in the skies. Tortoise trickishly made each "person" choose a salutation name for the foreign trip where identities must not be too frivolously revealed. By choosing the name "All-of-you" the Tortoise had an exclusive feast for himself since all entertainment was offered with the comment from the hosts "we offer this . . . (rice, palm-wine etc.) to all of you." The result was that the birds took all their feathers from Tortoise and he eventually had to fall back to Earth. An additional twist to the story is that Tortoise begged the birds to request his wife to leave out soft objects for him to fall on and they maliciously revenged on him by asking the wife to bring out her wooden mortars and iron pots and all things hard and bruising. Tortoise's fall from the sky onto these hard objects explains his splintered shell.

In the same community one may hear another story which says that when all the animals had killed and eaten their mothers in a famine, the squirrel had refused to kill his. The story partly shows the evil consequences of matricide since the famine continued and only the squirrel who had stashed away his mother in the sky continued to feed well by going occasionally to visit his mother. But the story continues into Tortoise's trickish discovery of the squirrel's secret, his attempt to benefit from the discovery to the discomfiture of the squirrel, and the eventual cracking of his shell when all the animals with whom he was climbing into the sky fell and landed hard on him. Two explanations but obviously what must be of paramount interest to the listeners would hardly be the etiological ending but the delight of invention and the moral lessons within the tales.

Most stories however do not set out to explain anything. There are animal tales in which animal characteristics are featured (many of them being about the tortoise – or spider in other African communities – and their tricks). There are animal tales in which the animals are endowed with human characteristics; stories abound which narrate activities of human characters; and we have stories in which supernatural creatures feature: spirits, ogres, deities.

This proliferation of stories serves the communities as means of entertainment, as avenues for the acculturation of the young ones, and as shorthand methods for adults to express ideas proverbially. The stories also provide the emotional release which is a function of literature. Each of these functions can quite easily be illustrated.

Entertainment derives from a variety of sources: the dramatic mode of performance of the tales, the verbal felicities and proverbial insertions which feature in narration by experts, from the escapist exploration of lands other than that of daylight reality and, above all, from the plot structures, especially those of dilemma tales and stories of clever rascals. Imaginative inventiveness is a pleasure and good stories told well provide marvellous entertainment.

For the young, and also sometimes for adults, the stories are told for their moral content. They therefore become teaching materials for acculturation. Society has used the stories as means of coating the bitter pills of dogmatic communal training of the moral and personality sensibilities of its members. To teach girls to marry suitors selected for them by their parents, they are told stories of girls who willfully made their own choice only to find that they had married monsters; behaviour patterns – greeting elders, hand work, modesty, lack of greed – are inculcated in stories which show the various rewards and punishment for good or bad behaviour. Those are stories which teach love between brothers and sisters, stories which warn wicked stepmothers about the evil consequences of their oppressive conduct towards their step-children, and so on.

Old men do not sit around and tell themselves folktales, that activity is reserved for children. But most tales could be used by the elders in conversation or in situations of admonition as extended proverbs or to introduce proverbs. The story of the wrestler who insisted on going on after great achievements till he has faced his *chi* and smashed in a throw is a proverbial warning in a situation where somebody is overstretching his ambition.[10] If somebody is too obstreperous in offering his opinions in every situation, and old man nearby could start telling the story of "The Calabash of Wisdom".

Finally, as a particular extension of their entertainment effect, stories constitute a communal medium for the excitation and purgation of the emotions. The late evening time of narration, the exclusive gathering around a light source or around the narrator (exclusive in the sence that the little group of narrator and audience hedges itself in and outside that circle, the dark night becomes a threatening presence), and the story itself combine for

[10] See footnote 3.

this effect. Some stories are, moreover, aimed directly in their plot structure to raise comic or tragic or pathetic suspense and to release the appropriate emotion at the end. The Xhosa hero story of "Sonyangaza and the Ogres" for example, sets up many suspenseful points of danger to the career of Bala and Balakazi, twin brother and sister, until, at the end, Bala, praise-named Sonyangaza, rescues his sister and her daughter from the ogres, to the great relief and joy of the audience.[11]

Folk Poetry

Much attention has been paid to folktales in the history of the study of oral literature, but it has become steadily clearer that it is in the area of song and dance and recitation that the best of any community's imaginative literature is to be found. In our context we must start with the lullabies that are recited for crying babies. They do not understand the words but they are soothed by the sounds and by the rhythms. Pleasant sounds, soothing or invigorating but regular rhythms, words of peculiarly strong effect — these go into the production of the poetry of the traditional African.

For various occasions, song and verse feature in their appropriate form and content in most African events, a child is born and the compound rings with the voices of ululating women who soon break into songs in which they praise motherhood, advise the child that is newly born, ask for the benefits which should accure to a successful mother, and warn the men to treat their wives properly.[12]

A boy or a girl matures and is being initiated or circumcized. The teaching that is to raise the person from immaturity to the new stage of maturity is transferred through song and symbol.[13]

[11] A. C. Jordan, *Tales from Southern Africa* (Berkeley: University of California Press, 1973), pp. 192–216.

[12] cf. D. Nwoga, "Mma Nwanyi Wu Nwa: Poetic Images of Childbirth among the Igbo." *Folklore*, 84 (1973), pp. 142–156.

[13] cf. for example, F. Deng, *The Dinka and Their Songs*, (Oxford: Clarenden Press); Gordon Innes "Mandinka Circumcision Songs," *African Language Review*, XIII (1972), pp. 88–112; John Blacking, "Songs, Dances, Mimes and Symbolism of Venda Girls' Initiation Schools," *Africa Studies*, XXVIII/1–4 (1969). Incidentally some of the language of the puberty songs can be quite uninhibited in its use of sexual expressions especially in Southern Africa.

A girl is getting married. She has to be taught by the women what she is supposed to do in her husband's home. The Abam women for example, sing:

Ọ wụ ife di mma	It is a good thing
Ada ọma, ada ndi Anaga	Beautiful daughter, daughter of Anaga
Ada ndi Ukwu, ada akụ	Daughter of the Great, daughter of wealth.
Ọ wụ ife ọma, meri je	It is a good thing, go ahead!
Otopusala, agbọghọ, anyi	She has matured, our virgin
Di gị sị gị ngwa, ge kwe	When your husband asks you to, do it.
Ụmụ, ọ wụ ife anyi chọrọ	Children, that is what we want.
Olu, olu, izi ejuo	One by one, the compound will fill up.
Ụmụ anyị ọ nnọ? Ehe Ehe	Our people, it is so, isn't it?

In their youth, boys and girls tend to make mistakes, and the society makes sure that it punishes and corrects them, whether it is for premarital affairs, for cowardice, for being too slow in getting married or for other kinds of misdemeanor. Some of the most entertaining songs come from this functional activity. Satire indeed constitutes a major genre of oral poetry and is not restricted to youths. The woman caught in adultery is a good target. But male failures are also attacked. Kings in their glory often receive snide poetic attacks. There is a special festival in Ghana in which satire is the vogue: attacks of one village by another, but even more it is the occasion on which people have the opportunity to tell their chiefs, with impunity, what they think of them.[14]

Current also is a steady perspective on the activities of politicians and administrators whom the folk take up in song as the occasion requires. This has been documented for South Africa and Okot Bitek has shown that this is true for Uganda among the Acholi. At the end of the Nigerian civil war a group of singers had this to say about the soldier – civilian relationship in

[14] For more details and for illustrations of these points: cf. D. Nwoga "The Concept and Practice of Satire among the Igbo," *Igbo Traditional Life Culture and Literature*, pp. 30–45; Oyin Ogunba, "The poetic content and form of Yoruba occasional Festival Songs," *African Notes*, VI/2, pp. 10–30; C. G. B. Gidley, "Yankamanci: to the Craft of the Hausa comedians," *African Language Studies*, VIII (1967), pp. 529–881; R. S. Rattray, *Ashanti*, pp. 100–163, esp. p. 161:

> Nkyi – Thursday is the great day when everybody is permitted to discharge his pent-up resentment. Early in the morning the queen-mother and her girls walk in procession . . . through the town, singing provocative songs and shaking their rattles, and in this way inform the people that they may now form themselves into two groups and start the traditional vituperations.

their town – and they sang this at the residence of the administrator:

Asika give us your ear
Asika our ruler there is a record we are going to give.
What is happening to Igbo people cannot but cause anger.
Any time we ride our bicycles we are knocked down.
Even when we walk we are knocked down.
What we sold to them becomes trouble for us.
What we did not sell becomes trouble for us.
The wives we married they have dragged away.
The daughters we bore they have taken over.
The wealth we made they have carried away.
Household property they have carried away.
Is this how to be one Nigeria?
Asika our ruler
Is this how to be one Nigeria?
Asika we ask you
Does this look as if things are alright with us?
Does this look as if things are alright with us?[15]

The mature person who has achieved status needs to be recognized by the community. Especially in hierarchically organized societies, we find a large corpus of salutation poetry in Africa. In some societies, the successful man has to praise himself adequately. Among the Bahima of Ankola unless a man praise himself successfully he cannot get a wife. The Igbo also have the habit of praising themselves as any of the examples in *Poetic Heritage* would show. The Hausa and the Yoruba hire and pay professional performers who go before them and chant their geneologies and achievements (and attack their opponents). Among the Zulu, the good salutation poems are retained in the memory of professionals so that there is a repertoire of historical praise poems. The praise-poem of Shaka, first king of Zululand who died in 1828, has been preserved in its great length of 450 lines. It is a good example of the sense and the following extracts will show some of the characteristics of the type:

Dlungwana son of Ndaba!
Ferocious one of the Mbelebele brigade,
Who raged among the large kraals,
So that until down the huts were being turned upside-down.

[15] Collected from Abigbo Mbaise in Imo State of Nigeria, 1971.

He who is famous as he sits, son of Menzi,
He who beats but is not beaten, unlike water,
Axe that surpasses other axes in sharpness;
Shaka, I fear to say he is Shaka,
Shaka, he is the chief of the Mashobas.
He of the shrill whistle, the lion;
He who armed in the forest, who is like a madman,
The madman who is in full view of the men.
He who trudged wearily the plain going to Mfene;
The voracious one of Senzangakhona,
Spear that is red even on the handle . . .
He is curved like the ocean
Which until dawn is rolling waves;
He is as rough as the ear of an elephant,
Like gruel made of inedible millet,
Like a pot of millipedes.
You are a wild animal! A leopard! A lion!
You are a horned viper! An elephant!
You are as big as the great mountains of . . . [16]

Salutation poems also abound which are sung or changed to towns, to cattle, to trees, to divining bones, and above all, to the deities of the people.[17]

A person, finally, dies and even the lamentation produces some excellent literature. It was thought so important that a person of standing should be mourned with beauty that some people have learnt the art of the dirge; they can be hired to perform at a funeral. When, for example Adekunle Fajuyi was killed along with Aguiyi Ironsi in the counter coup of July 29, a Yoruba woman of great reputation composed a dirge which lasted all of one hour.[18] Great pathos is normally generated where an effective performer sings a dirge – or a well brought up sister mourns her dead brother, or wife mourns her husband. The following extract is from a lament by a woman at the death of her father-in-law:

[16] Trevor Cape, *Izibongo, Zulu Praise Poems* (Oxford, 1968), pp. 83–117.

[17] H. F. Morris, *The Heroic Recitations of the Bahima of Ankole*: Schappera, *Praise Poem of Tswana Chiefs*; Daniel P. Kunene, *Heroic Poetry of the Basotho*, all in the Oxford Library of African Literature.

[18] R. G. Armstrong, Val Olanyemi and Babatunde Adu, "Ekiti Traditional Dirge of Lt. Colonel Adekunle Fajuyi's Funeral," *African Notes* V/2 (1969), pp. 63–87. This paper contains a transcription and translation of the dirge.

O – O – O – O – O; O – O – O – O – O.
Where have you gone, father of my husband
Father of my husband who married me.
Where have you gone, where have you gone, where have you gone?
I am looking for the father of my husband who married me
Has anyone seen my husband's father?
Amadioha Ọzụzụ
Did he come to your house?
Umumiri who owns the people of Onicha
Did he come to your house?
I am looking for the hand that breaks iron
Where has he gone, where has he gone?
He who breaks iron for firewood, father of my husband
I am calling you . . .
The root that holds the tree has fallen
The major branch of the tree has been broken
The wind has put off the fire that burns in the compound
The hawk will now fly in to carry the chicks
The pillar of the house has fallen o!
The house will now fall with it . . .
The tree on which birds perch has fallen
Your little birds will now fly away
O – O – O – O – O! O – O – O – !
The branch of *uzi* is broken on *orie*
The source of the stream has dried on *eke*
etc.[19]

It must be mentioned that not all oral poetry of Africa is tied to stages in people's lives. There are also historical poems, and poems in which comments are made about life. Work and war also have their own poetry which supply rhythm and encourage group bravery.

Proverbs and Riddles

Some of the longer forms that I have talked about make use of the wisdom of the past which has been encapsulated in succinct memorable forms known as proverbs. The standard definition which every African now knows is that

[19] Ibuoma Veronica Onyemerkeya, *The Content and Form of Glegiac Poetry in Ezinihitte Mbaise: A Critical Analysis*, unpublished B. A. Thesis, U. N., Nsukka, 1978, pp. 41–42.

"proverbs are the palm oil with which words are eaten". Riddles, on the other hand are merely items of expression the solvable meanings of which are standardized and may only be stated in the usual way. They take imagination to formulate but require only memory in their solution. Proverbs on the other hand require imagination in their usage[20] and they are best appreciated when used in the context in which they have their meaning.

The Igbo for example have a proverb that *Asawa mkpuru agadi nwanyi a sakwute ya nshi*, (If you wash an old woman's loin cloth persistently, you will come across shit). The respect in which women and the aged are held among the Igbo suggests that anybody who refers to the process of defecation with regard to an old woman is in a situation that is distressing. The point is that one does not want to be clearly conscious of all reality: everybody knows that everybody else does defecate but it is impolite to attach the idea to an old woman. An imaginative user of the Igbo language would introduce this proverb to warn a man to desist from pursuing a case too closely as he might discover that unravelling the details would bring him embarrassment.

Conclusion

In a brief exercise of this nature it is not possible to expand fully the concepts or illustrate adequately the variety, force, social impact, and imaginative beauty of the literature with which Africans have entertained and educated themselves in the past. A growing body of both texts and critical material is being steadily published on the subject.[21] Why should we develop an interest in this material?

With the changes that have taken place in our knowledge, in our social and political and religious organisation and objectives and in our mode of living, it is clear that traditional literature will not do for us what it did for our peoples. We cannot, for example, take seriously any story which suggests that death came into the world because the dog sent to ask God for eternal life dallied along the way so that the vengeful frog got to God first with a request that death be final.[22] The moral dictates that certain proverbs are likely to be subjected to the incredulity which results from a more complex

[20] cf. D. Nwoga, "The Appreciation of Igbo proverbs and Idioms," *Igbo Language and Culture*, pp. 186—204. Alsọ Ogbalu, *Ilu Igbo*, 1965, and Njubigbo, *Igbo in a New Setting*.

[21] Ruth Finnegan, *Oral Literature in Africa* (Oxford: Clarenden Press, 1970).

[22] R. U. Umeasiegbu, *The Way We Lived*, p. 94.

analytical attitude to moral issues. While the songs and incantations will continue to dazzle us for their imaginative virtuosity, we are also growing out of the situations which gave their statements validity. If we take, for example, one of the *ozo* praise-songs:

> I am:
> One who tills hills
> One who with yams challenges soil
> Knife that clears bushes
> Barn that is wide
> Bush that yields wealth
> Bush that is colossal
> Bush that is fearful
> Hoe-user untouched by hunger.[23]

While we receive exhilaration from the images and have a residual respect for the *ozo* man's achievement praised in the poem, we cannot but remember that the man's total wealth described as collosal here perhaps comes to somebody elses earning in one month today. And perhaps we no longer accept the attitude of self-declaratory praise.

Knowledge of traditional literature, however, in addition to the pleasure derived from all good literature, makes us aware of the extent to which traditional societies developed the area of intellect and imagination. In this regard they would appear to have been more fortunate than the modern elites (intellectual, political, economic) who have proved very limited in the development of their leisure activities — using diversions and vulgar frivolities to pass away their spare time which traditional societies filled with creative endeavours. So, one valid reason for the growth of an awareness of the role of folk-literature among our people is the need it should create in us to develop our own liesure activities of a parallel nature, something to awake in us the subconscious needs of our personality for beauty and order and creativity.

Traditional literature is also one of the most uninhibited media through which the culture of a people can be exposed because the composer/performer takes his culture for granted as the setting for the further exploration of people and situations. It also becomes progressively evident to a student of African traditional literature as he spreads his coverage over Africa, that there is an underlying similarity of archetypal structures in most African

[23] Egudu and Nwoga, *Poetic Heritage*, pp. 31, 33.

cultures. One brief illustration of this will suffice. A Sotho praise-poem for the lion says:

> Tawny one, brother of Mothebele, rise up,
> Tawny one, fawn-coloured king of the wilds.
> Why, you eat not what belongs to men.
> But eat, for your part, the sleeps-in-the-veld!
> A nephew bereft of uncles
> Kills and lays claim to all the botty!

The last two lines depend for their meaning on an aspect of Sotho culture: "The allusion here is to the custom whereby the spoils from the hunt, or the first earnings from paid work, or any first reward from any kind of employment, have to be handed over to the earner's maternal uncle, for him to retain as much as he wants and give back to the nephew what remains".[24] Most Africans, whether from patrilineal or matrilineal background, would recognize this peculiar relationship between a child and his maternal homeland as a crucial aspect of traditional culture. Its manifestations may vary but the basic archetype is there — the mother's home is a prime source of one's existence to be acknowledged as each tradition specifies.

Most of this essay has presented the types and functions of traditional literature. Analysis of linguistic and stylistic aspects has of necessity been very limited. A few analytical generalizations will now serve to conclude:

1. Although the literary arts played a subsidiary role on the purely aesthetic level to music, dance and the visual arts, they were highly regarded in the society and were more pervasive and important in their role of reinforcing and embellishing normal communication in other facets of life which were non-aesthetic. This meant that though African societies did not usually support financially a class of professional literary artists, the literary artist was well rewarded for his expertize and, more importantly, ability to use language creatively was demanded for social success in the community. For example, it was difficult for any one who could not use proverbs to be regarded as a wise man in any community. Imaginative creativity therefore appears to have been required as a part of total personality development in traditional Africa.

2. There was a scale of importance of literary types. The folktale to which much attention has been devoted by anthropologists and folklorists was

[24] D. P. Kunene, *Heroic Poetry of the Basotho*, p. 131.

largely regarded as children's literature. Gnomic and incanatory poetry was acknowledged as the peak of imaginative creativity.

3. Deeper study of traditional literature reveals a wide variety of compositional techniques and standard forms throughout Africa. Dynamism was part of the tradition of a living culture. Classification and determination of the characteristics of each type constitute a continuous challenge to scholarship. It would appear however that orality tends in one direction — towards memorability and this in turn demands some characteristics, namely, brevity, clarity, rhythm, and convolutions of emotive meaning. This, I believe, is why the praise or salutation name is the basic unit of all traditional African poetry.

4. Certain mythical structures appear to operate in all African traditional literature. The same stereotypes appear in various traditions.[25] The suggestion is unavoidable that a mythical approach to the study of African folk literature would yield valuable results. This would not only give some guidance with regard to migrations, cultural affinities and cross-cultural influences, but would yield some knowledge as to the psychology and social and political preoccupations of African peoples as well as establishing their traditions of literary perspective for modern generations.

We still have in the present, in the village and sometimes in towns, carriers of African's traditional literature. All the time too new literature is being created which fits into this tradition and increases its corpus. Hopefully we always learn to enjoy the old. Hopefully too we will enter into the spirit and participate in the creation of the new literature of Africa.

Bibliography

1. Okeke, Uche, *Tales of Land of Death: Igbo Folk Tales*. Doubleday, 1971.
2. Egudu, Romanus, *The Calabash of wisdom and other Igbo Stories* Nok., 1973.
3. Egudu, Romanus and Donatus Nwoga, *The Poetic Heritage: Igbo Traditional Verse*. Nwamife, 1971.
4. Abimbola, Wande, *IFA: an Exposition of Ifa Literary Corpus* Ibadan University Press, 1976.
5. Babalola, S. A., *The Content and Form of Yoruba Ijala*. Oxford: Clarendon Press 1966.
6. Beier, H. U. and Gbadamosi, *Not even God is Ripe Enough*. Heinemann, and *The Moon Cannot Fight: Yoruba Children's Poems* Mbari.

[25] Alagoa's paper "Stereotypes in Ijọ Oral Tradition," *Ikenga* I/1, reveals many similarities between Ijọ and Ibgo traditions.

7. Beier, H. U. *Yoruba Poetry, An Anthology of Traditional Poems.* Cambridge University Press, 1967.
8. Fuja, Abayomi, *1,400 cowries and other Yoruba Tales.* Oxford University Press, 1967.
9. Johnson H. A. S., *A selection of Hausa Stories.* Oxford: Clarendon Press, 1966.

Many more items are in less easily available media. The bibliography for Africa would stretch over 1,000 titles.

CHAPTER SIX

Writing in Pre-Colonial Africa: A Case Study of Nsibidi

Dr. O. U. Kalu

Senior Lecturer, Department of Religion, University of Nigeria, Nsukka

At the turn of the century, a Presbyterian missionary, Rev. J. K. Macgregor, was deployed to teach in Hope Waddel Training Institution, Calabar. In a typical ethnocentric fashion, he took the opportunity to declaim the heights of European civilization compared to the primitive state of Africans who had no writing. At one level, Macgregor's attitude betrayed the uncomfortable fact that Christian missionaries shared the dominant racist ideas of their age. But more crucial, in the culture contact with Europeans, Africans felt greatly disadvantaged because they had no comparable art of writing for storage, development and propagation of their civilization. In Liberia, an African employee of the American Firestone Company was so distraught by such strictures on his race that he took God to task. Wido Zogbo, as local tradition has it, querried why:

> God takes he no pity on the Tomas? Other races know writing. Only Tomas remain in their ignorance.

Apparently, God picked up the gauntlet and a discussion ensued. It went like this:

> God: I fear that when you are able to express yourselves you shall have no more respect for the beliefs and customs of your race.
>
> Wido: Not at all. We shall still keep living as in the past days. I promise it.
>
> God: If such is the case, I am willing to grant you the knowledge but take care never to show anything of it to a woman.

It is said that Wido Zogbo was then inspired to develop a form of writing. Arguments persist whether the use of the language was restricted to males or whether the last sentence was a later emendation. But the writing spread through Liberia, Toma and French Guinea. Headmen kept their records and communicated with this script. To a certain extent the script resembles both the older Vai and Mende scripts except that there is a greater use of Western alphabets.[1] A similar reaction to western ethnocentrism occurred in Ibibioland in 1936 when the wave of spiritualism produced a new script called "Oberi Ọkaime".[2]

Macgregor's students, however, did not react to the racial slur by producing a new script with some western alphabets. Rather, one of them introduced the teacher to an ancient script which existed before the Europeans came. It is called *nsibidi.*

In the current wave of African studies, frequent references are made to this script mostly from the same nationalistic spirit which produced the schoolboy's protest. Few have explored *nsibidi* as to its origin, meaning, nature, extent of the usage, functions and why it was never used to produce a literature.

This paper is a modest attempt to explore this ancient pictographic writing so as to answer some of the questions. The effort must, perforce, be modest because the script has been shrouded by secrecy. When Macgregor made initial enquiries, "people smiled . . . and declared that they knew nothing about it".[3] Elphinstone Daryell, a District Commissioner to Ikom, concurred that:

> the men who understand Nsibidi are very reticent about giving any information on the subject, and it is only through natives whom I have known several years that I have been able to obtain the signs now given.[4]

For the African scholar who may be a member of any of the societies and may, therefore, know some of the signs, the constraints are still immense both from the initiation oath and from nationalistic considerations.

There has been a debate about the origin of the *nsibidi* script. In 1909, J. K. Macgregor attributed it to the "great Ibo tribe which is said to number four million people and to cover about one-third of the Protectorate". But

[1] Theodore Monod, "A new West African Alphabet Used by the Toma, French Guinea and Liberia", *Man*, 43 (1943), item 85. For comparison, see G. Marin, "An Old PWO Karen Alphabet," *Man*, 43 (1943), item 5.

[2] R. F. G. Adams, "Oberi Ọkaime: A New African Language and Script," *Africa* XVII/1 (January, 1947), pp. 24–34.

[3] J. K. Macgregor, "Some Notes on Nsibidi," *Journal of Royal Anthropological Institute* 39 (1909), p. 210.

[4] Elphinstone Daryell, "Further Notes on Nsibidi Signs with their Meanings from the Ikom District, Southern Nigeria," *Journal of Royal Anthropological Institute* 41 (1911), p. 521.

then, he had discovered that the script was in use in the non-Igbo Calabar District. Besides, earlier missionaries, such as the linguist J. T. Dean, had known of *nsibidi* as an Efik word for the cuts made on calabashes. Macgregor quickly explained what he considered to be a form of cultural diffusion by alleging that:

> They [the Ibo] are a great artisan tribe, and their smiths are to be met in every village in this part of the country, and wherever a smith goes he carries with him the knowledge of nsibidi.[5]

This is the origin of the frequent assertion by writers that *nsibidi* is an Igbo contribution to the art of writing.

Years later, amateur ethnographers, such as M. D. W. Jeffreys, propagated the Igbo hypothesis but from a different ideological perspective. Jeffreys perhaps shared Palmer's Hamitic hypothesis and assumed that the Nri and Aro cultures must be non-Igbo influences on a more backward people. These external change-agents or leaven to the lump conquered and blended with their victims. Deeply impressed with the Aro, colonial officials turned them into a legendary race. So, writing on the *nsibidi* in 1928 and 1964, Jeffrey insisted that:

> This sign writing originated so far as can be ascertained among the Aros (on the Cross River) who call it Nsigidi and state that this was the name of a club that organized the writing and perpetuated it.[6]

Supposedly the club waned as the Aro aristocracy disintegrated following British conquest.

Macgregor obtained most of his information of the Igbos from two Abiriba students of Hope Waddell Training Institution, Onuoha Kalu and Ezikpe Agwu. They had fled as trading apprentices, were captured and found their way into mission employ and later school. Earlier, Macgregor had persuaded the boys to lead him to their village where he gamely tried to open a church and school. The enterprise failed in spite of Agwu Otisi's patronage as Abiriba traders on the Cross River warned the home folk against having any parley with white missionaries. But Macgregor took the opportunity to learn about the Abiriba people and collected a number of *nsibidi* signs with cross-

[5] Macgregor, p. 209.

[6] M. D. W. Jeffreys, "Corrections on *Man*, 1910 item 67: Nsibidi Writing," *Man* (1964), item 192. On Aro legend see A. E. Afigbo, "The Aro of South-Eastern Nigeria: A Socio-Historical Analysis of Legends of their Origin, Pt. II," *African Notes* VII/1.

checked interpretations. That was in 1907.[7] The following year, he collected other signs at Calabar and published these in the *Journal of the Royal Anthropological Institute*.

His assertions were made with so much hubris because the whites had just found their way into the Igbo hinterland in the aftermath of the Arochukwu Expedition. Likewise, T. D. Maxwell, a District Commissioner in Calabar, had in 1904 discovered the extensive use of the writing among the Efik.

In a study on native modes of thought, an ethnographic hobby which administrators were encouraged to undertake, Maxwell collected twenty-four *nsibidi* signs from a chief woman of the Henshaw family. He was encouraged to publish these on the Government Civil List for the Protectorate in July, 1905. But Maxwell had no inkling of the extent of the usage beyond his jurisdiction. Macgregor, thus, appeared to open a new vista on the study on *nsibidi*.

From such hypothesis it was a short step backwards to conjectures on the beginnings of *nsibidi*. Africans have a knack for weaving imaginative myths of origin and so folktales explain why the sun and moon look the way they do, how death came into the world, why the ram has long, pendulous testicles and the monkey a red bottom. Thus, when Macgregor investigated the origin of *nsibidi*, he was told that it started among the Ugwuakuma who live at Uyanga. The story is that the large baboons (idiok) were very rampant in that forest area lying a few miles off the mangroove swamp of the Cross River bank. If hunters made fire to warm themselves, the baboons would gate-crash and impose their uninvited company. The first reaction of the hunters was to scram but they soon noticed that the baboons would make some marks on the ground and in a pantomimic fashion act out the meaning of the signs. Ugwuakuma people detected a meaningful relationship between the signs and the pantomimic act, and they called the signs *nsibidi*. *Sibidi*, according to Macgregor, means *to play* "for they have learned these things through the playing of the *idiok*". Men improved on the signs by adding new symbols for new articles such as comb, money and so on.[8]

Within a comparative perspective, Macgregor's story sounds like other mysterious origins of the art of writing. For instance, the Vai script originated

[7] *Ibid.*, p. 210; National Archives, Enugu, Presbnig 1/1/5: Minute Book of the Presbytery of Biafra, Vol. 5, 1903–26; Oral Interview with Mr. O. A. Otisi aged 84 at Abiriba, 7/10/76. His father, Agwu Otisi was the first convert.

[8] Macgregor, p. 211.

from the dream of Dualu Bukele, a messenger for Europeans in Liberia. It is said that he was so deeply impressed by the fact that a piece of paper could convey a message that he:

> sat up night after night fasting and journeying, just to unravel the mystery. One night while Bukele was wrapped up in a dream a person draped in white appeared before him and said, "Dualu, I have brought you a script with which you, too, can now write your language".

Dualu woke up and wrote down the script.[9]

However, the obvious problem in Macgregor's hypothesis is why he erroneously classified Uyanga people as Igbo and alleged that *sibidi* is an Igbo word meaning, *to play*.

Within three years, Macgregor's conjectures were punctured at many points. First to strike was Elphinstone Daryell, a District Commissioner in Ikom. He found that the script was in use beyond Calabar District and Cross-River Igboland to much of Ikom District. Daryell had collected over fifty *nsibidi* signs from his jurisdiction and published these in 1910. His research into the extent and nature of the script was partially based on classification of tattoos on men and women. He regarded these tattoos as identity labels and epigrams which social clubs made on their members. Daryell kept a close tag on where the tattooed people came from. Some were Efik, others came from various parts of Ikom District, Obubra, Ekoi, Afikpo, Akunakuna, Bende and Edda. *Nsibidi* was, therefore, in use all over Cross-River Basin.

Besides, argued Daryell, *nsibidi* signs were devised by many social clubs. The script was to a large extent pictographic, thus, different social clubs easily devised their own symbols. For instance, in the Ikom District, the Egbo, Ukpotio, Ukwa and Isong Esil societies had their different symbols. However, over the years and with increased contacts along the Cross River, certain signs became conventional.

Finally, Daryell noticed that these signs were not just written but often acted out. For instance, one could enter a room full of people and make a pantomimic code either with the hands, toes or a variety of body movements and the initiated would understand. *Nsibidi* is not just a written script but a language "spoken" with body movement. With such a cloud of witnesses and

[9] Bai T. Moore, "Liberia's Contribution to the Science on Communication," in J. Okpaku, ed., *New African Literature and Arts*, Vol. III (New York: Third World Press, 1973), pp. 377–389.

exotic symbols, Daryell resorted to the same *Journal of the Royal Anthropological Institute* in 1911.[10]

These findings set the stage for P. A. Talbot's iconoclastic work in 1912 romantically entitled, *In the Shadow of the Bush.* It remained one of the few studies on the Ekoi until Daryll Forde studied the Yakurr.

Talbot argued that it was the Ekoi who originated *nsibidi*; that he found a "greater variety of signs . . . among the Ekoi of the interior than amid any other tribe". The Ekoi explain that *nsibidi* is a corrupt form of *Nchibbidy* which is derived from the verb *Nchibbi,* to turn. In usage, the word refers to agility of mind and, therefore, cunning or double meaning. *Nsibidi* was also the name of an ancient but defunct club whose membership was restricted to chiefs and which was charged with the execution of criminals. It antedated the Egbo or Ekpe society.

To buttress this, Talbot alleged that there was no trace of Macgregor's baboon legend among the Uyanga. With obvious exaggeration, in the hurry to deliver a *coup de grace*, he observed that:

> With regard to the Ibos, all of this nationality questioned by me deny the existence of any system of writing save that adopted from missionary sources, which has been modified to suit their convenience.[11]

Finally, he pointed to Dr. Mansfeld's work to show that *nsibidi* was used in the Cameroons and was not restricted to non-Bantu races. Mansfeld's work, dated 1908, had pointed to the use of *nsibidi* by "the Ekoi who live north-east of Calabar both in British and German territories".[12]

Talbot did not need exaggerated and spurious argumentation. The Ekoi origin is the most probable. This is deduced from a number of reasons: first, there is evidence of the diffusion of Ekoi culture throughout the Cross-River basin. It is obvious that the Ekoi for some inexplicable reason dispersed from the forest heartland. One could conjecture trade, civil war and survival instinct as probable causes. A group migrated to the Ikang area on the Nigerian border with the Cameroons. It is this group to which Mansfeld referred. Another party settled in Akim Qua. By their tradition, they arrived earlier and granted land to the Efiks.

[10] E. Daryell, "Some Nsibidi Signs," *Man,* X/8 (1910); E. Daryell, "Further Notes on Nsibidi Signs from the Ikom District, Southern Nigeria," *JRAI* XLI (1911), pp. 521–540.

[11] P. A. Talbot, *In the Shadow of the Bush* (London, 1912), p. 305.

[12] Macgregor footnoted that Mansfeld's work came too late to his attention. His own assertion was based on questionaires sent to fellow missionaries in the Cameroons.

A third group comprising of the Yakọ, Ugep, Nkpani, Nko, Idomi, Ekori and Assiga moved north of the ancestral home. A fourth cluster comprising of Ebiase, Akuna-Akuna, Okurike, Adim, Uyanga, Akankpa, Netim and Ojo moved to the bank of the Cross-River and now has a sizeable number of Ibibios within their communities. A core group made up of Iko, Iko Ekperum, Ikom Esai, Owai and Ekuri have remained in the ancestral home in small villages separated by formidable forests.[13]

With dispersion, the Ekoi spread their culture and purveyed the unifying cultural forms which identify Cross River culture area – even enveloping the neighbouring Igbo people. So pervasive is Ekoi cultural influence on the Cross River basin that Talbot argued that the Aro had a strong Ekoi origin.

Secondly, though various societies use *nsibidi*, the language has been preserved mostly by the Ekpe Society. The Ekpe society is definitely of Ekoi origin. An aspect of the initiation ritual into the higher Ekpe grades in Akim Qua entails a visit to the Ekoi ancestral home for proper education in Ekpe intricacies. The Ekpe Society has spawn a large number of *nsibidi* signs. Some of these appear on their cloth which is called *Ukara*, others are painted on the walls of Ekpe halls. Members identify themselves by making these signs with their fingers, head movements, standing postures and other gestures. A newcomer is quizzed with challenging signs and the higher one climbed in the ranks of the society, the more *nsibidi* he learned. Messages are passed among Ekpe societies with *nsibidi* signs cut or painted on split palm stems, wood or skin parchment. However, these are often short, telegraphic messages: a sign or two carried a load of meaning. Intricate questions would be answered verbally by the messenger when duly escorted to the society's hall.

Briefly, then, there is less difference between the hypotheses of Macgregor and Talbot than appears at first glance, Uyanga is Ekoi. Dealing with culture boundary areas, Macgregor mistook Uyanga people for an Igbo group. The Efik and Aro who dominated the pre-colonial trade routes in this area also spread the influence of Ekpe and *nsibidi* language.

Yet, the monopoly of *nsibidi* as the secret language of Ekpe society is probably the product of cultural change. For instance, in modern Cross-River communities, the symbolic passwords of lesser secret societies like *Obon*

[13] Oral interview with Chief O. Arikpo, Asst. Village Head, Betem, aged 95 years; Chief Ekpo Obam, Chief of Ekpo Society, Betem aged 85 years. Mr. O. A. Arikpo, Customary Court President of Ehom Clan, Akampa Division served as interpreter. Iko Ekperim: Chiefs Osam Aidam (85), Arong Okpo (80), Eyo Oyama (65), July, 1976.

and *Akang* are not usually referred to as *nsibidi*. This is a constriction in usage. In older days, many societies evolved their own elaborate *nsibidi* and thereby creating enormous complexity in the study of *nsibidi*. For instance, the same signs may stand for different things while different signs may stand for the same thing.[14]

Even more complicated, it does appear that *nsibidi* was not always restricted to the use of secret socieites. There was a secularist usage. Thus, when some Christians denied that they knew *nsibidi*, it was out of fear of being suspected for sexual immorality — and missionaries were apt to pass such judgements since they entertained low opinion of the sexual probity of their hosts. Written *nsibidi* was replete with signs which lovers used in passing sweet messages. To learn this art, one had to apprentice with professional female teachers (usually old women). The collection of *nsibidi* signs which Macgregor, Maxwell, Mansfeld, Daryell and others made describe every imaginable situation in a love affair from courting through intimate relationship to marriage. Pregnancy, divorce and illicit relationships were all duly represented in pictographic forms. It is probable that this amorous form of *nsibidi* withered leaving the corpus preserved by powerful secret societies like Ekpe.

In the cultural history of the Cross-River basin, *nsibidi* acquired at least four levels of meaning: it was once understood as the secret language of secret societies; it has become more associated with the secret language of the Ekpe Society; it once served as the secret code for transmitting amorous messages; and white ethnographers constantly applied it to the principles underlying decorative art.

The point, however, is that *nsibidi* served various functions in olden Cross-River communities: identity label, public notice, private warning, declaration of taboos, amorous messages, reckoning of goods and money, keeping of records and decorations. As the Ekpe/Okonko Club spread and acquired importance in government, *nsibidi* became quite important socially, economically and politically. The connection between the principles of decorative art and *nsibidi* needs some examination.

Talbot claimed that body decorations were often in *nsibidi* signs "and sometimes a girl's whole life-history is proclaimed in this manner. Such patterns are always traced by a female relative, usually the aunt of the person decorated".[15] As noted earlier, Daryell took tattoos for *nsibidi* signs.

[14] Macgregor, p. 211.

[15] Talbot, p. 320.

Recent studies of Igbo art have raised questions. Body decoration is an important aspect of Igbo aesthetics. For instance, an Igbo riddle poses the question:

> Who is the maiden
> Whose body was decorated with uli lines
> And roams the forest?
> The Python.

Uli art form is an elaborate method of decorative designs. The artist is usually a woman utilising stains from the pods of various plants and a quill feather. There is little need here to go into the details about the ingredients and materials. Of more relevance is the fact that the basic designs are abstracted from natural objects, local animals and vegetables. Certain abstract designs become conventional, for instance, a triangle for leopard's claw, circle for the moon, half circle for half-moon and wavy lines for the snake's movement. The artist would devise various designs following traditional usages.[16] Using leaves and camwood, girls would create designs on walls of a home and calabashes.

It must be pointed out that the decorative art form is not just typical of the Igbo. It is widespread. Talbot acknowledges that

> In the interior, [i.e. Ekoi] children and young girls still have their bodies painted with designs made by black vegetable dyes. The most usual of these is extracted from the rhizome of the little flower "Ibiri Nsi" much like a wild hyacinth.[17]

While his wife and sister-in-law collected numerous designs, neither went beyond the surface to understudy the basic conceptions in the decorative art form.

The problem, therefore, is the connection between *uli* art form and *nsibidi*. It does appear that the two traditions developed separately but as *nsibidi* spread in-land into Igboland, the two art forms intemixed in various ways: *uli* absorbed some of the *nsibidi* designs, while there was correlation in others since both used basically the same pictographic and descriptive principle. Also, *uli* forms were often used to express *nsibidi* signs. The admixture was most aided by the fact that both *nsibidi* and *uli* designs are

[16] Uche Okeke, "Igbo. Art," an unpublished Mss which the author kindly allowed me to see. Obiora Udechukwu, "Functionality, Symbolism and Decoration: Some Aspects of Traditional Igbo Art," *The Conch* III/2 (September, 1972), pp. 89–96.

[17] Talbot, p. 320.

derived from man's environment. Doubtlessly, all body decorations and designs on calabashes and walls were not *nsibidi*. For one, decorative art was a woman's job and the tendency was towards restricting *nsibidi* to males. Secondly, in spite of the tendency for African art to be religious and functional, some art forms were veritably imaginative creations to satisfy man's sense of beauty.

The confusion between mere decorative art and *nsibidi* by amateur ethnographers has bedevilled the study of *nsibidi*. For instance, only a few of the fifty-six signs collected by Mansfeld bear resemblance to other known *nsibidi* signs. Most must be body or utensil decorations.[18]

From a broader cultural perspective, one would like to speculate on why the *nsibidi* did not develop alphabets and a literary corpus. Obviously, the high premium placed on secrecy hindered the development of the language. With the incursion of white men, such secrecy became deeper in certain communities, restricting the fertilization of *nsibidi* by western art of writing. *Nsibidi* became a form of cultural resistance. This is quite different from the Liberian reaction to white racism. The Toma script had the possibility of development because each member of the community was under oath to teach the language to others. There were two other hinderances: firstly, the complexity in esoteric meanings created by different clubs and secondly there was a lack of order in writing which made the use of *nsibidi* in record-keeping difficult. Both Macgregor and Talbot claim to have seen court records kept in *nsibidi* though Macgregor denied ever seeing a letter in *nsibidi*. One is not certain whether those stories written in *nsibidi* and reproduced in an appendix by Talbot were contemporary creations inspired by the white man's inquiry or whether they were older creations. Generally, *nsibidi* accounts were written in pleats rather than in full-bodied accounts. Secrecy did not allow initiates to experiment imaginative stories with the script. But going through hundreds of the pictographs one gets involved into rich, albeit unordered, cameos of life.

[18] Alfred Mansfeld, *Urwarld Dokumente* (Berlin, 1908), Tafel IV/V.

CHAPTER SEVEN

Concept into Form: Religion and Aesthetics in African Art

Obiora Udechukwu
Department of Fine and Applied Arts,
University of Nigeria, Nsukka

African traditional art was the emotional and intellectual peg on which tribal cultures hung spiritual truth.

Dr. Lambo

The Christians do not have any physical representation of their *ikenga*. But we make ours and keep, so that we can see it always.

Mazi Ezeafulukwe of Oraifite

Introduction

Religion is defined by the Chambers Encyclopaedia as "the word generally used to describe man's relation to divine or superhuman powers and the various organized systems of belief and worship in which these relations have been expressed". It further states that the "belief in the existence of such relations is a general human conviction, common to all peoples and to all stages of culture". There is still confusion about the precise meaning of the word "aesthetics" but the Oxford English Dictionary regards aesthetics as "the philosophy or theory of taste, or of the perception of the beautiful in nature and art".

Having set forth these operational definitions, we shall delimit the scope of this short inquiry. It is, of course, impossible to cover the vast and diverse art cultures of Africa in a lecture. We intend, therefore, to use the Igbo society as an example for looking at the relationship between religion and art in traditional Africa. Even then, we shall not attempt to cover the entire spectrum of Igbo art which would be equally difficult, but merely touch certain key aspects of that system, and, with one or two examples, illustrate specific points and assertions.

Igbo World View

Western mode of cognition is generally regarded as analytical. Things are seen essentially in parts; life is broken down into near rigid compartments. On the other hand, the African recognizes units and sees the whole before the parts. Hence his own mode of cognition is said to be synthetic or holistic. For the African, the entire world is one fluid, coherent unit in which spirits, plants, animals, the elements, the dead and human beings interact. There is a thin line between any two sections of reality.

For man to survive in this world, to be able to live a successful and happy life and, upon death, to rejoin his ancestors, he strives at all times to maintain a harmonious relationship with all the forces that impinge on his life and being. This means a continuous quest for equilibrium, the wooing of benevolent forces and the keeping in check of malevolent ones, for duality is also a veritable aspect of this system. (cf. Igbo *ife dị abụa abụa.*)

Some years ago, when questioned, Okonkwo Ndeche, a well-known wood carver in Agulu, attributed creative intuition to *Chukwu* (the Great God), *Ajaana* (the Earth Principle) and *Ife Nwe Nka* (literally, "that which owns creativity or craftsmanship"). These three forces represent the different levels of relationship of man with the immaterial. The Supreme Being and creator of the world is transcendent and generally detached. Man recognizes his existence and pre-eminence but does not sufficiently understand him as to relate directly with him. Man, therefore, concentrates on the lesser deities, the most important of which is *Ana* (*Ala*, *Ani*, *Ali*), the earth, on which man stands, walks, builds his house, raises his crops, livestock and children, from which he derives his food and in which he is buried. His whole life, in effect, depends on the earth. Is it suprising, therefore, that the people's life, ethics, and art are closely bound up with and controlled by the earth principle? Lower down the ladder are innumerable spirits and forces that control every aspect of man's life and activities from birth to death. To get an idea of the intricacy of this system or how pervasive it is, some mischievous forces known as *umunnadi* are held to be responsible for things such as the breaking of pots.

Objectification of the Forces

With this elaborate pantheon of deities and spirits, it was logical that an equally elaborate symbol system should be developed by man to bring them, as it were, closer for more effective and daily communication as Ezeafulukwe rightly observed. This had given rise to those statues, statuettes and other man-made aesthetic objects that we have come to recognize as African art and which strongly influenced the direction of 20th century art, producing the phenomenon known as modern art.

In order to clarify a common misconception perpetrated by iconoclasts, it must be stated that these art objects were and are never worshipped. The producers and users never cease to recognize them as symbols for ideas and concepts, in much the same way that the Christian does not mistake a statue or picture of Christ, Mary or the Saints as the real things. For the Igbo and the Christian alike, the work of art is merely a focal point for concentration during worship.

Okafor Okefi, a wood carver in Agulu, made an observation that both clarifies this and at the same time reveals the intellectual origin of traditional art. Talking about *ikenga*, he insisted that every man had an *ikenga*, including Christians. The Christian did not commission a sculpted representation of his *ikenga*, said Okefi, but when he slaughtered a goat at Christmas, it was an indirect offering to his *ikenga* without whose help and wakefulness he would not have been successful enough to kill a goat at Christmas. So, the African recognizes the difference between the piece of wood, the work of art, and the concept it represents. Hence an ineffective *ikenga*, for instance, could be thrown away or destroyed or a communal *alusi* abandoned.

To get a clearer and more tangible idea of what we are talking about, let us imagine, for instance, a Mr. X who is very much within the traditional Igbo system and is about to set out on a journey to Nsukka to study. Being admitted into a university would be a thing of joy and achievement. What would be Mr. X's hopes? He would look forward to enhancing his social standing by obtaining a degree (something like a title), increasing the respect he commands, his fame and so on. Of course, there would be fears: an accident on the road, envy at home and at the university, fear of the unknown. Before he leaves his home in the village, he would invariably offer kolanuts, palm wine, kill a fowl or goat depending on his pocket, and offer thanks and pray to Ana and the following:

(a) his ancestors (represented by wooden statues known as *okpesi*). He would ask for their protection at all times.

(b) his *ikenga*, the individual achievement principle. He would thank it for what it had done and would do for him. Related to *ikenga* and sometimes incorporated on the *ikenga* figure are the other principles associated with the individual, namely *ufo* ("mention") which is responsible for fame, *iru* ("face") which controls influence, personality (cf. *iru a bana m ọfịa*), uhu (tongue) which controls persuasive eloquence.

(c) *ukwunije* (lit. "foot and journey"), cult of the limb. He would ask for its guidance on his journey to Nsukka and back, keeping at bay all *ọgbọnuke*. *Ukwunije* is also related to the day/week principle. Mr. X would probably consult a diviner (*dibia afa*) to find out what he should expect, what he should do, which *agwu* he should propitiate. *Agwu* are mischievous spirits and are usually represented by wooden figures in the paraphernalia of the *dibịa afa*.

Concept into Form

Now, how does the concept of *ikenga* influence eventuation of visual form? As already noted, *ikenga* is a symbol of individual achievement, strength, success. Two upthrusting protuberances are standard on most *ikenga* (Fig. 1).

There are divergent opinions as to what they stand for. Some people say that they represent the horns of a ram, meaning strength, power. This seems to be supported by the evidence of some *ikenga* figures whose horns are curved like those of a ram. Others maintain that they stand for the hands held up above the head and showing the palms, symbolizing straight-forwardness, uprightness and justice. This is the opinion of Okafor Okefi.

Beneath the horns is a face which may bear the *ichi* (facial sacrifications that show high rank). The face, though anthropomorphic, is not a human face. Some *ikenga* have a human body with the right hand wielding a matchet (*okala dimkpa* — "a man's half") with which man hacks his way through life, and the left holding a human skull symbolizing achievement, power, might a carry-over from the days of head hunting. The combination of knife and skull epitomize the fulfilled man. The figure sits on a carved stool.

This is the general form of an *ikenga*. But variations stretch from the very abstract ones with just the horns and a highly stylized *mpata* (stool) which some people interprete as a sign of the ancestors, to the very elaborate figures incorporating several other elements such as snakes, baboons, and other wild animals. The social standing of a man is often reflected by the size and iconography of his *ikenga*.

Animals and human elements have, as we have seen, been borrowed by the artist to create a potent and evocative symbol for something that is essentially conceptual. Function, therefore, is primary and determines the form. A further illustration of how function can influence form is the way the arms

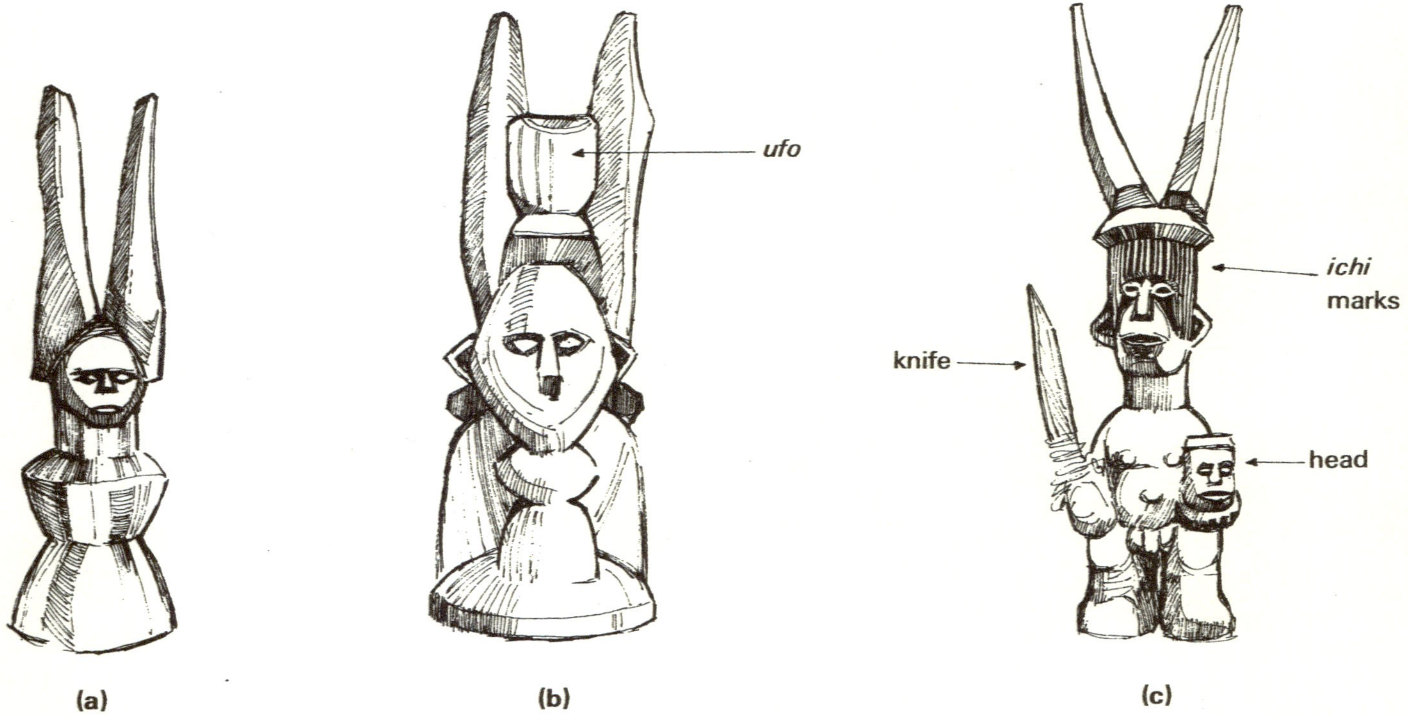

FIG. 1. *Ikenga figures:* **(a)** *and* **(b)** *carved by Ezeafụlụ of Oraifite,* **(c)** *carved by an artist from Agulu.*

have been rendered on the *ndiom agwu* figure by Ahaotu Mbagwu of Attah (Fig. 2).

The arms are stunted and end in receptacles for kolanuts during sacrifice. So, it is not as if the artist cannot sculpt a "proper" arm.

This *ndiom agwu* figure exhibits another quality of African sculpture that

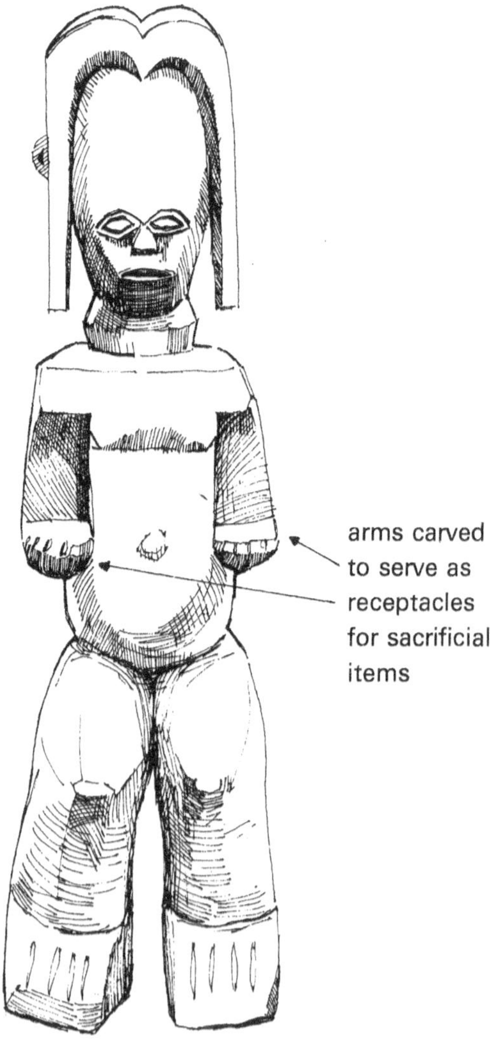

FIG. 2. *Ndiom Agwu, carved by Ahaotu Mbagwu of Attah.*

has often been commented on, namely, a sensitivity to or respect for material; one can still visualize the original form of the wood from which it is carved.

The Oxford Companion to Art (ed. Harold Osborne) states that "the most distinctive contribution of Africa to world art has often been considered to be its intuitive character and *direct, non-literary apprehension of form* which acts as a foil to what many authorities regard as an imbalance between intellect and intuition in the traditions of Western art". The italics are mine.

The keywords are, therefore, functionality, symbolism and sensitive apprehension of form. The work of art is recognized as a sign of something, not a reproduction of nature.

Masquerades

With the same kind of analysis one would be able to relate the forms of different Igbo masks to the concepts that inform them. The ethereal beauty of *Agboghomuo* is caught by the delicate feminine features, surmounted by the elaborate headgear decorated with *uli* motifs and mirrors. This beauty is enhanced by the brightly coloured applique costume and the delicate dance steps. On the other extreme, the raw, naked power or might of *Agaba Idu Mgbedike* is captured by the huge, awesome visage with very bold features and frightening teeth.

In a class of its own is the *Ijele* which appears once in every so many years. It is a spectacle, a sight that summarises majesty, grandeur and communal endeavour. All these it achieves by sheer size, colour and movement. Above all, almost anything one can think of, including other masquerades, is presented on an *Ijele*. (The *mbari* house which is a combination of architecture, sculpture and painting is in the same class as *Ijele*, in many ways related to it.)

Decorative Art: Painting

At this point, it should be stated that not every work of art produced by Africans is within a conceptual framework. During festivals the walls of shrines, and, in some places, private homes, are decorated with brilliant well-composed murals executed by women. These serve a purely decorative and artistic purpose and people look at them for aesthetic pleasure. Nevertheless, they still exhibit the schematization and simplification of forms that one observes in the sculpture. Well-known objects such as the kolanut, fruits, linoleum, reptiles and other animals are used as points of departure for creating geometric designs. One familiar with the symbol system would recognize the motifs used but without that knowledge one's enjoyment of the paintings *qua* paintings is in no way impaired.

Tradition and Originality

Is it possible for an artist to be original within this traditional system we have been discussing? *Nka di n' obu* (Lit. "creativity/craftsmanship is within the heart"), the concept of *akika obu* (intuition or lit. "design of the heart") would suggest an affirmative answer. Beyond the required symbols/motifs in any given context, the artist is usually free to express himself, to give full rein to his imagination. This is borne out by the incredible variety within a given form, for example the *ikenga*. It may be said, therefore, that the artist is only restricted in the area of primary symbol. But beyond that it would be a question of "*ife afịfia di n'anị gosili mmadu*" (lit. "what the grass on the earth reveals to man"), in the words of Okafor Okefi.

Conclusion

Much of African art is functional, tied to religion which is very much a part of the people's everyday life being an adaptive instrument in the quest of what Max Weber called "the problem of meaning". This is not, in anyway, to deny the importance of innate aesthetic impulses in the eventuation of the work of art. Rather, it is that religion provided the initial impetus or *raison d'etre*, and the artist the rest.

Though the artist resorts to anthropomorphic and zoomorphic forms to realize the concepts embodied by the works, the distinction between natural forms and art forms is recognized. Every attempt is made to avoid sculpting human beings because spirit or immaterial beings are the subjects. Furthermore, it is believed that if the sculpture piece resembles a living human being, the person so resembled will die. Even in the essentially decorative arts of drawing and painting, the divorce between the forms of nature and those of art, of imagination, is recognized.

The traditional African system recognizes and encourages individual talent and originality. Hence, artists receive commissions beyond their own villages, though occasionally with unfortunate results as in the case of the Umunze *ikoro*, where the villagers who commissioned it, waylaid the artist on his way home and killed him to prevent his carving an equally beautiful or even better one for any other community.

Bibliography

1. Aniakor, Chike, "Structuralism in Ikenga – An Ethnoaesthetic Approach," *Ikenga* (January, 1973), pp. 6–28, illus.
2. Igboanugo, C. P. S., "Decorative Designs as Essential Element in the Cultural Life of Oraifite," B.A. Thesis, University of Nigeria, 1972.
3. Okeke, Uche, "Traditional Igbo Art", mimeograph (unpublished).
4. Trowell, Margaret, *Classical African Sculpture,* 3rd revised edn. London: Faber & Faber, 1970.
5. Udechukwu, Obiora, "Functionality, Symbolism and Decoration: Some Aspects of Traditional Igbo Art," *The Conch* III/2 (September 1971), pp. 89–96, illus.
6. Willett, Frank, *African Art.* London: Thames and Hudson, 1971.

CHAPTER EIGHT

Modes of Communication

Dr. O. O. Oreh
Department of Mass Communication
University of Nigeria, Nsukka

What is Communication?

Some maintain the view that the word communication is dervied from the Latin verb "communicare" which means "to talk together, confer, discuss and consult one with another". Others believe it comes from a Latin noun "communus" which means "common". They say with justification that to communicate means to make the message of communication common.

It is however the meaning of the word — the sharing of ideas — not its origin that interests us here. For our purpose, therefore, we will accept that to communicate means to share our ideas or feelings or messages with another or others by making our message common property to them.

Technological developments have greatly widened both the scope and means of communication that even the original word "communication" has now been extended to accommodate these new meanings.

Systems of Communication

We discern:

1. *Human or social communication.* This is "the art of transmitting information, ideas and attitudes from one person to another"[1] by a variety of means such as spoken or written word (language) or gesture.

2. *Transport communication.* This includes aeroplanes, cars, ships and such other vehicles for travelling and transportation as are available to man.

[1] Edwin Emery *et al.*, *Introduction To Mass Communication*, 2nd edn. (New York: Dodd, Mead and Co., 1968).

3. *Tele-communication.* Communication at a distance only, cable telegraph, telephone or radio (c/f radio message).

4. *Mass communication.* This is the system whereby information, ideas, and attitudes are transmitted to a sizeable and diversified audience simultaneously through the use of a medium such as radio, television, newspapers or cinema.

Because of the use man makes of all four systems described above, our world has become, figuratively speaking, small. We can eat breakfast in Enugu, lunch in London and dinner in New York by jet.

We are present in a world-cup football match between Holland and Argentina in Buenos Aires, sitting by television in the comfort of our living rooms. We can telephone and confer with our overseas business partners about colour television receiver sets for Festac. Marshall McLuhan can speak of the global village because of television's ubiquitous presence as a medium of mass communication.

Because of the ever-growing means of sharing ideas and attitudes, it is now possible to speak of traditional and modern methods of communication, even if the latter is an enormous extension of the former.

To study theories of communication is to pursue knowledge that on the one hand dates back to the beginning of culture and on the other hand includes hypotheses so recent that they are still being tested and modified today. It includes *rhetoric*, the art and science of speech; *cybernetics*, the science of control and communication in animals and machines; *information theory*, which postulates that communication requires the transmission of energy; and now, *mass communication*. This chapter is, of necessity, restricted in scope and cannot, therefore, go into all the theories of communication; it is concerned with traditional and modern modes of communication as they relate to the way messages, attitudes and feelings are communicated among human beings.

Taken together, both the traditional and the modern means of communication are quite vast. They include all possible ways of attracting attention such as facial expression and gesture, touch, pictures, and visual signs, symbols, music, dance and words, both spoken and written.

The range of communication is as varied as the means. It stretches from simple commands, such as "go", "don't", "stop", which may be conveyed by verbal expression or gesture, pictorial signs, or flashing of lights of agreed or accepted and known meaning, to the most complex and lofty expressions of human thought and feeling. Drama, painting, sculpture, music and religious rituals are among such human expressions of lofty and complex ideas, emotions and feelings.

Traditional Modes of Communication

Traditional modes of communication can be divided into several categories: inter-personal or face-to-face type of communication, a broader level inter-group communication, and communication at the mass level. Distinction is made between verbal and non-verbal modes of communication and a combination of verbal and non-verbal. Each of these modes of communication sometimes suffer a certain degree of *noise** *poor fidelity*** and often total *break-down****.

A verbal or non-verbal mode would be used in each of the communication situations mentioned above depending upon what type would ensure message fidelity or complete and effective communication goal achievement.

Communication is perhaps man's second most important need after biological needs. In fact, to satisfy some biological needs man must employ verbal or non-verbal communication. This is why a face-to-face system, and, indeed, all other systems of communication developed in traditional African societies.

Non-Verbal Mode of Communication

In any given society, if two or more persons expect to understand each other, to hold some kind of meaningful discussion, they must have a common object or event to which they attach a mutually accepted meaning. Secondly, one universal purpose of communication is to influence/stimulate reaction (or feedback as it is now called) from the person the message is addressed. For these two reasons a variety of non-verbal modes of communication developed among Africans of early times.

* *Noise* in communication theory is anything which interferes with message fidelity.

** *Poor fidelity*. In communication theory if the message received is less than that sent or unclear at reception it is said to be of poor fidelity.

*** *Break-down*. If there is a misunderstanding of the message sent at reception, for any of many reasons, there is a break-down of communication. For example, if a person is addressed in a language he/she does not understand.

Instruments

In almost all parts of Igboland a number of instruments developed for this purpose are still in use today. They are *Talking Drums*, *Ikoro*, *Opi*, *Oja*, *Ekwe*, *Ogene*, *Egbe* (see diagrams on following pages). In all cases, each community attaches specific meanings to the sounds that these instruments make.

In Abam, Ohafia and Arochuku areas, as in other parts of Igboland, the *Ikoro* (a big tree trunk hollowed out and slit open in one small area which gives a "dum dum" sound when struck with a stick) represents what the telegraph is to the modern and industrialized world. To this day, it is still the quickest means of transmitting messages of community-wide importance. It serves on occasions such as festivals, funerals and emergencies. It occupies a central position in the governance of the community. It "sings" praises of tribal war heroes and people of distinguished achievements.

Beaten at night everybody in the community and in nearby villages and towns knows that something is amiss or that the moon has been sighted and the New Yam Festival is to commence, depending on the rhythm, intensity, and interval of the sound. This instrument is sacred and is not owned individually nor beaten for frivilous reasons. *Ikoro* is normally not approached by men who are not titled either as a result of bravery or great heroism, and never by women.

The *Ekwe* (a wooden gong, i.e. a piece of wood carved hollow, which when beaten with a small stick produces a dry sound) and the *Ogene* (a metal disc with a folded rim that gives a resonant sound when struck with a small stick) are used by towncriers in diseminating news. Their main function is to demand attention for verbal communication. When the gong is struck in any area (compound) of a community, usually at night, absolute quiet descends. The town crier then delivers his message. This is an example of the combination of verbal and non-verbal types of communication which is discussed later.

Another instrument of non-verbal communication used in traditional societies in Igboland is the *Talking Drum*. It comes in many shapes, sizes, and names in many parts of Africa. It is called *Ikpirikpe* in the Ohafia area already mentioned, *Igba* in the Awka area of Anambra State and *Iya Ilu* or *Ulu* in some areas of Yorubaland. This is a drum made of a hollow cylinder with leather parchment covering one or in some cases both ends. It plays a similar communication role to that of the *Ikoro*. The *Talking Drum* is, however, less sacred than the *Ikoro* in many parts of Igboland. It is mostly used to summon young men to communal labour or for praise singing.

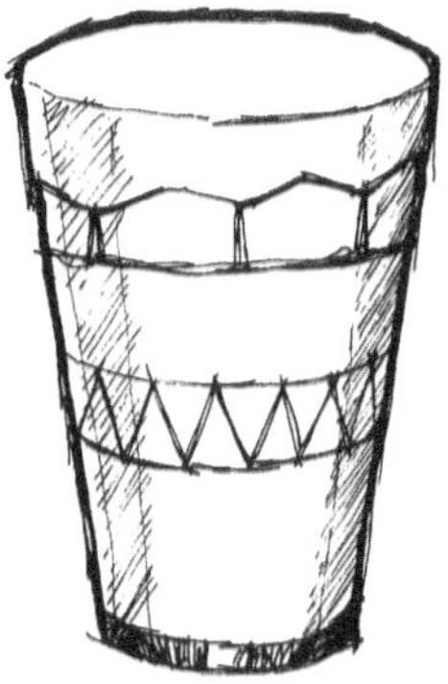

Igba, Ikpirikpe or *Talking Drum*

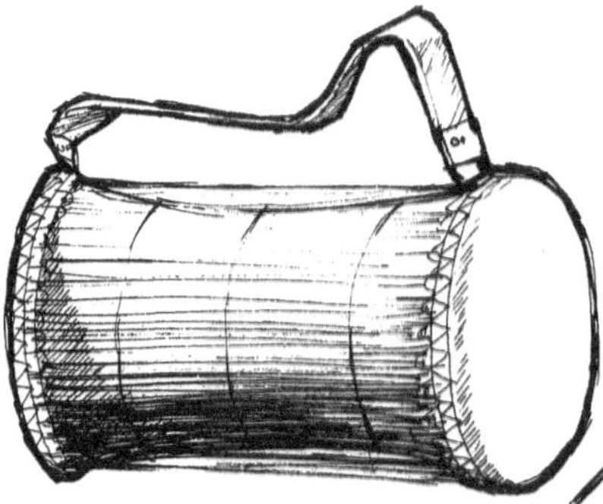

Iya Ilu or *Talking Drum* *Ukeke*

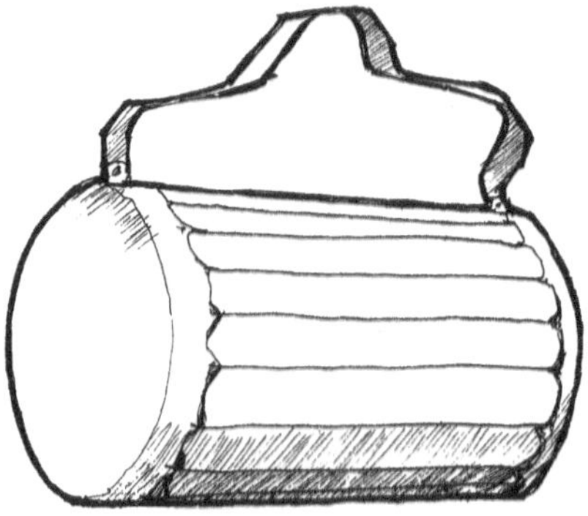

Akpema Olimi (Burial Ceremony Drum)

Ukpi

Ikoro

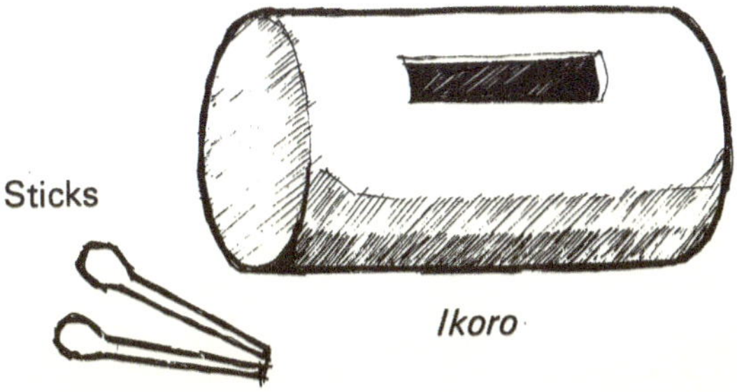

Ikoro

Ekwe

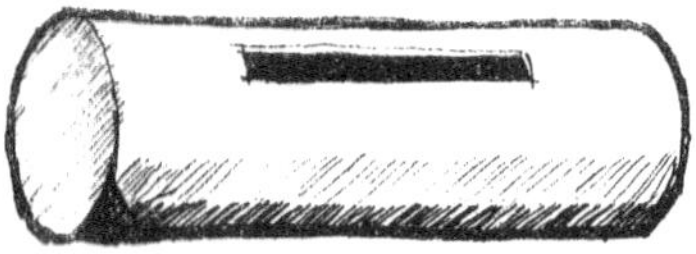

Ekwe

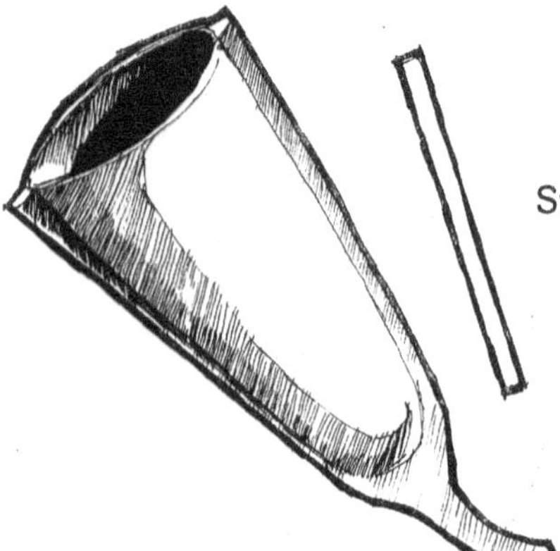

Ogene

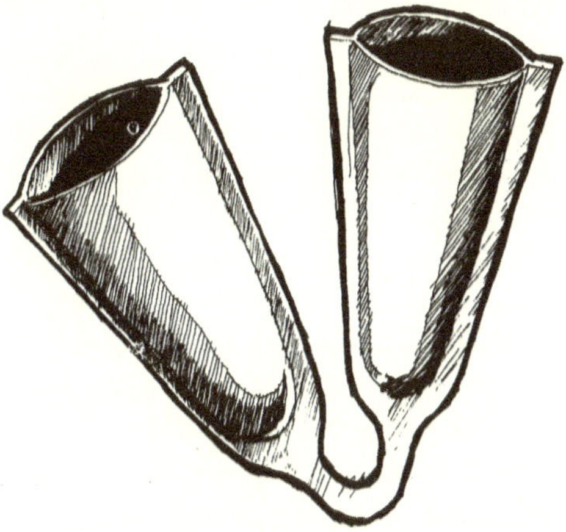

Ogene

Palm Frond (*Omu*)

There are two types of *Opi* (horns). The smaller one, the antelope horn, is used like the modern trumpet to summon the youth, encourage them during communal labour, and praise brave deeds during ceremonies. It conveys an emotional message, asking men to do and dare.[2]

The bigger kind of this type is the elephant horn. It is blown by titled men during burial ceremonies of titled and wealthy men. Men also blow these horns during festivals to show their wealth in that they were able to purchase them. In some areas of Igboland, Enugu, Nkanu, Awgu, the elephant tusk horn announces births and indicate the male sex by mentioning a masquerade.

The *Oja* (wooden flute) and *Ogene* (metalic gong) serve in much the same way as the *Opi*.

The gun is also one of the universal non-verbal instruments of communication throughout Igboland. A gun shot at night conveys the unmistakable message that an important person has died and that burial obsequies are to commence. The firing must be done repeatedly and at intervals and can last for days when a very important person dies.[3]

In some areas firing of a gun behind a woman being led to her father's compound by her husband means that she is being divorced; the man will never remarry her. This custom of communicating final divorce has an exact opposite in some other areas of Igboland. In Abam for instance, one gun shot when the bride goes into the compound of the bridegroom, concludes marriage ceremonies; it pronounces a man and a woman married.

Kurutu (canon – a type of explosives) buried beneath the surface of the earth and detonated to produce heavy and far reaching sound is the highest form of gun shooting used to convey to distant villages and communities that an illustrious son of a village from where the shooting is occuring has died and that final burial obsequies are in progress.

Other Symbols

Apart from instruments, other symbols of communication abound in traditional societies of Africa. These instruments include the *Omu*, facial tribal

[2] There is a story that once in Achalla, a town in Awka local government area of Anambra State, a man skilled at blowing this *Opi* was engaged to do so. While blowing it, he reached the compound where the ceremony was being held. Finding that the ceremony was for a dead woman, he put the *Opi* in his pocket and cried profusely. "The *Opi* is not meant to be blown for women," he said.

[3] The 21 gun salute which today normally heralds the arrival of visiting foreign heads of state to a friendly country may have derived its origins and significance (message) from this African use of gun shot as a mode of non-verbal communication.

marks, dress patterns, hair style, *Ugba* (Yoruba calabash with broomsticks in it), a pot of palm wine (with some leaves in it), beads, feathers (*Abuba Ugo* in Igbo), and chalk (black and white) among others.

If it takes a gun shot to convey the successful conclusion of marriage negotiations in some parts of Igboland and the same gun shot to convey the conclusion of divorce proceedings in some other parts, other forms of non-verbal communication exists for bride-price discussion and initiation of divorce proceedings.

In Nnewi area of Igboland, for instance, young girls at puberty communicate their readiness to marry by decorating their young supple bodies with *cam wood powder and beads*. They then troop out to the village square to entertain the men with *dance* and *looks* which say, "look at me, I could be yours if you play it right". The message is usually taken because by the next outing ceremony none of the same group of girls are usually still available.

If this outing ceremony took place among the Zulus and Swazis of southern Africa, the girls would then be "promised" to the boys. A new set of non-verbal kind of communication would ensue. This time it would be *beads* of different colours. At betrothal, the courting couple would exchange beads of different colours — called *ucu*. After the sealing ceremony the beads would become love letters. A string of red beads would mean "I love you", white ones would mean "I am proud of you", and green ones would convey the consoling message, "I am thinking of you".

Apparently the traditional methods of buying and selling by long bargaining in words is too shabby for the institution of marriage. So when the families of the courting bride and bridegroom meet to negotiate the bride price, it is forbidden to haggle with spoken words. Instead, haggling is conducted in a different style in Yorubaland, as in some parts of Igboland. On such occasions there is an exchange of *Ugba*, a calabash with a number of short pieces of broomsticks put inside it. The one from the bride's parents represents the unit of money they are asking for in exchange for their daughter, while the number of sticks in the calabash sent to them from the bridegroom's parents represents the amount they are prepared to pay for the bride. This exchange continues until an agreement is reached and the young Yoruba bride is married.

In another part of Igboland, Ozubulu for instance, if a man does not like the wife arranged for him by his parents, he gives her a pot of palm-wine stuffed with some green leaves to go home to her parents with. Anybody who sees her carrying this pot understands at once that she has been rejected by her husband and that divorce proceedings have just started. If she carried that pot of wine with another type of fresh leaves (chude) people would know that she has just been accepted by the man going to become her husband, and is going to tell her father so.

The most common symbol of non-verbal communication in most parts of Igboland is the *Omu* ("palm frond" (p. 103) as it is called here, the plume of oil palm tree). A knot of it in anyone's mouth means he will neither talk nor should he be talked to. On a lorry, it means the lorry is conveying home a dead body. If the messenger of an Arochuku chief offers an *Omu*, he has summoned the man to a meeting with the chief without fail. In yet another sense, *Omu* among raw food items in some other parts of Igboland means that those items are for sale.

Whereas some titled Igbomen (and women in some places) wear only a string or metal ring or beads on their ankles, others wear in addition, one or more *Ugo* (eagle) feathers on their caps to show that they are men of substance, an *Ozo* or chief of some rank. Their counterparts, the Obas, in Yorubaland wear voluminous embroidered gowns with many beads on their dresses and crowns. The Oba's messengers have one half of their hair cut lower than the other.

Traditional dress pattern in Nigeria, if not in most parts of Africa, indicates the tribe of the wearer. A more permanent tribal identity in some parts of Africa is, of course, the *tribal mark* that leaves long scars on some Yoruba people's faces, holes in Fulani noses, and holes with ear-rings in the ear of a Masai of East Africa.

Another symbol of wide use in traditional communication is white *chalk*. Restricted use of the white chalk is made by jujumen or native doctors. When chalk is rubbed across the left eye, it conveys the information to all, especially prospective clients that these men are oracles of great powers, able to divine hidden mysteries and also to remove evil spirits by remote control, by herbal medication, through talisman sacrifices of some eggs, or live animals. On the other hand, in a traditional home in many parts of Igboland white chalk is offered to a guest to rub on his wrist or foot as a mark of welcome. A woman visiting another who had just had a baby expresses her joy by rubbing her face with white chalk offered by the new mother. If a community wants to declare war on another, they send such a community black chalk. But a messenger of peace clutches white chalk instead of an olive branch.

Non-Verbal and Verbal Communication Combined

A combination of the verbal and the non-verbal type of traditional mode of communication commonly used is the *town crier* and his *Ekwe* (p. 102).

As mentioned before, the town crier beats his instrument to ask the people to pay attention. This they do, some by standing right in front of him, thus completing the communication process. He then announces by spoken word his real message of a pending meeting or new laws.

The town crier's gong or *Ogene* goes like this:

Go-gom! Go-gom!
Go-gom! Go-gom!
Men and women of Obodo-o Inyi-o
Hear the words of the ndi ichie!
Every able-bodied man, one big yam!
Every able-bodied man, one big yam!
Every woman, five cassava tubers!
Every woman, five cassava tubers!
Every village, one tin of palm oil!
Every village, one tin of palm oil!
First thing tomorrow morning!
All for our soldiers!
Whoever hears should spread the world!
Whoever hears should spread the word!
Go-gom! Go-gom!

If the town crier has announced communal work, he will also announce fines for absentees and such people will be duly fined since the town crier has specified the fine. Every sentence is repeated in order to lay emphasis. This type of communication is in two parts, verbal and non-verbal, but each segment is complete communication by itself.

Most Africans tug on their ear or point to their eyes for emphasis, which is an important factor in communication process when saying "I heard it first hand" and "I saw it happen myself". Body movement, which is constantly employed apart from relaxing the speaker and helping speech delivery, communicates thought and emotion among Africans.

Verbal Communication: Language

The three most important ingredients of language communication are thought, feelings and words, One must know (by thinking or feeling) what one wants to say and must have or know what symbols — words — to use in expressing one's thoughts and feelings. Writing as it is known today, is one of the skills of language communication which is a relatively recent communication acquisition. Although it had its early beginnings in Africa, when writing became a communication skill acquirable through formal education, Africans did not participate for a long time.

Today, as in the past, Africans express themselves in languages of numerous dialects. This is what communication theorists call verbal communication. This may take the form of spoken or sung communication. Communication that is spoken includes proverbs, riddles, narratives, simple commands, requests, exclamations, and statements of one or more words as mentioned already.

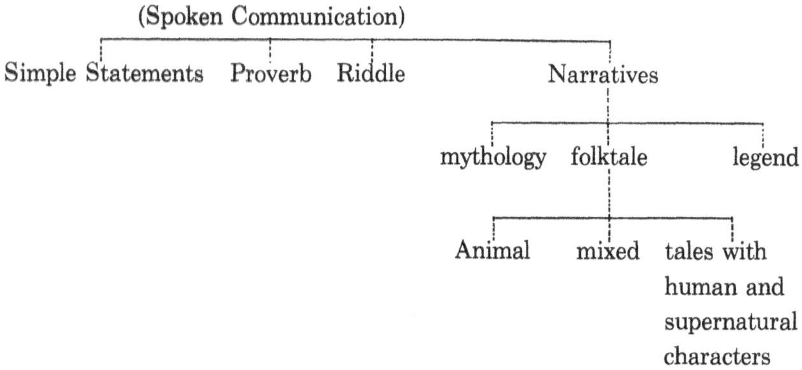

Sung communication as a mode of communication covers a large scope. Some songs are for mourning, war, or birth; others are used for title taking, praise, and festive occasions. A stranger approaching a funeral party does not need to be told that somebody has died as funeral songs convey a motif of sorrow, loss, search, anger, and grief.

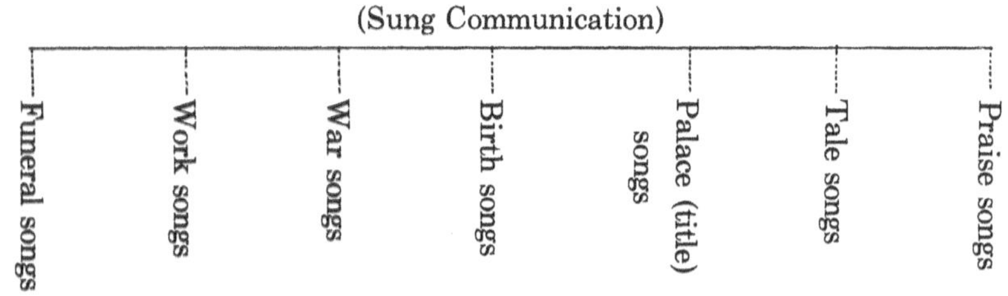

Work songs, often rendered with work tools such as cutlass or sawing machine, are used as labour accompaniments. They convey messages of strength, prowess, and dignity of labour.

War songs are used to encourage valor or hostile sentiments. Thus, the use of war songs are restricted to occasions of war, or celebration of victory. Abam, Ohafia and Bende war dances have become famous throughout Nigeria.

Birth songs announce the arrival of a new baby. This is first announced by an exclamation of joy by a woman –"O! weo wo! !" This repeated exclamation summons all women around to the scene of the joyous event. They sing, dance and shout the name of the husband of the woman inviting him to dance and entertain them. The man responds by firing a gun shot in the air. This response consolidates the amusement. He gives them palm wine, kola and some money.

Title songs are sung at title-taking ceremonies, the installation of chiefs and *ozo* men. Such songs convey the message of respect and loyalty.

Praise songs are used to welcome war heroes, men of achievement and eminence. Such terms as *Isam* ("coral"), *ugo*, ("eagle bird"), *ola edo* ("gold ring"), constitute words of praise.

Proverbs

The communicative ability of proverbs in African usage can best be explained by the saying popularized by a Nigerian novelist, Chinua Achebe, that "proverbs are the palm oil with which we eat words". Proverbs are used in giving information, advice, rebuke, praise and lament. The reason may be because of their subtlety, brevity and precision. For instance, a proverb user who says "onye ara na uche ya yi", ("The madman is accompanied by his senses") has communicated an important message which should not be taken literally. This proverb means "the actor knows what he is doing".

The *riddle*, like the proverb, makes conscious use of words for literary effect. The audience of a riddle is a youthful one, but it is supposed that adults coined the riddles for such use. To children, riddles mean more than aesthetic enjoyment. It is a complete language; it is communication that calls for man's wit and a perception of the world around him. Example:

Proposition: Gwa-m Gwa-m Gwa-m
Ekpete Chukwu kere
Answer: Afo

Proposition: Tell me Tell me Tell me
A drum made by God
Answer: Belly

This brand of communication is popular among African children and is used in socialization (teaching).

Narratives (story telling) are modes of communication too. Here, the speaker gives his message in simple direct statement. He may talk of daily events, myths, folktale or legends. With myths he answers questions about world order and epistemology. In traditional societies, myths explain creation and geographical phenomena. They propagate a world view; the universe instills fear by extolling conformity to social norms through the powers of witchcraft, magic, spirits, and other supernatural beings that defies nature in much the same way as present-day organized foreign and imported religion does.

Folktales are moonlight recreations. Stories are told on any subject, animals, human and supernatural characters. Such stories invoke the special qualities of some animals mentioned.

Example: The tortoise (Mbe) is known as a trickster
The leopard (Agu) and the lion (Odum) are associated withh brutal force.
The antelope is known for fear.
The spider is also known for tricks.

Thus in our daily traditional communication, these names, when used to describe people, convey a message by signifying what the animals are noted for. This is a high form of language communication.

Modern Modes of Communication

"At what point for, example," asks Doob "does a community or society in a developing continent like Africa begin rapidly to abandon traditional media of communication and to adapt modern mass media?"[4] Schram thinks that such a time is "when a society begins to modernize . . ."[5]

Some traditional modes of communication are today still used in their

[4] Leonard W. Doob, *Communication in Africa: A Search for Boundaries* (New Haven, Conn., Yale University Press, 1961), p. 370.

[5] Wilbur Schram, *Mass Media and National Development* (Stanford University Press; Stanford, Cal.: Paris: UNESCO, 1964), p. 79.

own right and independently. Others have found their place in the mass media of communication. Some others no longer serve any function in the present state of communication. The *Ikoro* and *Talking Drum* are used in broadcasting for station and time identification. Our languages are the spoken and written languages of our electronic and print media.

In other words, although Africa is in short supply of newspapers, magazines, cinema seats, radio and television sets, she nevertheless uses these modern media of communication and has found them to be useful tool of modernization and development.

Communication Model

The communication model for traditional modes of communication when compared with the model for the modern methods is rather simple, has no intervening channel, and the response or feedback of the message is often more immediate.

Wilbur Schram has noted that "in a completely traditional and illiterate society, the effective environment extends about as far as one can see, although it does include folk wisdom and religious beliefs handed down from parent to child or priest to believer [whereas] with [a] larger world comes a profound psychological change [and man] is shown a world in which he has to depend on others to tell him about".[6]

Both modes of communication have the same basic ingredients and the same purpose, that is, the aim of communication in each mode is to affect others. The concept of meaning is central in each case. This meaning of the message and its purpose acts as a link between the communicator and the receiver as our diagram below shows.

Graphically, typical models of communication look like this:

(I) Face-to-face (inter-personal) in traditional communication.

Here the link between the communicator and the recipient is the content or meaning of the message. It is this concept of meaning that the receiver "expresses" in his response or feedback.

[6] *Ibid.*, p. 79.

(II)

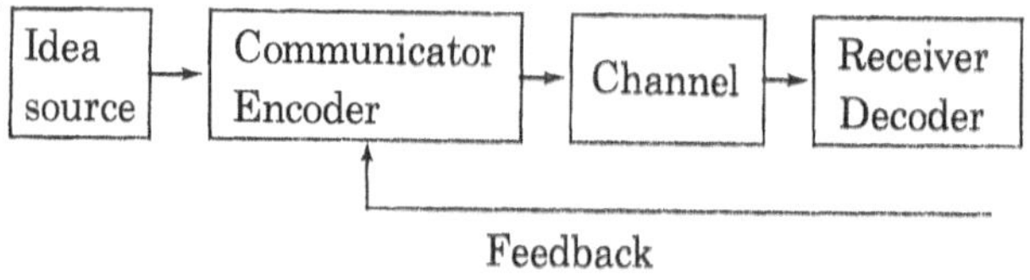

1. Source = Origin of the idea to be transmitted.
2. Communicator = The one who encodes the idea (transmits).
3. Channel = Media: radio, newspaper, T.V., film, etc.
4. Receiver = One who hears, reads, sees or perceives meaning and encoder.
5. ——→ = Idea, message, meaning, encoded transmitted, received, decoded and perceived.
6. ——→ = Feedback, response, reaction, occasioned by meaning perceived.
7. ——→ ——→ ——→ = Noise. This can occur at any communication process.

The modern media of mass communication is new in Africa. The first newspaper established in the West Coast of Africa "was the *Sierra Leone Gazette* which was founded by officers of the Sierra Leone Company and which experienced alterations and restorations of name until 1827 when it was given up".[7] In 1822 the *Gold Coast Gazette* was established in Accra and patterned after the *Freetown Newsheet*.[8] The Loveday Mission of South Africa established the *Indaba (News)* newspaper in South Africa in the Kafir language in 1841. In 1859, the *Iwe Irohin fun awon ara Egba ati Yoruba*, "a newspaper for the Egba and the (Oyo) Yoruba", was established by Rev. Townshend in Abeokuta.[9] By 1939, a weekly, the *Nigerian Catholic Herald*, was established in Calabar (Nigeria) and in Enugu, the *Eastern outlook*, was established in May, 1951.

Cinema came to Lagos, Nigeria in 1903, while radio broadcasting came in 1932 as a result of the British Broadcasting Corporation's empire service for West Africa.

Television broadcasting was first established in Morocco in 1956 and failed for want of money. In 1959 it was established in Ibadan, Nigeria.

[7] Fred I. A. Omu, "The Iwe Irohin (1859—1867)," in the *Journal of the Historical Society of Nigeria* IV/1 (December, 1967), pp. 35—44.

[8] *Ibid.*, p. 35—44.

[9] *Ibid.*, p. 35—44.

Today newspapers are being printed by fascimile methods enabling the *New Nigerian* to publish its daily issue in Lagos and Zaria simultaneously for quicker circulation. Today there are colour television by satellite, coaxial cables and tethered aerostat balloon transmission in Africa. Today Nigerians are asking for and getting multi-channel TV transmission and FM radio broadcast.

Africa of the 20th century has joined the "global village" and its concomitant world culture. She is no more the dark continent nor is she still the white man's grave, if she ever was in any objective sense.

Why?

Why and how did this transition from ancient to modern modes of communication occur?

It can be said that traditional modes of communication are no longer able to satisfy all present communication needs. These needs include: (1) socialization (transmission of the social heritage from one generation to the next); (2) surveillance (informing us of what happens in both our immediate environment and the larger world society); and (3) entertainment. Traditional modes of communication did all these successfully, but with urbanization, the erstwhile closely-knit community or society is losing the ability to enforce its social norms. The modern modes of communication are now better able to carry on these functions.

When one amalgamates diverse communities into nations, when one must speak to plural societies of hetrogenous peoples in a common "world dialect" as it were, when one must try, with hope, the laws of combined development; one needs a technical form of communication which permits rapid transmission of information publicly to large, heterogeneous and impersonal audiences almost simultaneously. The technical form of communication that can do this is the modern mode of communication the mass media. Mass media has taken over the role of the town crier because African societies are now large, complex, and diverse and information needs now require the sophistication of modern modes of communication.

In places such as the Ivory Coast and the Cameroons, television and radio are being used effectively for education and information, hence for development. What now remains to be done is for Africa to exploit her media of communication for cultural, social, economic and political development in greater detail.

Bibliography

1. Barry, Sir Gerald, *et al.*, *Communication and Language*. New York: Doubleday, 1965.
2. Dickens, M., *Speech, Dynamic Communication*, 2nd edn. New York: Harcourt, Brace and World, 1963.
3. Emery, E., *et al.*, *Introduction to Mass Communication*, New York: Dodd, Mead and Co. 1968.
4. Wright, C. R., *Mass Communication: A Sociological Perspective*. Berkeley: University of California Press; New York: L. A. Random House, 1965.

PART III:

Colonial Society

CHAPTER NINE

Education and Socialization

Dr. U. Onwuka
Department of Education,
University of Nigeria, Nsukka

An American psychologist, M. K. Harlow, carried out a number of experiments with monkeys and found out that monkeys reared in social isolation showed marked anti-social traits. These traits include apathy, unresponsiveness, and heightened anxiety. In addition, the general appearance was dull, shrivelled, or flaccid.[1]

If a human baby could be taken away at birth from the mother and somehow raised in complete isolation, such an individual would lack the essential attributes of a human being. Based upon this theory, it can be asserted that *man without man cannot be human*. It is the fact of living together that makes man truly human, for man is a social animal. Hence Aristotle, long ago, observed that "man is by nature an animal intended to live in polis. He who is without a polis, by reason of his own nature and not of some accident, is either a poor sort of being, or a being higher than man . . ."[2] In other words, such a being is either a beast or a superhuman. This prefatory merely underlines the fact that man must live together with his fellow man.

Living together is by no means easy. But to be man, man must live and grow up among his fellow man in a given group: family, nation, or generation. In order to survive, he must share or, at least for some time, accept some of the sentiments, norms and values of the group in which he finds himself. Survival also demands that man must be able to satisfy his needs or continuously tackle the tasks and face the problems involved in securing the

[1] See Gregory A. Kimble and Norman Garmazy, *Principles of General Psychology*, 3rd edn. (New York: The Ronald Press Company, 1968), p. 419.

[2] See *The Politics of Aristotle*, translated with notes by Ernest Barker (Oxford: Clarendon Press, 1957), p. 6.

necessities of life in society. The task of making an individual fit in and play his part in society is the function of education and socialization.

This chapter examines the role of education in the process of socialization. It seeks to define education and socialization, and to study the relationship between them. It briefly describes the various stages of socialization as well as the processes involved in the course of socialization and education. It touches upon some fundamental concepts which must be understood in order to assess the degree of success of socialization in any particular society, especially the socializing influence of the educational effort in Nigeria. In the light of the following discussion, the reader should be able to make some recommendations for more effective socialization and education in this country.

Because it is many-faceted, "education" defies any single, precise, all-embracing definition. The term could refer to the work done in schools and all institutions of learning. It could refer to the specialized study in departments or colleges of education regarding the preparation of teachers or various personnel engaged in educational services. Thus, it is often said that someone is reading "education". Two definitions of education that embrace the broad aspects of the term regard education as "*all of man's activities which enable him to realize himself and to live fully as a human being*", or as "*a process of influencing the young and inexperienced so that they may become worthy human beings and citizens*".[3]

Education can further be defined as "the process of relating the individual to society, so as *to secure the development of personality* and social welfare"[4] or as the process of remaking or transforming the quality of experience to enable the individual to partake in the interests, purposes, and ideas current in the social group.[5] It can then be accepted as the process of harmonizing the individual with a given environment in such a manner as to enable him to develop his physical, mental, emotional and volitional capacities for the happiness and welfare of all. It is the means by which the older and more experienced bring their influence to bear upon the young, or more immature, and inexperienced members of society.

[3] See U. Onwuka, "Interplay of Education and Administration in Development," *Universitas* (University of Ghana) IV/2 (May, 1975), pp. 106–107.

[4] Paul Monroe, *A Text-book in the History of Education* (New York: The Macmillan Company, 1957), p. 754.

[5] See John Dewey, *Education and Democracy* (New York: Free Press Paperback edition, 1966), p. 11.

Socialization can be defined as learning that enables the learner to perform his various roles in his group. Thus, it is learning to participate as a member of a group. It is the process by which young people acquire the already existing culture of the group or groups in which they are associate.[6] Any learning or preparation that contributes to the individual's ability to perform social roles is socialization. P. H. Mussen and others have defined socialization as "the whole process by which an individual, born with behavioural potentialities of an enormously wide range, is led to develop actual behaviour which is confined within a much narrower range — the range of what is customary and acceptable for him according to the standards of his group".[7] They see it as the process by which the individual becomes a member of his social group through acquisition of the group's values, motives, and behaviours.[8]

It can now be stated that education and socialization are, simply, processes which enable people in any society to form their young into social beings. In other words, they are the means by which young people acquire the already existing culture of groups in which they live.

Upon what criteria can the two terms be differentiated? Both involve learning, and all learning involves some change in the individual. Nevertheless, "not all learning is socialization, since . . . some learning is irrelevant to the motivation and ability necessary for participation in social systems".[9] It is possible to be schooled without being socialized. While socialization implies conformity, education involves deliberate modification.

Education and socialization are both deliberate processes, carried out by specific agents and based upon previously determined norms. Who are these agents, and what are the norms? Agents of socialization and education are adults and experienced members of the society. They include the family (parents and other members of the family, nuclear or extended), peer-groups, teachers and a host of other responsible members of the society. It is the parents that lead the way in helping children develop the different types of acceptable behaviour in any society. The norms are based on the culture

[6] Harry M. Johnson, *Sociology: A Systematic Introduction* (London: Routledge and Kegan Paul Ltd., 1963), p. 82.

[7] Paul Henry Hussen, John Janeway Gonger, and Jerome Kegan, *Child Development and Personality*, 3rd edn. (New York: Evanston and London: Harper and Row Publisher, 1969), pp. 242–243.

[8] *Ibid.*

[9] Harry M. Johnson, *op. cit.*, p. 110.

and value system of the group. Since the agents must train the children or the immature and inexperienced members in accordance with ways of life of the society they belong to, they must, themselves, understand the culture of the group. They must also be loyal to the society and its institutions as well as its values. Where they hold these in contempt, they ignore them, bringing about a situation in which those undergoing the socialization process learn little or nothing of the society in which they live. Other societies about which they read or learn provide their reference pattern. What occurs in such a situation is "anticipatory socialization".

Anticipatory socialization is a kind of socialization in which the value system of the society in which an individual lives does not represent the individual's reference norms. An individual may live in circumstances of a close combination of kinship, religious or lower-class norms. Yet, by the virtue of his exposure through schools, television, or outside visits, he may become deeply influenced by the norms of a social group alien to his own. What happens is referred to as *anticipatory socialization* because the norms of the reference group that the individual aspires to belong to in the future are dominant in his life. Such a reference group may become the source of a radical break with native conditions.[10]

In order to be effective the agents of socialization must understand what they are trying to accomplish. But the effectiveness of their attempts ultimately depends upon the maturation of the "pupil". The pupil must be physically, mentally, and emotionally mature and ready for whatever social roles he is expected to perform. The pupil must internalize the roles he will be expected to perform as well as the roles of the other persons with whom he will interact. Timing is important in socialization. At each stage the pupil must internalize a set of roles. We shall now consider the stages of socialization.

Stages of Socialization

The process of socialization can be described under four stages corresponding with the development of the individual human being. The first is the *oral stage*, directly followed by the *anal stage*, the *oedipal stage*, and the *adolescence stage*.

[10] See Robert A. Nisbet, *The Social Bond, An Introduction to the Study of Society* (New York: Alfred Knoff, Inc., 1970), p. 110.

Stage I

The *oral stage* lasts up to the first year of life. The foetus (fetus) was warm and comfortable in the womb, but at birth it faces crises and frustrations. Whereas in the womb, it depended for its breathing upon the mother, at birth, it struggles to breathe on its own. The new baby must himself be fed, covered, cleaned and kept dry in order to be comfortable. Struggle for survival has begun.

At this stage, the child is almost wholly dependent upon the mother or "mother representative". He is not involved in the family as a whole, but with only a sub-system consisting of himself and the mother. Other members merely share with the mother in caring for the infant. In that way, they are said to be performing the role of "mother".

The child draws attention to his needs and gratifies himself through the mouth. He cries. He grasps with the mouth. The mouth is about the most active organ at this stage. Hence, the term *oral stage*.

This *oral stage* of development has two levels. The first level is the *passive-receptive* oral phase. The child at this stage is so passive relative to the mother that Freud refers to this stage as the period of "primary identification".[11] He is no more than a "possession". The child has no choice at all in what happens to him. Apart from crying, he cannot do anything as his senses are not yet developed. This level lasts until the child becomes able to reach actively for objects.

The second level is the *active-incorporative* oral phase. This is characterized by attempts at mastery through incorporation. He bites everything within his reach. His receptive tendency is charged with aggression directed toward the mother. He discharges his tension by means of "crying fit" and he bites the nipple with force and suckles with greed.

From the point of view of socialization, this is a very important stage. Some important traits of the individual's character develop at this stage. If the mother does not succeed in pacifying the crying infant, his physiological tension increase, and the need for incorporation becomes more and more charged with energy. This is referred to as hostile incorporation.

Obviously, the child cannot at this stage be said to be hostile. But the model of hostility is so formed. The crying infant alienates the helpless mother who subconsciously feels rejected by her child. On his part, the child feels

[11] Harry M. Johnson, pp. 124—125.

more "annihilated" by the sense of frustration which leads to exhaustion.[12]

It is at this oral stage that the child learns to differentiate what causes pain and learns to avoid it. He also learns which of his actions earns the mother's and others' approval and expressions of love and those which bring about disapproval and withdrawal of love. This is the beginning of the reality situation which ushers in the second stage, the *anal-sadistic* stage of development.[13]

Stage II

The second phase is the *anal stage*. This stage occurs from about the end of the first to the third year of life. During this stage, the double functions of the anus (retention and elimination) become the centre of interest as well as the source of pleasure. Of course, the urinary elimination and retention together with the pleasure or displeasure derived from them are included in this period of "anal" crisis.

A crucial learning situation is toilet training. The mother imposes some demands upon the child. H. M. Johnson asserts that the faeces are, to the child, a gift. It is a symbol of the child's love for the mother. Withholding it, or releasing it at "wrong" times is an expression of aggression or defiance. The positive sanction for correct performances is the mother's love.[14] In some cases, punishment of some sort is used to discourage incorrect performance. In every society, however, the mother encourages the child to discriminate between correct and incorrect performances. This is usually done by presenting cues and rewarding correct performance and not rewarding incorrect performance. If the training is pursued with severity and punishment, the incorporated prohibitions appear to be strictly punitive. The child rebels against them and tries to turn the hostility back onto the mother.

At this stage, the child internalizes two roles: his own and his mother's. The two are now clearly separate. He is no longer almost one and the same with the mother. The child receives love and care. In return, he gives love. But if the mother is severe, the child returns it with defiance and hostile self-assertion during toilet training. The ambivalence (love and hate, in this

[12] Therese Benedek, "Personality Development," in Franz Alexander & Helen Ross, eds., *The Impact of Freudian Psychiatry* (Chicago and London: University of Chicago Press, 1969), p. 40.

[13] *Ibid.*, p. 41.

[14] Harry M. Johnson, p. 125.

case) creates a vicious cycle. It increases the child's conflict with his environment. At the same time, it increases the conflict within himself.[15]

While trying to manifest his separate personality, no longer part of the mother, the child at the same time tries to identify himself with the mother as when he imitates some of his mother's activities. Freud refers to this characteristic as *anaclitic identification.*[16]

Already, by the second half of the first year of life, the child had become aware of other people in his orbit aside of the mother. But it is about the second year that these individuals begin to play definite roles in his life. Self-assertion then begins to manifest itself. The child begins to learn that he is expected to move from self-centred dependence to independent co-existence. Boys and girls become aware of their sex differences physiologically. They also begin to learn that in certain situations only certain types of behaviour are appropriate, and that some time in early life, people around them expect males and females to engage in different types of behaviour. From then on (two-years olds), owing to socializing influences, behaviour manifestations which are decidely masculine or feminine begin to appear. The girl begins to identify herself with the mother. The boy begins to compare himself with the father. If he is positively attracted to him, he identifies himself with him. Freud refers to this tendency of boys and girls identifying themselves with their fathers and mothers respectively as *defensive identification.* The boy, for instance, realizes that the father is more powerful and so he begins to identify with the "aggressor" and to become more like him. In this way, the boy defends himself against anxiety.[17] This tendency continues until the next stage when the rivalry between parent and child develops and influences the child's behaviour.

Stage III

The third period is the *oedipal stage.* This stage consists of two parts: the oedipal phase and latency. The first phase manifests itself during the fourth or fifth year of life, while the latency period follows and continues until about the age of twelve or thirteen.

The first part of this stage is characterized by what Freud popularized as

[15] Therese Benedek, p. 42.

[16] Robert F. Beihler, *Child Development: An Introduction* (Boston: Houghton/Mifflin Company, 1976), p. 344.

[17] *Ibid.*

the "oedipal complex".[18] Oedipus complex refers to the sexual attraction to the parent of the opposite sex and hostility for the parent of the same sex. Freud's belief is supported by the common "preference of the mother for the son, and of the father for his daughter".[19] The boy wants to possess his mother and remove his father, while the girl has a feeling of jealously toward her mother because of their rivalry for the father. Some psychologists refer to the girl's sexual attraction to the father as "electra complex". But the use of this term has not become general.[20]

It needs to be borne in mind that many of the actions and reactions of children which Freud attributes to sex seem to be quite unconnected with sex. The child becomes conscious of his sex organ and fondles it. Generally, parents take no notice of this and, by ignoring it, they keep the oedipal tendencies of the child in check.

During the first part of the third stage, the child becomes very fond of the mother. Indeed the mother still remains the most important socializing agent. The child clings to the mother and is unhappy to share the mother's attention with other siblings.

Many social pressures begin to force the child to identify with the appropriate sex. Boys and girls begin to be rewarded for acting out the expected roles of their sex. Some fail to make the proper identification until much later but, whenever this identification takes place, it gives rise to jealousy for the parent of the same sex. The child's behaviour is characterized, too, by some degree of ambivalence. The boy of four or five unconsciously wants the father dead. He "does not merely hate the father; he loves him as well, admires him, and has long taken him as the model to be imitated".[21]

From about the age of six or seven (possibly, later in some cases), the child begins to settle down to mastering many new demands for independence. "In many situations he must learn to get along without the immediate

[18] The term "oedipus" derives from the legendary Oedipus Rex, lame hero of Greek legend. He was the King of Thebes who unknowingly quarrelled with, and slew, his father. For freeing a Theban city of a long-standing pest, he was proclaimed king and given the widowed queen, his mother, to wife. So, he committed incest with his mother, Jocasta. He had had four children before he realized the truth. In despair, he put out his eye and lived miserably in exile. (See Robert S. Woodworth, *Contemporary Schools of Psychology* (London: Methuen & Co. Ltd., 1959), p. 179.

[19] *Ibid.*, p. 179.

[20] Therese Benedek, pp. 49—50.

[21] Robert S. Woodworth, p. 180.

guidance and support of his family."[22] Interest in the opposite sex tends to be suppressed in favour of devotion to the problems-mastering skills. In their struggle with the task of being *boys*, boys reject girls. Girls, too, lose interest in boys. Interest in the opposite sex becomes relatively latent (hidden or inactive). It does not surface again until the fourth stage of development.

Stage IV

The fourth stage is the period of adolescence. In every society this is a very difficult stage. It is a period of intense physiological and emotional disturbance to the boy or girl. It is time in the teens when the individual approaches the peak of his physical and mental growth and becomes capable of reproduction.[23] But society does not usually permit free sexual activity because the individual at this stage is not mature enough to take on the full responsibility of adulthood – namely, the raising of a family, etc. The social restriction is often very disturbing to the individual, for he is usually expected to play the part of a child for a few more years. He has to accept the advice and decisions of adults. "Thus he is apt to scrutinize and criticize his parents and teachers, to flout their opinions, and disregard their authority."[24]

The degree and method of restriction vary from society to society. In indigenous African societies, life at this stage used to be different. Initiatory rites and different age-set demands and regulated marriage systems helped keep adolescents busy. They played their normal civic parts without disturbance. The individual is, more often than not, in the company of his equals, age-grades. He abides by their rules which are, in turn, guided by the norms of the society. Much happens during this stage, initiatory rites, circumcision, fattening (in the case of girls) for marriage and home-making, etc. Following this stage, the individual graduates into adulthood.

In any culture, the home, at this stage, is of the greatest importance to the adolescent. A good home provides love and security. The home transmits to the adolescent the mores and standards of society. The home also helps him in his adjustments to the outside world. Indeed, the attitude of parents affects the growing up process. Yet, the individual does not naturally confide in the parents, often preferring to confide in outsiders. In boarding schools, the

[22] Harry M. Johnson, p. 128.

[23] K. Lorell, *Educational Psychology and Children* (London: University of London Press Ltd., 1962), p. 214.

[24] *Ibid.*, p. 216.

pupils at this stage are more influenced by the attitudes of teachers than in day schools.[25]

Throughout those four stages, the process of socialization demands that the individual should be able to make certain distinctions as circumstances present themselves. Socialization requires four basic important distinctions to which our attention will now turn.

Fundamental Distinctions in Socialization

The first task of socialization is to bring the biological drives, such as hunger and thirst, under control and to substitute for them needs that bind the individual more closely to his fellows in social life. He gradually becomes sensitized to the approval and disapproval of others. His successful socialization involves ability to make necessary distinctions at each stage and in every situation. He must be able to choose from every one of four pairs of possibilities (or values of a pattern variable) referred to here as *fundamental distinctions in socialization*.

1. *Diffuseness-specificity*

In his reaction with any other person, the occupant of a role may have strictly limited and specified obligations toward the other person. On the other hand, he may have an indefinitely large number of obligations. Much depends upon the demands of the occasion. Consider, for instance, the role of a medical doctor in relation to his patient, the role of a landlord toward his tenant, the role of a hair-dresser toward her client/customers, or that of a mathematics teacher toward his pupil. The roles in each of these examples are relatively specific and definite. The doctor, the landlord, the hair-dresser, or the mathematics teacher knows exactly what to do in each situation.

On the other hand, there are roles that have relatively diffuse responsibilities. Consider the role of a husband or wife, mother or father, the role of a friend or the role of a political leader to his followers. In each of these, the pattern of obligation is not defined. There are no specific legal expectations. Thus, a friend, (a real friend, not a casual acquaintance) is expected to do whatever he can for a friend. Indeed, all family roles are diffuse. As the individual passes through the four stages, he learns to distinguish between the specific and diffuse roles.

[25] *Ibid.*

2. *Affectivity-neutrality*

Another pattern variable is *affectivity-neutrality*. This variable is concerned with the expression of feeling (affect) or the withholding or keeping in check of those feelings in any given situation. "Expression of feeling is a form of self-gratification or enjoyment"[26] in any given situation.

In the course of interacting with others, situations for expressing various feelings present themselves. The individual may laugh or cry; the individual may show signs of pain or signs of sympathy. There are situations in which he may really enjoy eating or freely romance. On the other hand, there are situations when he is expected to keep these feelings in check. This distinction is highly relative. So, the individual must be able to determine when to indulge in self-gratification and when to submit to discipline. Discipline, here, refers to self-control.

Children in the pre-oedipal stage are not expected to have any inner restraint or self-control. But, gradually, they begin to be rewarded for certain kinds of self-control and scolded or not rewarded for others. Societies differ in this respect as some are more permissive than others. For example, in western society, children are freer to express themselves to their elders or parents as they like. Culture in the traditional African societies places more restrictions on children or younger persons.

Generally, from oedipal stage, the child begins to learn to forego the pleasure of affectivity in the interest of attaining some goals. One must do some relatively unpleasant things for *deferred rewards*. The adult must distinguish between occasions in which to relax and occasions when they must attend to business. Indeed, any adult role requires self-control. Some roles present opportunities for the person to indulge his impulses or maintain a strong affective-neutrality. Persons employed as salesmen or public servants must practise affective neutrality. The affective-neutrality pattern variable resembles the next pattern variable, *universalism-particularism*.

3. *Universalism-particularism*

The values of this pattern variable answer the question whether an occupant of a given role in a given situation should give preferential treatment to persons with whom he interacts because they are members of some group to which he belongs. In other words, the values demand whether a man in any given position should pay special or particular attention to people

[26] Harry M. Johnson, p. 137.

because of their special status or close relationship with him, or should he treat all persons alike irrespective of who they are.

Some positions permit discriminatory treatment to the public depending upon whether or not the members of the public attended to are members of the group providing the service. Other positions have no room for discrimination; they provide universal treatment regardless of group membership. Indeed, some obligations are derived from the fact that the other person occupies a certain social position while some arise from the application of general criteria having nothing to do with social position. For example, the obligations of a son toward his father depends upon the social position the father occupies in relation to the son; they do not depend upon the kind of man the father is. Such obligations are particularistic while all public positions are expected to be universalistic.

The obligations of a judge must be strictly "universalistic". He must (or is expected to) make decisions not on the basis of social position of the persons before the bench, but on the basis of impersonal criteria of justice. Teachers and clerks as well as other public servants must be universalistic in their service in order to effectively carry out their obligations. A person in any position should be able to make the distinction.

Until the time a child joins his peer group outside the family the child has few opportunities to distinguish between particularism and universalism. However, during the latency period, he has to go to school where he is (or is expected to be) treated according to standards that apply to all students irrespective of their family background. All pupils are classified by the teacher according to their scholastic ability. Peer groups help to establish the distinction between particularism and universalism. It is only when individuals are able to make this distinction that they can participate fully in group games. Games help to develop the ability to make this distinction. The basic rules of the game guarantee that each player has the same rights as the other players.

In peer groups, the child learns that he cannot win an argument or dispute by appealing to the authority of the father, for among equals, no particular father has authority over the whole group. So, the age-set or age-grade system in indigenous African societies is very important in fostering universalism-particularism.

4. *Quality-performance*

The final pair of pattern variables is quality-performance distinction. This has to do with the aspect of a role that the individual pays more attention to.

It is during adolescence that this distinction is more and more expected of the individual.

A role occupant emphasizes "quality" if he reacts to some objective characteristics such as age, sex, group membership, academic qualification, weight, height, or any other predetermined quality. The assumption here is that every possessor of such "qualities" is capable of carrying out certain tasks or doing certain things. The emphasis is not on whether or not the task is properly performed but that the occupant of the position has the requisite quality.

On the other hand, a role occupant emphasizes "performance" if he pays attention to how well he wants something to be done regardless of age, sex, group membership, qualification, etc. This distinction between "quality" and "performance" resembles that between "ascribed" and "achieved" roles. Most roles in the family are "ascribed". One is treated as the first or second son or daughter merely because one happens to have been born in that order. One is treated as a father, uncle, etc., not as a result of any particular achievement, but owing to one's hierarchical position. Likewise the role of a hereditary king is ascribed; the occupant automatically acquires the position.[27]

In schools where "automatic" promotion is practised, "grades" or "classes" are ascribed. In contrast to this are schools where pupils are assigned to classes on the basis of their performance in examinations. The emphasis in the latter category is "performance." Membership of any age-group is "ascribed" but the position a person ultimately occupies in society depends upon one's civic performance.

In summary, education and socialization have been presented as deliberate processes by means of which society turns its young and inexperienced members into worthy human beings. Socialization is an instrument of conformity while education involves conformity and change. Any successful education must, in addition to making the individual a worthy and knowledgeable citizen, equip him to constantly recreate or modify his environment with a view to making it congenial for him to live and work in.

Thus, any effective educational system can equip members of a society to constantly examine their society against the background of their line of development. If, from their findings, the existing value system and general pattern of life militate against real development, such retrogressive or static values can be replaced with more positive ones. Such is the function of

[27] *Ibid.*, pp. 136–141 for the *fundamental* distinctions in socialization.

dynamic education. Once a new pattern of life has been accepted, the process of socialization then popularizes and propagates it.

Emphasis has been placed on one aspect of education, socialization, which is the whole process by which an individual is led by the adult or experienced members of a community to develop acceptable behaviour. Effective socialization depends upon the maturation of the "pupil", i.e., the individual becoming socialized. The process passes through four stages. The first stage is the *oral stage*, when the child's identity is manifested principally through the instrumentality of the mouth. The second is the *anal stage*, when the crucial learning centres around toilet training. Then follows the third stage which is broken into two phases. The first phase is the *oedipal stage*, characterized by the attraction of the child to the parent of the opposite sex and a degree of rivalry between the child and the parent of the same sex. The second phase of the third stage occurs when the individual identifies himself with the parent of the same sex and incorporates the characteristics and values of that parent. Interest in the opposite sex becomes relatively dormant and "latent". Hence it is referred to as the *period of latency.*

The final stage is *adolescence*, a very difficult and trying time. The teenager is now approaching the peak of his physiological and mental growth. Society maintains a number of restrictions on the individual who, in his effort to assert his independence from parental control, becomes very critical of adult ways of life. The role of the family at this stage cannot be overstressed. Nevertheless, the adolescent does not really confide in his parents.

Through the various stages of socialization, the individual learns to make vital distinctions which have been referred to as *fundamental distinctions of socialization*. Any social role at any stage demands the ability on the part of the individual to choose any variable out of any pair. There are four such pairs of possibilities.

The first pair is *diffuseness-specificity*. The choice to be made here depends upon whether the individual's role in relation to others with whom he interacts embraces an indefinitely large number of obligations or whether the obligations are strictly limited. The obligations of a father to a son are limitless whereas those of a geography teacher to a geography student are limited to the teaching of the subject. Another pattern variable, *affectivity-neutrality*, demands whether the individual should indulge in self-gratification or submit to discipline, self-control. A third pair, *universalism-particularism*, requires the individual to decide whether to observe some universal norms applicable to everybody with whom he reacts, or to treat the person in a particular way because of what that person is in relation to the individual or the social role that the other person occupies. The last pair deals with what a role occupant, the individual lays emphasis on, qualification, achievement, or capability. This pair is referred to as *quality-performance*.

Education and socialization are vital in every society. There is, therefore, need for societies to be particularly concerned with the nature and quality of their education and socialization, for upon them hinge the rate and degree of their development.

CHAPTER TEN

Education, Urbanization and Social Change in Colonial Africa

A. E. Afigbo
Professor of History,
University of Nigeria, Nsukka

Change and Continuity

In the rival mythologies of European imperialism and colonial nationalist, *change* was one of the many vital innovations which European rule introduced into what is usually described as traditional societies. If imperial apologists were to compile a dictionary of their own, in it the word change, as applied to colonial peoples, would be defined approvingly as *progress*, a dramatic and benefitial linear transition from a static and unproductive traditional culture to a dynamic and limitless modernism. But to the myth-makers of colonial nationalism, the word connotes "disruption", the process by which unsympathetic and uncomprehending imperialists shattered the idyllic and happy indigenous way of life of colonial peoples, substituting in its place turmoil, instability and uncertainty.

But in spite of their differing attitudes to change, the two groups subscribe equally to a number of assumptions regarding change in traditional societies. These assumptions include the belief that traditional societies are static and unchanging, that traditional societies and modern values are polar opposites as a result of which the natural relationship between them is one of conflict, that new values, attitudes and structures necessarily displace their traditional counterparts once they come into contact and that, in any given colony or even geographic region, traditional societies respond uniformly to the impact of European culture.[1]

In the course of the last twenty years or so, scholars working in Africa have

[1] J. F. A. Ajayi, "The Continuity of African Institutions Under Colonialism", in T. Ranger, ed., *Emerging Themes of African History* (London, 1968), pp. 191–192. J. R. Gusfield, "Tradition and Modernity: Misplaced Polarities in the Study of Social Change," in J. L. Finkle, and R. W. Cable, eds., *Political Development and Social Change* (New York, 1971) pp. 15–26.

shown that as far as that continent is concerned the above assumptions are popular fallacies. For instance, it has been shown that the societies upon which, from about 1800, European nations imposed their rule were not "traditional" in the sense of being static. On the contrary, they were themselves the products of generations, or even millennia, of change brought about by forces which were at times elemental and at other times man-made. The alternation of pluvials with dry periods, the degeneration of vegetation from high savanna and forest to desert and poor steppe, the neolithic revolution, the dawn of the metal (especially iron) age, regional or localized population pressures caused either by natural increase or by the activities of more powerful neighbours leading to migration in search of new living room, the rise and disintegration of state systems, the penetration of Africa by early Christianity and then by Islam, the Hilalian invasion, the drawing of Africa into the orbit of the western world in consequence of the geographical revolution, the slave trade, the introduction of new food crops and new weapons of destruction, these were some of the many forces which made the history of pre-colonial Africa one of continuing adjustment.

Nor is the "traditional-modern" polar model, with all its attendant implications of conflict and incompatibility, applicable to the African experience of social change under colonialism. The research of various African authorities show that there were "manifold variations" in the relation between traditional African culture and Western innovations. Not only have certain customs and beliefs been discarded or modified, but some have been retained by one level of society at the same time as new alternatives were being accepted on another level. Thus, while human sacrifice, the slave trade, and the killing of twins have been discarded, and old and new ideas have been amalgamated in the sphere of religion; the European ideal of monogamous marriage accepted by the Christianized elite exists side by side under the law with the institution of polygamy among the urban and rural masses.

With regard to the ease with which indigenous African ideas tend to survive the impact of, or even to blend with, alien European values, Mrs. Leith-Ross in 1937 drew attention to the case of the Igbo, often regarded as examplary in the way they embraced Western ways. According to her, with disengaging facility, an Igbo attends communion at the same time as he believes in the potency of traditional magic; he ties up in the same handkerchief the rosary and the traditional talisman and "plants side by side in the garden round his new cement and pan-roofed house the hibiscus of 'civilization' and the *ogirisi* tree of pagan family rites".[2] Professor Ajayi has

[2] S. Leith-Ross, *African Women* (London, 1939), pp. 292–93.

also recently given the example of the African who:

> gets himself baptised a christian, sends his children to school, comes to terms with modern technology by buying a lorry and learning to drive it, and yet insists that the lorry is not just a mechanical device but also a force whose control properly belongs to god of iron whose emblems and charms he therefore displays on the lorry.[3]

The fact is that Africans were probably not unaware of the elementary fact that the acceptance of "new forms may only increase the range of alternatives"[4] available to them.

Thus, any simple generalization on the response of African societies to European impact is bound to be misleading. In this regard one must bear in mind the vastness of the African continent, the rich diversity and variation of African societies, of individual and group temperaments and psychologies, and thus, of the fact that response to even similar stimuli was bound to vary not only from society to society but even from time to time within the same society. In Nigeria, for instance, authorities in this field of study have been impressed by the differing responses of the Igbo, the Yoruba and the Fulani to the policy of indirect rule. In East Africa while the Kikuyu of Kenya responded positively to European values, many of their neighbours are said to have "followed the opposite course".[5]

In light of the foregoing discussion, therefore, one can subscribe to the view that there is no African culture which was not affected by European contact or which has completely crumbled before it. In studying social change in Africa under colonial rule the task of scholarship is thus not to repeat the myth of the displacement of indigenous cultures by European values and forms. Rather, it is to determine and analyse the extent and mechanism of change and adjustment within each integral social unit, and to compare and contrast any findings made with what obtained in neighbouring societies.

The Spread of Western Education

Social change in colonial Africa was brought about largely by the imposition of Western education, Western Christianity, Western economic forces and Western political structures and ideas. Of these new forces the effects of

[3] J. F. A. Ajayi *The Continuity of African Institutions*, p. 200.

[4] J. R. Gusfield, p. 19

[5] W. R. Bascom, and M. J. Herskovits, *Continuity and Change in African Cultures* (Chicago, 1965), p. 4.

Christianity and education would appear to have been more revolutionary than any other and, although the two were for the most part intimately linked, in this chapter education will be treated separately from Christianity.

The introduction of Western education into Africa, at least to the coastal regions of the continent, preceded the imposition of colonial rule, though the latter event helped to create conditions and incentives which accelerated its spread. It is now known that in Ghana, Western educational institutions were introduced as early as 1644. But the real beginning of modern education in Africa lay in the nineteenth century and came as part of the evangelical and humanitarian drive to "civilize" Africa and to destroy the slave trade through planting Christianity and spreading general Western civilization. To such an extent was the pitching of the missionary tent synonymous with the establishment of schools for teaching the three R's, that the date of the advent of the missionary into any African society could, for that community, safely be taken as the date marking the introduction of Western education. For West Africa, South Africa, Egypt and the Maghreb, the crucial years for the introduction of education along the coast and into a few centres in the interior were the first five decades of the 19th century. For East Africa, and what later became French Equatorial Africa (A.E.F.), solid beginnings were hardly made until the 1860's and the 1870's.

The Christian missions thus played a key role in the introduction of Western education into most of Africa and in its subsequent expansion. To understand the missions' role in this matter, it is necessary to understand that though they did not see the spread of Western education as an end in itself, they saw it as the main means to what they considered a very vital end: the Christianization of Africa and the creation there of a new and higher moral order. It is not only that they recognized the school as a very effective instrument of recruitment or proselytization, but also that they believed it was the only means by which they could give permanence to their work. Convinced that they were in no position to work for very long periods in Africa and that they had to revolutionize African society to give Christianity firm root, the missionaries set about creating self-perpetuating congregations whose members could read and produce the Bible as well as preach the gospel message. The way to achieve this was through creating a local African *elite* through an imaginative and energetic educational programme.[6] The missions remained an important bastion of Western education throughout colonial Africa.

[6] J. F. A. Ajayi, *Christian Missions in Nigeria 1841–1891* (Longman, 1965), pp. 126–65.

However, the spread of education in Africa in the period under consideration cannot be satisfactorily explained solely by reference to missionary commitment and achievement for there were at least two other participants in the venture. Next to the missions in importance were the various colonial governments which, from the 1880's, increasingly took over responsibility for the political destiny of the continent. Like the missions, the governments did not see their main business in Africa as the spread of Western education. On the contrary, they were concerned with creating such conditions — political, economic, social, moral, etc. — as would enable European business men to exploit as fully as possible the hitherto untapped resources of the continent. As part of this programme they had to conquer the continent, maintain law and order, and introduce improved means of communication.

One result of the new political settlement was that it enabled the missions and their educational institutions to spread from the coast (to which they had been largely confined for decades) to the far interior. A look at any map of Africa showing the expansion of the missions and their schools shows that interior penetration, except probably in Yorubaland and one or two other places, coincided with or came after the establishment of the new political settlement. In West Africa, for example, whereas the establishment of the new centres of learning along the coast dated mainly from 1800 to 1855, the interior posts date from 1885 onwards. In East and Central Africa inland penetration came even later.

But the contribution of colonial governments to education in Africa was not limited to this incidental service for they saw themselves also as having an important part to play in the so-called programme to bring about moral regeneration in Africa. This meant that they accepted some responsibility for the introduction of certain Western values, techniques and methods, and believed that it could be achieved only through formal instruction. Furthermore, the governments found it cheaper and wiser to use local people to staff the lower cadres of their administrative services — clerks, interpreters, messengers, teachers, etc. — than to import them from Europe. Again, in order to do this they had to promote education.

These were some of the considerations which forced the colonial governments to intervene in education, at first rather half-heartedly, but later with varying degrees of firmness. In the French and British colonies particularly, this intervention initially meant giving the missions some support in their educational effort either through limited or even token financial grants, or by introducing some order and uniformity of standards into the hitherto uncoordinated missionary educational efforts by setting up conditions which mission schools had to attain to qualify for government support.[7] At times some governments did both. But as time went on, many colonial governments found it necessary to intervene directly in education through the establishment of government schools which, unlike the mission schools, were open to all, irrespective of religious persuasion.

In the British colonies such schools were intended to be shining examples of high educational and moral standards, and of direct social relevance. It was hoped that through watching and emulating these, the sectarian schools would improve their performance. These were ideals which for the most part eluded British colonial governments. This was especially so with regard to the ideal of social relevance where the logic of colonial society at different times and places forced the government schools to patronise curricula as academic as those of the mission schools or parish.

The French lay school programme, launched by General Faidherbe, was motivated on the other hand less by the streak of anti-clericalism infused into French national temper by the Great Revolution as by a desire for the centralization and rationalization of administrative methods, procedures, and systems.

The Germans in Tanganyika (now part of the Republic of Tanzania) appear to have set out from the beginning to establish and run state schools as they considered this a more efficient and practical method of raising from the local population the administrative subalterns they needed. Governor von Soden, for example, would not entrust this work to the missions whom he felt were inclined to retain the best pupils as teachers while letting the government meet its needs from the less abled.[8]

In another special sense the establishment of lay or government schools promoted the spread of Western education in Africa, especially with reference to the Muslim areas. Since the missions saw their schools as instruments for winning converts, their institutions could hardly meet the needs of Muslims for Western education as Muslims generally remained very jealous of their religion and culture. Lay schools thus offered them their chance to obtain western education without running the risk of having their religion subverted

[7] R. Clignet, "Education and Elite Formation," in J. Paden and E. Soja, eds., *The African Experience*, Vol. 1 (Chicago: Northwestern University Press, 1970), pp. 304—330. A. E. Afigbo, "The Background to the Southern Nigerian Education Code of 1903," *Journal of the Historical Society of Nigeria* IV/2 (June, 1968), pp. 198—225.

[8] O. W. Furley, "Education and the Chiefs in East Africa in the Inter-War Period", *Trans-african Journal of History* I/1 (January, 1971), pp. 60—83.

in the process. This was particularly important in French West Africa, Northern Nigeria, the Maghreb and Egypt. In Northern Nigeria the British pursued a deliberate policy of excluding the educational and other activities of the missions from the emirates, except perhaps from Zaria, and thus had to take the main responsibility for providing Western education.[9]

Yet even in those areas where the governments pursued an independent line on educational matters, either instead of or in addition to supporting the efforts of the missions, the latter managed to retain some responsibility for the education of a not inconsiderable number of students as shown by available statistics. In Northern Nigeria, for example, whereas by 1929 the government had 106 schools with a total of 4,549 pupils on roll, the missions ran 152 schools with a total enrolment of 4,446 pupils. By 1910 in French West Africa while the state schools had 11,484 pupils on roll, the mission and other private schools had 2,962. By 1937/38 the ratio had widened to 56,135 pupils in the lay schools and 12,281 in the mission schools. Again in A.E.F., the mission schools which had 12,605 pupils on roll in 1929 were said to be far ahead of the state schools in the number of pupils they taught.[10]

Apart from the missions and colonial governments, local initiative was also of some importance in the propagation of Western education in the period. Even long before the formal onset of colonial rule, Muhammad Ali of Egypt had introduced a strong push for Western education into his adopted country as part of a many-sided effort to modernize that ancient state.

But much more relevant to the period covered in this work was the effort, from the 1920's, by some culturally nationalistic Kikuyu to establish and run their own schools. By that time, the Kikuyu had had cause to believe that the missions were bent on destroying indigenous Kikuyu culture. Also the Kikuyu had come to view the attempt to insist on the teaching of Swahili as aimed at subordinating them perpetually to the settlers through giving them an inferior education.

For these reasons there emerged among the Kikuyu in this period the

[9] S. F. Graham, *Government and Mission Education In Northern Nigeria 1900—1919* (Ibadan University Press, 1966), pp. xxviii, 192. Lord, Hailey, *An African Survey* (Oxford, 1957), pp. 1193—1197. N. A. Ziddeh, *Origins of Nationalism in Tunisia* (Beirut, 1962), pp. 52—54. D. L. Ling, *Tunisia: From Protectorate to Republic* (Indianapolis: Indiana University Press, 1967), pp. 93—95. G. A. Williams, "Education and Government in Northern Nigeria," *Presence Africaine* No. 87 (1973).

[10] G. A. Williams, pp. 173—174. Lord Hailey, p. 1197. V. Thompson and R. Adloff, *The Emerging States of French Equatorial Africa* (Stanford, California: Stanford University Press, 1960), pp. 281—282.

independent schools movement of which there were two factions. The one was the Kikuyu Independent Schools Association (K.I.S.A.) which, though bent on preserving Kikuyu values and operating independent of mission control, was prepared to allow some cooperation with the central and local governments, at least to the extent of accepting grants from them. The other, the more radical and the more uncompromising, was the Kikuyu Karinga Educational Association (K.K.E.A.) which would not even accept grants from central and local governments. In spite of the many problems which it faced, especially with regard to finding qualified staff (a problem which remained intractable until the Kikuyu established their own teacher training college in 1939), the Kikuyu independent schools movement helped to supplement the efforts of the missions and the colonial government in promoting Western education in Kenya.[11]

Elsewhere in Africa, local initiative in education took the form of local rulers and elders joining with colonial governments or with missions to finance schools and run them. This was so in Southern Nigeria and in East Africa, especially in Uganda.[12]

Though missions and colonial governments, the two agencies most responsible for the triumph of Western education in Africa, were active in all parts of Africa, the spread of education was far from even throughout the continent; not even in any particular geographic region nor in all the colonics under the same colonial power was the distribution equal.

Taking the geographical regions first, West Africa would appear to have witnessed the greatest advances in education, followed by Egypt and the Maghreb, South Africa, East Africa and then Central Africa. But if we consider the colonial blocks instead, greater progress was made in the British territories, followed by the French and the Portuguese with the Belgian Congo limping far behind. Within the British territories there was also differential performance in education. Here the territories where substantial progress was registered included Egypt, Ghana, Southern Nigeria, Uganda and Sierra Leone, with Northern Nigeria, Kenya and the Rhodesias (including what is now Zambia) coming after. In Francophonic Africa, the West African territories would come first followed by the North African territories and then the A. E. F. Within French West Africa, Senegal and Dahomey led the way while the other territories lagged rather far behind.

[11] J. Middleton, "Kenya: Administration and Changes in African Life 1912–45", in V. Harlow and E. M. Chilver, eds. *History of East Africa* Vol. II (Oxford, 1965), pp. 365–370.

[12] A. E. Afigbo, O. W. Furley, pp. 60–83.

The fact is that the spread of education was controlled by many factors and no mission, colonial government or African group was in any position to master them all. First there was the question of the length and extent of the contact which the particular territory had had with Europe by the time colonial rule was imposed. West and South Africa, for instance, had enjoyed contact with Europe since the 16th century. By the beginning of the 19th century, therefore, quasi-urban conditions of life had come into existence at several points along the western half of the continent, at St. Louis, Banjul (what used to be Barthust) Accra, Lagos, the Oil Rivers ports, Luanda, and at the Cape. These points therefore provided good stepping stones for the missions in their bid to penetrate the interior with Christianity and Western education. The northern coast of the continent, on the other hand, came under such regular and sustained contact only early in the 19th century, while for the eastern coast this was not even the case until about the 1870's.

This, of course, meant that Western education was introduced much earlier into West, South and North Africa than it was into East and Central Africa. This is very important in any attempt to account for the differential spread of education in these areas. The portion of the 19th century which preceded the imposition of European rule could be described as the most liberal phase of Europe's relationship with Africa taking into account the entire period from 1500 to the 1960's. Before Europe thought of conquering and ruling the entire continent, she was willing to encourage the emergence of a group of Africans equipped to co-operate with her in the business of "civilizing" the continent through the introduction of Christianity, Western education and modern commerce. This meant that in this period there was no question of hindering the extension of education of Africans or of watering down the type of education they got, or of frustrating those who had successfully gone through the prescribed course of instruction. Those regions of Africa where the missionary educational programme was in operation in this period thus gained immensely.

But with the imposition of colonial rule which was followed by the triumph of conservative racial policies, the amount and quality of education extended to Africans came under more rigorous control than before while educated Africans faced increasing discrimination. As a result, regions such as East and Central Africa where the earlier liberal policies had not taken firm root before the onset of alien rule, found themselves greatly handicapped in the spread of education.

With the dawn of this phase, the official policy and attitude of the colonial power which ruled a particular territory became a very important factor in determining the kind and the amount of education it received. Scholars have often compared and contrasted French and British policies in education. French policy is said to have been based on assimilationist principles and to have aimed at the creation of a small group of highly educated and Gallicized elite, while British policy is said to have been anti-pathetic to the creation of an elite group. Recent and more penetrating studies,[13] however, suggest that there is very little difference between British and French colonial education policies, though, owing to the working of other factors, they produced differing results. To a greater extent than has so far been generally realized, the two powers were guided in their educational policies by practical considerations rather than by *a priori* doctrines. Both were suspicious of highly educated colonials, especially those whose education, being largely of an academic kind, had exposed them to the radical democratic ideas of the West. Also both were anxious to ensure that the schools did not turn out more graduates than colonial society could usefully employ.

It was out of fear for the political harm which highly educated persons could do that some French thinkers warned: "the more you educate individuals in this [colonial] situation, the more they hate you".[14] And to control the production of such men, in fact to limit it to a minimum, the French edged out the missions from the centre of the educational arena, imposed restrictions on their activities and set up state schools under government control. They went further to ensure that these lay schools were largely vocational in orientation with rural schools emphasizing training in agriculture and rural crafts, and the urban schools the training of skilled low-grade teachers, interpreters, mechanics and inspectors. The first academic secondary school in French West Africa, the *Lycee Faidherbe*, was not established until 1920. Others came in 1940 and 1945. Lord Hailey admitted that the *Lycees* were intended mainly for Europeans though they admitted a certain number of African students.[15]

The French, like the British, thus favoured an educational system which did not alienate colonials from their natural environment. Hence, in the period covered here, the French created very few links between the educational system they established in their African colonies and that obtaining in the metropoles. The diplomas they awarded to the graduates of the more

[13] R. Clignet, pp. 304–330.

[14] *Ibid.*

[15] Lord, Hailey, p. 1195.

advanced schools were purely local. According to Virginia Thompson and Richard Adloff, French educational policy in this period is aptly summarized by the slogan, then current: "Better to train tens of thousands of artisans . . . than a dozen bachelors of arts".[16] The Second World War, effected some changes in this, as in other aspects of French colonial policy.

The British also did what they could to fight the uncontrolled spread of education in their colonies. They fulminated against the missions for building too many schools, for emphasizing academic training and they tried to hold the missions back by denying financial grants and supervision to these schools that did not meet the conditions the government wanted to impose. They espoused the superiority of vocational training over academic education and the advantages of sound mastery of indigenous languages over indifferent knowledge of English. And where possible, they created obstacles on the road to too much education.[17] In Uganda, for instance, they sought to supplant the mission secondary schools with the state junior secondary schools which emphasized vocational training. Upon taking over the control of Egypt they cut down the financial aid which the state gave to students. They did this partly because Egyptian finances were bad, but also because they wished to make sure that the schools did not turn out more graduates than the economy could absorb. British performance in Northern Nigeria was also along similar conservative lines.

However, even though they pursued basically similar policies, except in the area of language where the French authorities prescribed sound knowledge of French for all, they achieved different results. Education made greater progress in British than in French territories. The main explanation of this is that the French were firmer with the missions than the British were; the French intervened earlier and therefore more decisively in education. By the time the British colonial authorities decided to fight some of what they considered the undesirable aspects of the liberal education policy of the missions, the latter had already spread out too far and wide to be easily smothered.

The other factor which influenced the spread of Western education in colonial Africa was the presence of white settlers. There were no European

[16] V. Thompson and R. Adloff, p. 279.

[17] R. C. Pratt, "Administration and Politics in Uganda, 1919–1945", in V. Harlow and E. M. Chilver, *History of East Africa* Vol. II, pp. 521–525. Tignor, R. L., *Modernisation and British Colonial Rule in Egypt* Princeton, N. J.: Princeton University Press, 1966), pp. 322–348.

settlers in West Africa and this to some extent explains the impressive progress made by education there. But these settlers were present in force in Algeria, Kenya, the Rhodesias and South Africa. These settlers had a more racist attitude toward the indigenes than the colonial authorities as their interests clashed in many vital respects with those of Africans. Specifically, they competed with Africans for land, political rights, and places in the administrative and commercial establishments. Since the colonial government was, in general, prejudiced in their favour, it gave more time and more money to the solution of their problems. The settlers thus had better schools and were given first choice in employment. Through their inability to influence the administration, Africans were denied fair access to education so that they would perpetually remain in subjection to the settler class. In South Africa, for instance, the authorities were still arguing in 1936 that the education of the white child should prepare him for life in a dominant society while that of the black child should prepare him for a subordinate place.[18]

Finally, there was the fact of the response of different African peoples and strata of society to the prospects of Western education. In Nigeria, for instance, the Igbo accepted Western education more enthusiastically than the Islamized Hausa and Fulani did. In Kenya, the Kikuyu would appear to have seen the advantages of Western education long before their neigbours. In Uganda, the Baganda, through the enlightened attitude of their rulers, also went to school in large numbers from the late 19th century. Along the West African coast, the presence of ex-slaves and repatriates would also appear to have had something to do with the rapid spread of education because they already had some idea of what difference Western education could make to the life of any society. The presence of these men must be taken into account in explaining the expansion of education in Sierra Leone, Liberia, Dahomey and Yorubaland. In Senegal, an important factor should be recognized in the four communes which, by the mid-19th century, already housed men considered sufficiently cultured as to be admitted to the privileges of French citizenship.

Islamic cultural arrogance and resistance, especially in the Western Sudan, tended to hinder the spread of education. But in North Africa and Egypt the reaction was somewhat different. Though some Muslims there retreated into orthodox and intolerant Islamism in response to the challenge of the West, a significant fraction sought to ensure the survival of

[18] Lord, Hailey, p. 1144.

the Islamic heritage through the introduction of Western science and technology. This later group in time proved to be the more providential force in North African Islam. Their movement led to a fruitful marriage of Islamic culture and Western sceintific thought, and was responsible for the emergence there of an important new group of elite, Islamic in culture but Western in education.[19]

By the time this revolution in thought was taking place in Egypt and the Maghreb, the Western Sudan was already losing contact with supra-Saharan Africa and turning its gaze towards the Atlantic coast. When the British and the French imposed their rule there, they found the Western Sudanese Muslims ill-prepared to meet the challenges posed by the West. As a result, it was possible for these two colonial powers to decide in their wisdom what kind and how much of Western education was suitable to the conditions of the Muslim communities of most of West Africa.

The Impact of Western Education

As already mentioned above, Western education was only one out of many new forces causing social change in colonial Africa. It is thus not easy to delimit precisely the changes, if any, which could be correctly attributed solely to the impact of Western education. Still some attempt has to be made, keeping in mind the earlier discussion.

For the non-Muslim areas probably the most important single innovation of Western education was the introduction of literacy in the Roman script. Even for the Islamized areas, the challenge of Western education tended to give a new impetus to Muslim education. There too it spread literacy in the Roman script. It is difficult to appreciate fully the impression which the ability to read and write made on African peoples. It was a new magic, and was, in many societies, sought after as much and at all cost as it opened the treasure house of the modern world, a world into which Africans were fully drawn with the imposition of colonial rule. Familiarity with the amount of power, authority and influence which the first generations of African clerks, interpreters and teachers exercised largely because they were literate helps to give some idea of the spell which literacy cast on many African peoples.

And it was the quest for literacy that made many an African family send their children to school even after having sworn to live and die by the traditional culture. But literacy and the school merely served to open the flood-

[19] N. A. Ziadeh, *Origins of Nationalism in Tunisia* (Beirut, 1962), pp. 167.

gates of many far-reaching social changes. There in school, the children acquired a whole body of new teaching touching on all aspects of human existence and these were openly and widely advertised as antithetical to the African way of life. In this sense Western education occupied a place of primary importance among the forces that brought changes to colonial Africa for it caught the children before they had been fully inducted into the culture of Africa and laid the foundation of their intellect with Western ways of life and thought.

Beyond all this, Western education contributed in other respects to change many facets of African social life. Thus, it added to the problem of rural-urban disparity, a problem which either came into existence or worsened with colonial rule. For example, in the early years of colonial rule when post-primary schools were few and far between, most of the existing ones were sited in the urban or budding urban centres for a variety of good reasons. Consequently, promising rural children who had the will and the means to pursue their education beyond the primary school, had to make the pilgrimage to the towns. Because most of the children in these schools came from distant homes, each school had a boarding house attached to it. There the children spent most of their early years, except for brief occasional holidays which they might, or might not, spend with their family in the rural areas.[20] As a result, by the time the children graduated they had acquired a taste for urban life. Furthermore, advantages of literacy which they had acquired were to be found in the towns where their services were sought often and well renumerated. This contributed to the flight of skilled manpower from the rural areas.

In this way, too, Western education tended to wean African children from the control and influence of their families. The child who had stayed away from for so long, had acquired the art of reading and writing, had learnt the language of the colonising power, had acquired new dress habits and new food tastes and had learned explanations different from those of the elders for old familiar phenomena was bound to be isolated from his kinsmen who had never been to school. If such a child was ostentatious, as most of the first graduates of the schools were inclined to be, the tendency to parade this new knowledge was bound to create problems of communication between him and his people.

It was largely through this tendency to set its products apart from the rest of society that Western education had one of its most outstanding effects on African social structures by bringing about the rise of a new elite.

[20] C. Fisher, "Education" in S. Diamond, and F. G. Burke, eds., *The Transformation of East Africa* (New York, 1966), pp. 501–508.

Precolonial African societies had their elites. Among these were traditional chiefs, priests and war-leaders many of whom normally owed their elite status to birth. But, in addition, there were successful farmers and businessmen who generally owed their leading position to achievement. Now colonial rule created new challenges which the traditional elite were ill-equipped to meet, but which the graduates of the Western-oriented schools could easily cope with. As a result, these men came to assert their claim to leadership in the new situation and with time came to be looked upon by the masses as leaders and pace-setters.

For most members of the new elite their advantage lay in their education which gave them access to the scientific skill and social thought of the Western world, equipped them to enter into dialogue with the colonial authorities on the destiny of the colony, and familiarized them with the social fashions of Europe, all of which made thier life-style an example to be emulated by their countrymen.

But not all these classified as new elite in colonial Africa had education, nor were all those who had it educated to the same degree. As Professor Lucy Mair has shown, especially for the nationalist era, some of them gained admission to this rank either because they had made money from large-scale farming or business and could help finance the political agitation of their better educated but poorer brethren, or they controlled mass organizations such as labour unions, and could give the better educated elite the kind of mass support which they needed to convince the colonial power that they spoke for the people.[21] It is largely this wide variation in their qualifications that makes it so difficult to define precisely who were the new elite of colonial Africa.

But there can be no doubt that elite status in Africa from this period, to the present was and has been closely connected with Western education. In short, one can justifiably argue that the issue of the rise of a new elite among any African people in the colonial era was largely a question of what amount and what type of educational facilities were available to the people and how far they put those facilities to effective use. All the studies so far carried out on the matter show that regions or colonies which witnessed the most intensive efforts in the propagation of Western education produced the largest number of people of elite status.[22]

[21] L. Mair, "New Elites in East and West Africa," in V. Turner, ed., *Colonialism in Africa, 1870–1960* Vol. III (Cambridge University Press, 1971), p. 171.

[22] P. C. Lloyd, ed., *The New Elites of Tropical Africa* (London: Oxford University Press, 1966),

Also, in many parts of Africa many members of the elite came from the group which, in pre-colonial times, would have been classified as commoners. Some were even of the servile class due to the practice that it was often members of these classes who were first made to embrace Western education, while the traditional elite for the most part stood back. But as soon as the benefits of Western education were demonstrated, members of the traditional elite also joined in. Many colonial powers, especially France and Britain, deliberately set out with varying results to encourage this class by establishing special schools for them.[23] With the wealth they derived from their estates and/or salaries as local authorities they were usually able to train their younger sons not only locally but also in higher institutions in Europe and America.

In some parts of Africa, however, the traditional elite responded early to the call of Western education. In Egypt, it was this class who, in fact, took the lead in establishing Western-type institutions. In Buganda this same class quickly recognized the advantages of missionary enterprise and co-operated fully with the missions in establishing schools. In Ethiopia reaction was similar, the traditional elite sending many of their children to Europe and America to be educated. In this way they have been able to retain the leadership of their countries.

Thus the ranks of the new elite contained people from different strata of society making it responsible to talk in general terms of conflict between the new elite and the traditional rulers. In Sierra Leone and Liberia where, for much of the period, the elite class was made up of people who were not indigenous to these territories, there was an understandable tendency for the elite communities of the coast to be in conflict and competition with the traditional societies of the interior. The former were inclined to be contemptuous of the latter who, in turn, harboured an abiding suspicion of them. In 19th-century Gold Coast (modern Ghana) and in Yorubaland, the founding members of the new elite group were, or at least believed they were, related by blood to the peoples of the interior.

p. 390. P. C. Lloyd, *Africa in Social Change* (Baltimore, Maryland, 1969), pp. 125–56. J. F. A. Ajayi and J. B. Webster, "The Emergence of a New Elite in Africa," in J. C. Anene and G. N. Brown, eds., *Africa in the Nineteenth and Twentieth Centuries*, (Ibadan: Ibadan University Press and Nelson, 1966), pp. 149–162.

[23] Lord Hailey, pp. 1180, 1200. M. Kilson, "Emergent Elites of Black Africa 1900–1950," in L. H. Gann, and P. Duignan, *Colonialism in Africa 1870–1960* Vol. II (Cambridge University Press, 1970), pp. 358–359.

Elsewhere in Africa where the first elites did not include repatriates the ethnic and cultural tie was even closer. The result was that throughout the nineteenth century, and even into the early part of this century, the new and old elites built up a tradition of cooperation, the new elite being regarded as those who mediated between their indigenous societies and Western culture. After all they had been sent to school to learn new techniques in order to increase the ability of their people to meet the problems posed by the European presence. In the Gold Coast and in Egbaland (Nigeria) they worked closely with the traditional elite in an effort to build a new society and ward off European rule. But these efforts failed.

However, as colonial rule took deeper root, strains and stresses appeared in the relationship of the two groups. The new elite had wrongly hoped that Europe was out to modernise Africa and would use members of their group as the instruments for achieving that goal since they were well fitted for it. Apart from being African, they had acquired Western skills, techniques, and ideas and believed they could best introduce these of their less informed brethren. But under colonial rule it was European bureacrats who assumed the role which the new elite had cut out for themselves. And instead of taking the new elite into partnership, the administration preferred the traditional rulers whom they relegated to the area of local government. This was particulary so in British Africa where a determined effort was made to preserve the old ruling families. Even in the French territories where the great paramounticies were destroyed, the old ruling families survived in attenuated forms. When people who had no traditional status were used, they were labelled "chiefs" and assigned the same functions in the local government.

Because of their exclusion, the new elite went into open opposition against the colonial powers. They were both aggrieved and equipped by their education to do so. In this open opposition the traditional rulers could not join them. Their continued survival depended on the colonial power and this tied their hands. Also, for the most part they were not sufficiently educated to participate meaningfully in the debate. If they accepted the arguments of the new elite, they would be consigning themselves to second or even third place. For these weighty reasons they could not side with the new elite who, therefore, regarded them as the lackeys of imperialism. They, in turn, regarded the new elite as revolutionaries who wanted to destroy immemorial custom and turn the world upside down.

To make matters worse, the two were driven by imperialist propaganda into engaging in a struggle over who spoke for the people. The new elite said they did. This the traditional rulers denied, claiming the honour for themselves.

The colonial administration agreed with them. The kind of acrimony which this disagreement at times generated is evident in the dispute between Chief Nana Ofori Atta and the leaders of the National Congress of British West Africa. It can also be seen in the quarrel between Harry Thuku's Young Kikuyu Association on the one hand, and the Kikuyu Association dominated by the traditional rulers on the other.[24]

Yet one cannot conclude from the foregoing that during the period 1880 to 1935 the normal relationship between the new elite and the traditional rulers was invariably one of conflict. The nature of the relationship varied both in place and in time. In the French territories, neither the new elite nor the traditional rulers fluorished under alien rule, and, when after the Second World War the stranglehold of colonial autocracy came to be progressively relaxed, those who emerged as the leaders of French African nationalism included traditional chiefs like Houphet-Boigny of the Ivory Coast and N'Daw of Senegal, as well as descendants of chiefs such as Sekou Toure of Guinea.

In the Gold Coast the leading political party until the ascendancy of Nkrumah represented some kind of rapproachment between the new and traditional elites. In countries such as Ethiopia, Egypt, and Buganda where the traditional rulers had taken control of Western education and more or less converted into an instrument of their ascendancy, no logical conflict developed. It was the same in societies like that of the Igbo where the traditional elite had not the kind of stature that survived far into the colonial period. In any case the new elite were not all the "uprooted natives" of imperialist mythology, nor were all the traditional rulers the obscurantist apponents of change of later-day nationalist damagogy. Both groups had more in common than was often admitted in the evanescent heat of occasional debate.

New Association

Apart from creating the conditions for the rise of the new elite, colonial rule introduced other changes in the structure of African society. Here we

[24] D. Kimble, *A Political History of Ghana, 1850–1928* (London: Oxford University Press, 1963), pp. 389–396. K. Ingham, *A History of East Africa* (Longman, 1962), pp. 280–284. K. G. King, "The Nationalism of Harry Ihuku: A Study in the Beginnings of African Politics," *Transafrican Journal of History* I/1 (January, 1971), pp. 39–59.

have in mind the rise of new organizations which helped to mediate the adjustment of many individuals and their rural homes to the new demands and norms of colonial society. These new organizations have generally been described as "voluntary" by social scientists. They are "voluntary" in the sense that people are not born into them as they are born into lineages, villages or ethnic groups. But closer analysis shows that for some of them, especially the ethnic-based welfare or improvement associations, membership is not really voluntary since the practical alternative to membership generally means ostracism from society.

It has been found that the social conditions that brought these organizations into being generally originated in the new urban centres, although some of these associations, especially the ethnic-based ones, in time established home branches. The fact was that, as Professor Wallerstein has aptly put it, migration from "the traditional rural to the modern urban area" led to "dislocation and disorientation for the individual".[25] Since neither the traditional society nor the colonial administration had the means to meet the new needs of such migrants, they had to evolve their own institutions, systems and norms for achieving meaningful existence in the strange and heady social environment of the town.

The studies of Gordon Wilson in East Africa have shown that there was a clear correlation between the pressure of colonial society and the formation of these voluntary associations. Thus Kenyan Africans, whose traditional culture came under unusally severe pressure from colonial rule and settler aggressiveness, had stronger, and many more, ethnic associations than neighbouring territories such as Tanzania and Uganda.[26] There was thus a strong desire for individual and group protection in the formation of the voluntary associations. Furthermore, urban conditions of existence created opportunities that made it relatively easy to form such organizations since, as Professor Thomas Hodgkin has put it, it provided "physical centres where men and women, with particular interests in common, can collide with one another".[27]

Though it has been correctly pointed out that it is difficult to group the different voluntary organizations into clear-cut categories, especially owing

[25] I. Wallerstein, "Voluntary Associations," in J. S. Coleman and C. G. Rosberg, eds., *Political Parties and National Integration in Tropical Africa* (Berkeley: University of California Press, 1970), p. 319.

[26] G. M. Wilson, "The African Elite" in S. Diamond and F. G. Burke, eds., *The Transformation of East Africa*.

[27] T. Hodgkin, *Nationalism in Colonial Africa* (New York: University Press, 1967), p. 84.

to their functional versatility,[28] we shall here distinguish between three kinds. In group one we have those organisations which could be described as purely "social", that is devoted to promoting conviviality and relaxation. These were made necessary by the absence in the towns of the traditional forms of amusement, relaxation, and citizenship training such as the masquerades, age-grade associations and traditional festivities. There was also the attraction of forms of modern European social life as advertised in the life of the European community in each colony. In this category were the football clubs, scout and girl-guide movements, debating societies and alumni associations.

In the second group are the ethnic unions. These were an extension of rural ethnicity or "tribalism" to the urban area. There were different hierachies of the unions: village, clan and "tribal" unions. These had two main functions. One was to help the individual who had migrated newly to the town to adjust as smoothly as possible to the conditions of urban life. Thus when a migrant first reached town, he usually made his first contacts with members of his village or clan union who would help to find him accommodation, to introduce him to employers of labour or master-craftsmen, and to teach him modern skills. They also taught him how to comport himself in the city. Through such associations members received help when in difficulty. They could get loans to continue their business if they sustained crippling losses. Funeral, marriage, and other expenses approved by the association could also be met with loans or donations from the group.[29]

The other function of the ethnic unions was "to provide a channel for progressive public opinion at home",[30] especially through maintaining an organized link between the sons at home and the sons abroad."[31] To do this the unions had to take an interest in the political and social development of their homes. This at first won these associations the opposition and obstruction of suspicious European officers. In time, however, the

[28] *Ibid.*, p. 85.

[29] For a very good analysis of the rise and function of a voluntary association of the ethnic-based type see M. Banton, "Adaptation and Integration in the Social System of Temne Immigrants in Freetown," in I. Wallerstein ed., *Social Change: the Colonial Situation*, pp. 402–419, See also S. Ottenberg, "Improvement Associations Among the Afikpo Ibo," *Africa* XXV/1 (January, 1955), pp. 1–25.

[30] T. Hodgkin, p. 86.

[31] T. M. Yesufu, *An Introduction to Industrial Relations in Nigeria* (London: Oxford University Press, 1962), pp. ix, 190. W. Ananaba, *The Trade Union Movement in Nigeria* (London, 1969), pp. xi, 336. R. H. Bates, *Unions, Parties and Political Development: A Survey of Mineworkers In Zambia* (New Haven, Conn: Yale University Press, 1971), p. ix, 291.

latter recognized their capacity for good and began consulting them in matters such as taxation, education, and community development.

In the third group were the trade unions which came into being largely for economic bargaining. For the most part, modern urban centres grew up at vital commercial, mining, and communication points which had openings for the employment of skilled and unskilled workers. In these towns, therefore, there soon came to be concentrations of people who earned their living mainly by means of salaried or wage employment. These men, especially those at the lowest rungs of the labour ladder, have often been referred to rather inappropriately by Marxist-oriented analysts as proleterians. Apart from those who were bound by the wage nexus to the big employers (the colonial government, the commercial and mining firms, the missions, etc.) there were also the self-employed artisans who supplied certain of the needs of the urban population.

The life of these urban dwellers was tied to the vagaries of the world economy and market whose structure and behaviour they did not understand. To protect themselves in this unfamiliar economic world, those in wage or salaried employment formed trade unions for the purpose of effective negotiation with their employers for higher pay and better conditions of work. The self-employed craftsmen also formed craft guilds which helped to fix prices, standards, conditions of apprenticeships. etc. The trade unions and craft guilds also functioned at times as friendly societies, helping members in difficulty with money and advice, providing fitting funerals, educational facilities, scholarships, and occasional feasts.

The years 1880—1935 saw something of the beginnings of these voluntary associations. Professor Kilson has, in a recent summary, shown that by 1937 there were all kinds of tradesmen's and workers' organizations in Nigeria, Sierra Leone, Kenya and elsewhere. But his and other studies such as Professor Kimble's in Ghana, Professor Yesufu's and Mr. Ananaba's Nigeria, Thompson and Adolff's in French Equatorial Africa and Bates' in Zambia clearly show that the golden age of these organizations did not arrive until after the Second World War.[32]

The reasons for this were many. These associations depended to some extent on the spread of education, and the impact of this and of urbanism took time to manifest. Outside the coastal areas of West Africa, the Maghreb, Egypt and Kenya this generally took more than three decades. While in South Africa where the conditions were ideal owing to an early industrial and communications revolution, the gorwing harshness of Boer nationalism stifled

[32] T. Hodgkin, p. 119.

African initiative. The rise of these associations also depended to some extent on the development of a capitalist economy, but colonial Africa is said to have had only "a rudimentary capitalist economy"[33] which depended substantially on migrant workers, a species of labour which is said to be very resistant to trade union organization. Even then there were very few wage-earners in colonial Africa. In the 1950's their number was estimated at between four and five million. Finally, there were the many prohibitions associated with the autocratic and exploitative colonial regimes which, for the most part, did not accord legal recognition to trade unions until the 1940's.

In summary then, the period 1880 to 1935 was a crucial one in the evolution of modern African society. These years witnessed the penetration of traditional Africa by the revolutionary forces of Western education, Western Christianity, Western commerce, a new and radical urbanism and modern communications media. Under the impact of these forces African society did not wither away, as was once erroneously thought, but made a number of important adjustments. Among other things, it gave birth to the new elite and the voluntary associations which subsequently became largely reponsible for bringing about the dismantling of the colonial political structure.

[33] *Ibid.*, pp. 118–119.

CHAPTER ELEVEN

Cultural Nationalism in the Colonial Period

R. L. Okonkwo

Division of General Studies,

University of Nigeria, Nsukka

With the advent of colonialism, as was described in Chapter VIII, the traditional society was disrupted by Christianity, Western education, and other forces. European influences seemed to have swept away the African culture before it. Missionaries saw little of value in the African way of life and sought to re-make their wards into Europeans or black Englishmen. Whereas the Africans seemed willing pupils, ready to copy the European models at first, the cultural nationalists later rebelled against the denationalization of the African by the missionaries and the colonial authorities.

The cultural nationalist movement, which grew up at the end of the nineteenth century in West Africa, exhorted Africans to regain touch with their own culture. The cultural nationalists studied the institutions of the traditional society and sought, as much as possible, to cast off the European life style and to live according to African traditions.

The difficulties this first generation of African nationalists faced in restoring their African nationality was a sign of the everbearing influence European education had had. In their attempt to define the African personality and portray the true African culture, the nationalists could not divorce themselves completely from Western influences. They remained hybrids, a mixture of European and African influences. They could never identify completely with the uncontaminated African.[1]

The problem of the loss of African identity which the cultural nationalists first brought to light is as timely today as it was in the early part of the century. When Western education and religion first spread to the interior, pupils experienced conflicts of culture. Today, in reaction to western-oriented university education, Africans are turning more and more to the study of

[1] E. A. Ayandele, *Holy Johnson Pioneer of African Nationalism* (London: Frank Cass, 1970), p. 287.

themselves. They wish to study the traditions of their ancestors, to know the institutions and values which are peculiar to Africa and which should be retained in any move towards modernization.

It may be that the earlier generation of cultural nationalists were too intellectual in their attitudes to the traditional society. Their backgrounds were, in fact, unique in the degree to which they severed their ties to the village society. On the other hand, the Europeanization of the African life style has become more and more widespread with the urbanization of the interior. Otonti Nduka's book, *Western Education and the Nigerian Cultural Background*, highlights the fact that even after independence, Africa still needs emancipation from European culture. Nduka calls for the preservation of indigenous values and institutions and a blending of Western and African culture.[2]

Origins of Cultural Nationalism

Cultural nationalism was a movement of the western-educated elite of West Africa. The type of education the European missionaries gave their nineteenth-century pupils was at the root of the grievances of the cultural nationalists. The missionaries conceived that the teaching of Christianity and the skills of reading, writing, and arithmetic had to be accompanied by the adoption of Western dress names, food and life style. They insisted that a good Christian must drink tea and take walks with his wife. They could see little but barbarism in the traditional African institutions and sought to destroy the vestiges of African culture.

Sierra Leone was the first centre of missionary activity in British West Africa. Fourah Bay College, established in 1827, was the only institution of higher learning of that time in West Africa. Thus, Nigerians, Ghanaians, Gambians, as well as Creoles, came to Freetown to study. Their common education and friendships created a class of West African intellectuals who had more in common with each other than with their brothers in the interior. Thus, cultural nationalism was not actually a movement within any one nation, but was a response of the West African educated elite who had shared similar experiences at the hands of the ethnocentric missionaries.

The first generation of educated Nigerians were known as the *Saros*. They were originally captured as slaves in the tribal wars of the early nineteenth

[2] Otonti Nduka, *Western Education and the Nigerian Cultural Background* (London: Oxford University Press, 1975), p. vi.

century. The British Navy, which was patrolling the Atlantic in an effort to stop the iniquitous slave trade, recaptured the slaves and sent them to Sierra Leone. The liberated Africans were so grateful to their British mentors for saving them from slavery, that they willingly adopted European civilization along with the Christian religion.

In the 1840's the recaptives began returning to Nigeria to re-establish ties with their families. With the advantages of Western education and a knowledge of English, they became leaders in the society. They were valuable to the Europeans and traditional rulers as middlemen between the two groups. The Saros settled mainly in Lagos and Abeokuta, Calabar, Opobo and other coastal areas where, as doctors, lawyers, traders, and clergymen, they emerged as leaders.[3] The Saros came with the European names given to them by the missionaries. They included Thomas Babington Macaulay, father of Herbert Macaulay, Samuel Crowther, John Randall, and James Johnson. With such English-sounding names, they saw themselves more as Europeans than Africans.

Michael Echeruo's recent book, *Victorian Lagos*, described the extent to which the Saros imitated the European life style. Their entertainment included races, fancy dress balls, cricket, musical and dramatic concerts, levees, soirees, conversaziones, and at-homes.[4] They held elaborate weddings, with dresses complete with plumes, stockings, gloves, fans, and parasols. The wedding gifts included Morocco visiting cards and gold cheese dishes.[5]

It was from this class of Saros that the cultural nationalists recruited their supporters. The impetus for a re-examination of their European life styles came from two quarters, from the attitudes of the Europeans and from the indigenes. The ridicule of the Europeans was a great blow to their erstwhile pupils; the Europeans found the Africans dressing up in Victorian top hats and spats a caricature and a mockery. Lord Lugard, for example, refused to recognize the African elite as spokesmen for the traditional rulers and considered them dangerous spoilers of the traditional society.[6]

The Saros, who craved acceptance in European society, were deeply hurt

[3] For more about the Saros see Jean Herskovits Kopytoff *A Preface to Modern Nigeria: The "Sierra Leoneans" in Yoruba, 1830–1890* (Madison: University of Wisconsin Press, 1965).

[4] Michael Echeruo, *Victorian Lagos: Aspects of Nineteenth Century Lagos Life* (London: Macmillan, 1977), p. 30.

[5] *Ibid.*, p. 31

[6] James Coleman, *Nigeria: Background to Nationalism* (Berkeley: University of California Press, 1958), p. 156.

by the growing movement towards racial discrimination and segregation at the turn of the century. Whereas in the earlier period, the two groups had socialized freely, in the 1890's, the racial climate changed. The increasing racial prejudice was revealed in the attempt to make Christ Church a colonial church for whites only, and in the harsh treatment of Bishop Samuel Ajayi Crowther, a Saro who was the first black bishop in West Africa and a symbol of the potential of the black man to rise in the European church. The educated African also suffered discrimination in civil serivce promotions. Some, such as Herbert Macaulay, resigned from the government service during this due to unfair treatment. The scorn and humiliation they suffered caused the Saros to question their association with the European way of life. They began to see their destinies as allied to their brothers in the interior.

The second impetus to cultural nationalism came from the reaction of the indigenes to the Victorian Africans. At first the Saros were condescending to the natives, and the natives were hostile to them. After they became disillusioned with the whites, the Saros allied with the Africans. By 1910, the old Lagos society had changed into two groups, the whites and the blacks.[7]

Cultural Renaissance

Cultural nationalism thus grew up in the late 19th century in West Africa as a reaction to increasing discrimination against educated Africans in the church and colonial government. The movement embraced the elite in the major coastal cities, Freetown, Cape Coast, Accra, and Lagos. It was marked by a cultural renaissance, a re-awakening of interest in traditional African culture.

As an important symbol of their new sense of African identity, the elite abandoned their European names given them by the missionaries and took African names. In Nigeria, Rev. David B. Vincent became Majola Agbebi. Others retained their surnames, but adopted African first names. George William Johnson became Oshokale Tejumade Johnson and J. Augustus Payne baceme J. Otonba Payne, and in Freetown, William J. Davis took the name Orishatukeh Faduma.

Another important sign of the new African awareness was the wearing of African traditional dress instead of the Victorian heavy woolen suits. In Freetown, the Creoles organized a Dress Reform society in 1887 to encourage

[7] Patrick Cole, *Modern and Traditional Elites in the Politics of Lagos* (Cambridge: Cambridge University Press, 1975), p. 75.

others to abandon European dress, which was not only unsuitable for the climate, but made the African an object of ridicule. Mrs. Adelaide Casely Hayford, a Creole, was one of the few women who wore traditional dress, the buba and lappah, to all formal occasions.[8] Rev. Mojola Agbebi wore traditional dress in Europe and America, as well as at home in Nigeria, and became an international symbol of the African personality.[9]

The cultural nationalists took a renewed interest in the achievements of the traditional African society and wrote many learned books on African art, religion and history. Mojola Agbebi, for example, published a collection of Yoruba riddles in Yoruba, and began a Yoruba dictionary. Some of the published histories are still important sources for the modern historian, such as Samuel Johnson's *History of the Yorubas*, J. O. George's *Historical Notes on the Yoruba Country and its Tribes*, and Otonba Payne's *Tables of Principal Events in Yoruba History*. In the Gold Coast, J. E. Casely Hayford wrote *Gold Coast Native Institutions*, a study of the political institutions of the traditional Fanti society and J. Mensah Sarbah was the author of a book, entitled *Fanti Customary Laws*.

Education was an area of crucial importance to the cultural nationalists. They sought to run their own schools, which would teach traditional culture, the native languages, and African history. African-run schools were the answer to the denationalizing effects of the missionary and colonial government education.

Adelaide Casely Hayford founded the Girls' Vocational School in Freetown, 1923–1940, to give to the pupils a pride in their race and a love for their country. She introduced the teaching of traditional crafts such as spinning and weaving to foster and appreciate of African art which she deemed one of Africa's original contributions to the world. Mrs. Hayford lamented that the urban woman had lost the artistic skills of her grandmother as well as an appreciation of the beauty of African art work. The Creole women preferred to import cloth to decorate their homes rather than use the fine native materials. Mrs. Hayford encouraged her pupils to wear African dress and to learn the songs and dances. She sought to foster creativity as well as practical skills which were being lost in urban society.[10]

[8] R. L. Okonkwo, "Adelaide Casely Hayford: Cultural Nationalist and Feminist," unpublished paper submitted to the 23rd Annual Congress of the Historical Society of Nigeria, Zaria, April, 1978.

[9] E. A. Ayandele, *A Visionary of the African Church: Mojola Agbebi* (Nairobi: East Africa Publishing House, 1971) p. 13.

[10] R. L. Okonkwo, *op. cit.*

J. H. Casely Hayford, husband to Adelaide, stressed the need for an African university. He wanted to situate the university in the interior, closer to the true African culture. Hayford called for professorships of Arican history and African languages.[11] Edward Wilmot Blyden of Liberia stressed the importance of an indigenous university to counteract the harmful effects of Africans travelling abroad for higher studies, believing overseas travel to be harmful to health and the preservation of African identity. Education should take place in Africa, amid the scenes of future labours, with more access to the people of the interior.[12]

As many of the early cultural nationalists were clergymen, their reforms centred around the church. Edward Wilmot Blyden (1832–1912), often called the Father of Cultural Nationalism, spoke against the attempts of the European missionaries to destroy African culture. In his famous speech, "The Return of the Exiles and the West African Church", delivered during his visit to Lagos in early 1891, Blyden called for the Lagosians to organise an independent African church, free from European control and missionaries. He spoke of the need for Africans to convert Africans with a truer understanding of the African's deep religious instincts which only needed to be shown the way to salvation. Blyden believed Christianity was universal and could be adapted to the African culture.[13]

As part of the cultural nationalist movement, the Lagosians organized the United Native African Church in August, 1891. There were four independent churches established in Nigeria before 1917. They accepted polygamy and other traditional institutions which was judged compatible with the universal tenets of Christianity. They held services in the vernacular and wrote African hymns and songs.[14]

In addition to the clergy, African newspapers were an important force in cultural nationalism. *The Sierra Leone Weekly News*, *The Gold Coast Leader*, and in Lagos, *The Lagos Weekly Record* and *The Lagos Standard* exhorted the educated elite to abandon their servile imitation of European culture and become Africans. John Payne Jackson, editor of the *Lagos Weekly*

[11] J. E. Casely Hayford, *Ethiopia Unbound: Studies in Race Emancipation* (London: Frank Cass, 1969), p. 95.

[12] E. W. Blyden, "Aims of Liberia College," quoted in M. Echeruo, p. 65.

[13] E. W. Blyden, "The Return of the Exiles and the West African Church," in H. Lynch, ed., *Black Spokesman: Selected Published Writings of Edward Wilmot Blyden* (London: Frank Cass, 1971), pp. 191–194.

[14] For more information about independent churches in Yorubaland, see J. B. Webster, *The African Churches Among the Yoruba 1888–1922* (Oxford: Clarendon Press, 1964).

Record called the Europeanized African, "a non-descript, a libel on his country, and a blot on civilization".[15]

The cultural nationalists were forerunners of the poets of the Negritude movement in their attempt to define the "African personality". The cultural nationalists believed that the Africans were not backward or inferior to the whites. Each race was unique and had an independent destiny and contribution to make to world civilization. The greatest danger to the educated African was that he would lose his special African genius.

What was the "African personality"? Blyden stressed that the African was a spiritual being. The African's deeply religious nature and his humanitarianism would serve as an antidote to the materialism of the West. The African way of life was, in many ways, superior to that of the European. Blyden applauded the cooperative principles of African village life. "We, not I, is the law of African life."[16] In traditional African society, wrote Blyden, there were no hospitals as the family was responsible for its sick. There were no thieves and no paupers as everyone had enough. Blyden's idyllic picture was an antidote to the European view of the primitive and barbaric practices of traditional society.

J. E. Casely Hayford echoed Blyden's emphasis on the peculiar spirituality of the African, seeing Africa as a moral force to bring peace to the world.[17] The cultural nationalists continually quoted the passage, "Ethiopia shall stretch forth her hands unto God" as proof of the relgious destiny of the African race.

The concept of the "African personality", originated by the cultural nationalists, was later used by Kwame Nkrumah as a force in the stuggle for freedom from colonialism. Nkrumah also stressed the humanistic principles of traditional African society, the communalism in which members cooperated for the well-being of all.[18]

The Legacy of Cultural Nationalism

The cultural nationalists were never a large group among the educated classes. Yet, through the church and newspapers, they publicized their ideas

[15] *Lagos Weekly Record* (March, 1896), quoted in M. Echeruo, p. 35.

[16] E. W. Blyden, *African Life and Customs* (London: African Publication Society, 1969), p. 30.

[17] J. E. Casely Hayford, p. 208.

[18] Afari-Gyan, *Political Ideas of Kwame Nkrumah* (New York African Heritage Studies, 1970), p. 220.

and gradually molded a new national consciousness among the people. The first generation of nationalists were Saros. As education spread to the interior, other groups joined in the protest against the imposition of Western-oriented institutions. Dr. Nnamdi Azikiwe and Mazi Mbonu Ojike were important cultural nationalists of a later period. Ojike's slogan, "Boycott the boycottables" sought to induce Africans to use African products rather than imported articles.[19]

Cultural nationalism has been viewed as the first step in the growth of the nationalist movements which eventually demanded independence from the colonial authorities.[20] Consciousness of belonging to a nationality preceded the political movements which came later in the twentieth century. While political nationalism took prominence from 1940 to 1960, cultural nationalism has again assumed importance following independence. Western incursions into Africa have continued to threaten the African heritage, and latterday cultural nationalists continue the fight to preserve the traditional institutions and the African identity.

[19] P. M. Mbaeyi, "Culture in Nigerian Nationalism," unpublished paper delivered at the 22nd Annual Congress of the Historical Society of Nigeria, Benin, March 1977, pp. 15–16.

[20] D. Kimble, *A Political History of Ghana: The Rise of Gold Coast Nationalism* (Oxford: Clarendon Press, 1963), p. 506.

CHAPTER TWELVE

The Press and Cultural Development: A Historical Perspective

Dr. R. Chude Okonkwor
Department of Mass Communication,
University of Nigeria, Nsukka

This chapter is an attempt to examine the role of the press in the cultural development of Nigeria. A discussion such as this envisages can easily run into a definitional thicket. It will, therefore, be necessary to clarify the operational terms.

Culture, for example, has been defined in various ways by social scientists as "that part of the environment that is the creation of man".[1] Tylor sees it as "that complex whole which includes knowledge, belief, art, morals, law, custom and any other capabilities and habits acquired by man as a member of society".[2] Since Tylor, many other authors have sharpened the definition but among all attempts to understand the concept are some common attributes.

Chief among these attributes are perceptions of culture as a configuration of patterns and understanding, of patterns for behaviour and of understandings concerning the meaning and value of things, ideas, emotions, and actions. In other words, culture can be regarded as a social heritage, a learned behaviour shared by members of a group and transmitted from one generation to the next. This interaction among members of a group leads to ideal patterns of behaviour and expectations that assume normative quality. Diffusion of the ideal patterns among the members tends to engender the adaptive and integrative qualities of culture without which social stability becomes impossible.

Subsumed under the cultural attributes is the importance of language and communication. The ability of man to create and use symbols can be said to be the basis of societies and, for that matter, of nations. If we agree with

[1] Clyde Kluckhohn, *Mirror for Man: The Relation of Anthropology to Modern Life* (New York: McGraw Hill), 1949, p. 17.

[2] E. B. Tylor, *Primitive Culture* (London: John Murray Publishers Ltd.), 1871, p. 21.

McIver and Page that "a symbol is a representation of a meaning or a value, an external sign or gesture which by association conveys an idea or stimulates a feeling",[3] then we must also agree as Schramm mentions, that "communication is fundamental to all social process".[4] A society will cease to exist if the members do not interact. In developing societies, interaction takes the form of face-to-face communication and the employment of agents when the information is meant for all the members of the society. That is why such societies have town criers who inform the group about what they should know, watchmen who scan the horizon during wars and report to the home army, and old/wise men who not only take policy decisions but also teach the younger ones about the beliefs, customs, laws, and the necessary skills needed for living in the group.

In developed societies, the functions of watching the horizon and making available information upon which decisions are based have been taken over by the media of communication which include the press, radio, television, the cinema, and books. These also help in the work of socialization formerly the preserve of the elderly and the wise. The media of information are, therefore, at the very centre of existence for any society, developing or developed. The existence of the media is imposed by the sheer force of the demands and needs of the society in which they operate. Communication, therefore, is basic to any social process.

In 19th-century Nigeria, what formed the press were newspapers which were concentrated in the cities. Such dailies as existed, were urban phenomena because the city was the centre of life for the new social and political leadership. The city was also the centre for intensive acculturation. Contacts between Nigerians and Europeans or between the rural folk and the educated and sophisticated Africans were possible and it was in cities that new tastes and wants were created, new values adopted and emulative urges propagated. It is no wonder that these cities also were bases for newspapers. During the period, radio and television were non-existent and magazines were few.

The aim of this study is to discuss the role of the press, that is newspapers, in the creation, nurturing, and development of objects, ideas, knowledge, habits, values, and attitudes of Nigerians from 1859, the year the first news-

[3] R. M. McIver and C. H. Page, *Society: An Introductory Analysis* (New York: Rinehart), 1949, p. 153.

[4] Wilbur Schramm, *Masi Media and National Development* (California: Stanford University Press), 1964, p. 44.

paper appeared in the country, until 1959 when other media such as radio and television started playing major roles in the interaction process of Nigerians. The time for this study was chosen not only to focus attention on a distinctive period in the development of social and political cultures in the country but also so that it can form a basis for any comparative study of the pre- and post-independence cultural growth in Nigeria.

Viewed against mid-19th-century Nigerian history, the significance of the establishment of the *Iwe Irohin*, the first newspaper in Nigeria, is sometimes buried among the series of contributions made by the British and the missionaries in the anti-slavery movement. While it is not the intention to play down these contributions, the establishment of the *Iwe Irohin* in 1859 by the Rev. Henry Townsend at Abeokuta must be seen as a link in the chain of those missionary journalists who sought to encourage education and enlightenment. Townsend saw his role not only in the specialized evangelical terms of conversion but in helping the people of Abeokuta and its environs to develop their resources by bringing knowledge to the ignorant and health care to the sick.

Perhaps the claim by Townsend that he established the *Iwe Irohin* to engender in the Egba people the habit of seeking for information by reading not only sets the proselyting tone prevalent at the time but also portrays the immense power attributed to the newspaper. Townsend believed in this power and so included in his newspaper such content that justified the editor's aims. Apart from carrying church news such as the movements of missionaries, the number of baptisms and confirmations, deaths and births, the newspapers also made space regularly available for advertisements, commercial news about producer prices of palm oil and cotton, announcements from local chiefs and from the government of Lagos Colony, news about the arrival and departure of governors, and movement of commercial representaives.

The *Iwe Irohin* got so involved in the activities of the society in which it was based that its comments on the political and social issues became an influence no chief or government functionary could ignore. For example, the role the newspaper played in the Ijaye war between the Egbas and Ibadan not only enhanced the prestige of Townsend but made the newspaper a very important aspect of the Egba war effort.

It is important to note the sterling pioneering qualities of the didactic essays carried in the *Iwe Irohin*. The subjects covered ranged from simple tips on how to live a clean life, through world geography, to lessons on spelling. For example, just as Nigerian youths today seem to be confused about what to wear, the *Iwe Irohin* as early as 18 July, 1864 charged that it was better for Nigerians to choose from among the clothing of Europeans such as best suited their environment:

> To wear a shirt without trousers [sic] and jacket looks odd; to wear a jacket or coat without a shirt looks still more singular and out of place. It does not look well to see a soldier's helmet or any other head dress worn with country clothes or a soldier's red jacket with naked legs and feet. The wearing of the clothes of the country as the people are accustomed to do shows better taste than the mixing of European clothes with it oddly, does.[5]

The paper frowned at what it called the uncivilized custom of women walking about with their breasts uncovered and clothes so badly put on that they need to be readjusted every few minutes. It condemned the habit whereby the best clothes were preserved for Sundays while people, especially children would walk about in the worst of clothes. It declared:

> If we follow one of those sprucely dressed young men (to their homes) perhaps you will see the house unswept, the *agidi* leaves of the week cast outside the door for the wind to sweep away when dry . . . In our opinion, the native who wears his country clothes clean and tidy, and keeps his house well swept, his cooking vessels washed and put away, that has a clean mat to spread on clean ground for a visitor, a clean cup . . . and clean cold water to put into it . . . shows the better civilization.[6]

An example of the sort of blackboard journalism in which the newspaper engaged is the following lesson on errors in spelling. On 5 September, 1863, the newspaper carried the following:

> Proper names should either be spelt exactly the same as they are in the language from which they are taken, or at least, altered according to rule. It was an instance of spelling run wild to write Tamahana for Thompson, Wiremu for Williams, Piripi for Philip.[7]

The important thing to note is that the *Iwe Irohin* not only kept alive the printing trade that the missionaries had established in Abeokuta but also introduced many Nigerians to what formed the basis of enlightened society in Europe and other lands. Its insistence on education and all the good that could accrue from it prepared the grounds for the struggle for rights which

[5] *Iwe Irohin*, 18 July, 1864, Appendix, p. 1.

[6] *Ibid.*

[7] *Ibid.*, 5 September, 1863.

newspapers championed. The *Iwe Irohin* inspired the establishment in Lagos of other newspapers such as the *Anglo-African*. Zik said of this newspaper: "It carried news of local and overseas interest and its editorial columns were devoted to a critical appraisal of the problems of the times".

This comment can be made of other newspapers that were established towards the end of the 19th and early 20th centuries. Some of them were *The Lagos Observer*, *The Times of Nigeria*, *The Lagos Times* and *Gold Coast Colony Advertiser*, *The Lagos Times*, *The Lagos Weekly Record* and the *Lagos Standard*. These newspapers severally and collectively attacked what they deemed obnoxious in the British administration. They did not do this blindly, however, as when the *Nigerian Times* refused to support the agitation against the imposition of water rates in Lagos because it thought the measure essentially right.

Another example of when the Lagos press did not go out of its way to condemn the activities of Britain was the so-called pacification of the hinterland, that is the Yorubaland, north of Lagos and the eastern section of the country. Pacification was no more than Britain installing a government of her own making in those areas that were vital to her trading interests. In order to do this, Britain had to subjugate the existing native polities. This, naturally, engendered hostility between the British and the native princes. The hostility also brought out a seeming contradiction. While the traditional rulers tried to safeguard their sovereignty and prevent British intrusion, most of the educated elite, including some of the newspapers, saw a remedy in the British government's mediation. The *Record*, for example, strongly advocated British intervention. The newspaper's attitude on the issue was spelt out in these words:

> Convinced that the opening and maintenance of interior routes will confer a great and lasting benefit upon the country at large, we cannot permit our sentiments of patriotism to impair our judgments or deaden our instincts of right reason; we are therefore bound to give our adhesion and support to measures calculated to produce the greatest good, or to promote the interest of the largest majority. And we feel confident that in this determination we have the endorsement and sympathy of all right-minded intelligent natives.[8]

In the spirit of the times, one would expect newspapers to attack everything British ranging from ideas to activities. There is no doubt that they did this profusely but the *Record's* attitude raises some interesting points. The

[8] *The Lagos Weekly Record*, 5 March, 1892.

cardinal one is that most of the educated Nigerians thought the British role would be that of a disinterested arbitrator who would usher in peace and, consequently, enable Christianity to win converts in the land. Foremost in this belief was the Rev. James Johnson, who was convinced that Christianity and African nationalism were interdependent and that the former should provide the superstructure for the latter. Christianity, to him, was not just the pure milk of the gospel but was, as well, the most potent political instrument that could and should be employed in the creation of a virile, independent Nigerian nation state.[9]

Another point to note is that even where newspapers attacked the British policies, they always expressed surprise that the British were capable of evil. For example, in 1894, the newspapers condemned the expedition against Chief Nana of Benin River which led to his trial and deportation to the Gold Coast. The *Record* observed that to the African anxious for the perpetration of his race, the hunting down of native chiefs and their being made fugitives in their homeland by civilized nations armed with murderous weapons of modern warfare, can only draw the severest of censures. Continuing, the newspaper said:

> All intelligent Africans would desire that the native potentates should continue to maintain their ancestral position and status under the light and influence of civilized government and must therefore regret whenever this prospect is removed by some untoward circumstances.[10]

The *Weekly Times* had earlier condemned what the British did to King Jaja of Opobo and emphasized the incompatibility of the action with the honour and dignity of the British Government.[11] In a similar fashion, the *Record* flayed those who advocated the "smash up" of Benin. It regarded such suggestions as "wild-brained" and that a policy of retaliation detracted from the Christian principles which were supposed "to actuate and influence civilized governments".[12]

This respect for British humanitarianism soon started to fade when educated Nigerians saw beyond that garb which was the most potent weapon

[9] E. A. Ayandele, "The Political and Social Implications of Missionary Enterprise in the Evolution of Modern Nigeria," unpublished Ph.D Thesis, University of London, 1964, Chapter 2.

[10] *The Record*, 8 September, 1894.

[11] 11 October, 1840.

[12] 23 January, 1897.

of 19th-century imperial Britian. The educated Nigerians had embraced education because it Europeanized them, gave them status, good employment, and, above all, broadened their outlook. With time, this development meant competition with the Europeans for jobs. Those whose work meant association with the Europeans showed much enthusiasm in being given the opportunity to show what they could do.

The association, however, became a basis for friction later for as Ajayi said:

> There was often competition for office, and on such occasions, the missionaries on the spot cautioned the officials at home not to go too fast about promoting Africans to positions of responsibility on the grounds that there were limitations to their capabilities, weakenesses to their character, and defects to their Christianity.[13]

Even Rev. Henry Townsend, editor of *Iwe Irohin*, denied the basis of equality upon which the missions were supposed to be working. In opposing the appointment of Crowther to the rank of Bishop, Townsend said of the Negro, he

> feels a great respect for the whiteman (and) God gives a great talent to the white man in trust to be used for the Negro's good . . . Shall we shift the responsibility? Can we do it without sin?[14]

More than the missionaries, European traders and government officials used arguments such as the above to keep Nigerians from positions of responsibility. They began to show that they were not in the country just for philanthropy; they had interests to protect and that where African welfare clashed with both their personal and national interests, they had to choose theirs. Under these circumstances, Nigerians became frustrated and began to change their opinions of the intentions and the benevolence of the Europeans.

The frustration engendered by the contemptuous ways the Europeans dealt with the Negroes, the alleged organic inferiority of the Negro race, and the idea of the incapability of Africans to govern themselves manifested itself in two ways. First, it led to agitation within the church which led eventually to the establishment of native African churches. Sensitized by comments in

[13] J. F. Ade Ajayi, "Nineteenth Century Origins of the Nigerian Nationalism," *Journal of Historical Association of Nigeria* II/4 (December, 1961), p. 203.

[14] Correspondence from Henry Townsend to Venn, 18 October, 1858; 3 November, 1859; 18 February, 1860; CMS CA 2/085.

the newspapers and buttressed by the powerful personality of Edward Blyden, Nigerians caused schisms in the churches. The Native Baptist Church was founded in April, 1888 as the first African church in Nigeria. It was such unanimity in the protest of West African Christians that forced the parent committee of the Church Missionary Society to reinstate most of the Africans dismissed or suspended. The United Native African Church which Blyden advocated was set up in August, 1891.

Secondly, it is perhaps in the cultural nationalism which arose out of the Europeans' disdain for the African that one can see the significance of the European missionary enterprise in Nigeria. Here, ironically, it was the failure of the missionaries to accept as equals those they had trained in various fields of endeavour that cuased the disharmony. In the words of a Lagos newspaper:

> They were not accepted into the European community despite their education. In the Civil Service, educated Africans with British degrees were placed under Europeans whose experience and educational standing did not equal theirs.[15]

It was not, however, until after 1895 that the change of attitude of many educated Africans to European civilisation became emphatic and universal. The repudiation of European culture, hitherto regarded as civilization *par excellence*, was quite revolutionary. Educated Africans began to have pride in African customs and institutions and regretted the avidity with which they had accepted alien forms of culture.

This regret took many forms. It began with the discarding of European clothes and European names. George William Johnson became Oshokale Tejumade Johnson; David B. Vincent, one of the leaders of The Baptist Church Schism, became Majola Agbebi. The Reverend, later Bishop James Johnson, did not discard his own name but refused to baptise children with foreign names.[16] On the social side, the educated Africans began to take interest in indigenous dancing. On the religious side, they demanded the use of local airs in their church worship, and some reform of the liturgy to take into account the deep knowledge of God found in the indigenous religions. On the aesthetic side, African art forms began to be better appreciated instead of being dismissed as outward signs of inward paganism.

Above all, the cultural nationalism of this period took the form of literary

[15] *Lagos Times*, 23 May, 1883.

[16] J. F. Ade Ajyai, p. 207.

resurgence. Educated Africans began to take interest in the politics and history of the indigenous peoples. They read the accounts of the various explorers intimately and constructed their own theories of African history. Samuel Johnson's *History of Yorubas* was perhaps the best known of these books and pamphlets.[17]

The place of cultural nationalism in the evolution of modern Nigeria must be strongly emphasized. It provided sufficient scope for articulation of nationalist sentiment among the educated Africans. Its significance can also be seen from the fact that practically all important figures who had anything to do with the achievement of Nigerian independence, returned to some African customs, however incompletely, or advocated return. This was why most of British administrative measures before 1914 were criticized by the press in the light of preservation of indigenous culture and institutions. *The Lagos Times* seemed to summarize the mood of the times when it declared:

> We respect and reverence the country of Wilberforce and Buxton and of most of our missionaries, but we are not Englishmen, we are Africans, and have no wish to be other than Africans.[18]

On the same day, while protesting the introduction of a Lagos Government Education Bill which made it mandatory for all teaching to be done in English before any school could receive a government grant, the newspaper declared:

> Is the ulterior object of the Education Bill to promote the conquest of West Africa by England morally through the English language and secure morally that which African fevers perhaps prevent acquiring physically . . . we shall not sit tamely to witness the murder, death and burial of one of those important distinguishing national and racial marks that God has given us . . . Surely the way to elevate a people is not first to teach them to entertain the lowest ideas of themselves and make them servile imitators of others.[19]

Although cultural nationalism provided an opportunity to Nigerians to articulate their grievances through the newspapers, their unpreparedness for immediate political control made it impossible for them to turn this opportunity into a distinctly political movement. This was a period when the colonial administrator and the missionary assumed the virtues of their Christian civilisation to be absolute in relation to African "savagery" and

[17] London: G. Routledge, 1921 (completed in 1897).

[18] *Lagos Time*, 12 July, 1882.

[19] *Ibid.*

"darkness". These high moral convictions fueled imperialism but devastated the self-respect of young Africans. Instead of accepting the situation as it was, the newspapers became totally involved and committed to sensitizing the educated Nigerians of the injustice called colonialism. Ainslie, for example, said of the editor of the *Record* that "Jackson attacked white hypocrisy, white arrogance wherever he saw it and so perhaps helped soothe the wounded pride of his compatriots, and give them courage to fight back".[20]

Just as the newspapers spearheaded the work of acculturation and education between the years 1859 and 1936, they also, from 1937, turned to the task of organizing and mobilizing the populace. The newspapers were in a privileged position for this task because of their ability to reach the growing numbers of literate individuals emerging from the expanding school system. On these literate individuals fell the responsibilities of secretaries, chairmen and members of the executive committees of local organizations. The new type of journalism spearheaded by the Zik group with its provincial subsidiaries, shattered the myth of information for the privileged few. It was, therefore, through these newspapers aided by various associations that the work of mobilization for nationalism was begun, paving the way for a smooth transition to the formation of political parties.

The founders of the political parties at that time had all been involved with the press in one way or the other. Through the newspapers, they had become associated with the struggle for rights, freedom from and opposition to colonial domination. One can say also that they were close enough to the colonial administration to know of the British predisposition to hand over power to the natives of her colonies. They were also aware of the British preference and, more often than not, insistence on handing over power to well-established groups through the Westminster model of the democratic process.

On their part, the colonial administrators' acceptance of the early journalists and editors as leaders of opinion conferred on them an influence they wielded in the task of organising political association. For example, Herbert Macaulay, as editor of the *Lagos Daily News*, was able to mobilize the local market women and other Lagos organisations from whom he drew support. With the entry into the Lagos political scene of the new intelligentsia, the power of the press became more pronounced. The editors, therefore, had little difficulty organising their respective followers into political parties through

[20] Rosalynde Ainslie, *The Press in Africa: Communication Past and Present* (London: Victor Gollanez Ltd., 1962), p. 30.

which the ideas propagated through the press were crystallized and articulated.

The role played by newspapers and their editors in the formation of the various political parties then in the country can easily be identified. The Nigerian National Democratic Party (NNDP), formed in 1923 and regarded as "the first and best organized political party in British West Africa",[21] was co-founded by Horatio Jackson, editor of the *Lagos Weekly Record* and Herbert Macaulay of the *Lagos Daily News*. How deeply involved the *Record* was in the formation can be gleaned from the May 26, 1923 issue of the newspaper where Jackson suggested that:

> following the practice in other countries, it will, undoubtedly be necessary to form a political party, give it some convenient identification tag or label, define the principles that are supposed to govern its conduct in affairs political and construct the various planks in its political platform, i.e. the programme of work which it proposes to carry out, if its nominees are placed on a very favourable position or are sufficiently supported at the polls in order to secure their election. Within the next few weeks, we hope to be able to formulate our own political party for the coming elections.[22]

From its inception, the party had the support of jouranlists and newspapers. When in 1927, the *Lagos Daily News* was taken over by Herbert Macaulay, for example, it became the official organ of the party. A confirmation of the influence of the *Record* in the formation of the NNDP can be seen from its editorial of June 7, 1930:

> Even the christening of the party as "National Democratic Party" was our handiwork though a collaborator (Macaulay) added the word "Nigerian"... which we thought was somewhat superflous ... Even the very constitution and rules of the Party were drafted by ourselves.[23]

The influence of the press and journalists did not end with the formation of the early political parties. It extended to the three main parties in the country before the advent of the military regime in 1966. The National Council of Nigeria and the Cameroons (NCNC) and the Action Group (AG) came into being as a result of the feud among journalist politicians on the one hand and between supporting newspapers and the other.

[21] Tekene N. Tamuno, *Nigeria and Elective Representation 1923–1947* (London: Heinemann), 1966, p. 46.

[22] 26 May, 1923.

[23] 7 June, 1930.

When, for instance, the Lagos Youth Movement was changed in 1936 to the Nigerian Youth Movement at the instigation of Duse Mohamed Ali, editor of the *Comet*, it attracted men of substance in law, business, medicine and journalism. These included Zik, H. O. Davies, Ernest Ikoli, and Adetokunboh Ademola who later became the Chief Justice of Nigeria. The aims and objectives of the movement were so realistic and far-reaching that they were described by Coleman as "the first major step in the Nigerianization of the nationalist movement".[24]

The West African Pilot, although an independent commercial newspaper, was used to espouse the cause of the Youth Movement. A decision by the movement to publish *the Daily Service* as an official organ for the party was seen by Zik as an unnecessary competition for the comparatively small reading public.[25] After this Zik's enthusiasm about the NYM cooled down considerably to the extent that in 1939, he resigned from its executive committee. The press war between the *Pilot* and *Service* which these actions occasioned polarized Nigerians into supporters of both newspapers and predisposed Zik to think of founding another political party. Coleman reports that the "educated non-Yoruba (and) youths of all tribes" were increasingly attracted to Zik through his newspapers while "the emergent middle class in the cocoa areas of the Yoruba provinces" slowly followed the leadership of Obafemi Awolowo.[26]

This explains why, when some students of King's College, Lagos asked for Zik's leadership, that request was used as an opportunity to found a "national council to weld the heterogeneous masses of the country into one solid block".[27] At the inaugural meeting on August 26, 1944, which was chaired by Duse Mohamed Ali, Herbert Macaulay was elected president and Zik, the first General Secretary of the NCNC.

The press war of 1941 had highlighted the tribal differences between the Igbos and Yorubas. It demonstrated, according to Post, that the Yoruba "were unorganized and were lacking in concerted programmes and effective leadership".[28] This led to the formation of *Egbe Omo Oduduwa* ("Society of

[24] James Coleman, *Nigeria: Background to Nationalism* (Berkeley: University of California Press), 1963, p. 225.

[25] Zik was the founder and first editor of the *West African Pilot*.

[26] Coleman, p. 229.

[27] *Ibid.*, p. 264.

[28] K. W. J. Post, "The National Council of Nigeria and the Cameroon: The Decision of December 1959," in J. P. Mackintosh, *Nigerian Government and Politics* (Evanston: Northwestern University Press, 1966), p. 428.

the Descendants of Oduduwa"), a Yoruba cultural organization. Oduduwa is regarded as the culture hero and mythical progenitor of the Yorubas. The "Egbe Omo Oduduwa" had a political understanding with the NYM which had been predominantly Yoruba since 1941. The Action Group (AG) was, therefore, the exuberant protrusion of the alliance of the Egbe and the NYM.

Unlike the formation of its southern counterparts, the Northern Peoples Congress (NPC) was mainly a reaction to the imagined domination of the north by the south. The attitude of the northern elite can be seen from the fact that in the 1943 press delegation to London, the editor of *Gaskiya Ta Fi Kwabo* ("Truth is worth more than a penny"), a government-owned newspaper and the only one in the north, was the only member who did not sign the memorandum presented to the Secretary of State for the colonies. On that occasion, the editor had said:

> We despise each other, . . . we call each other ignorant; the South is proud of Western knowledge and culture; we are proud of Eastern (culture) . . . To tell you the plain truth, the common people of the North put more confidence in the white man than in either their black southern brothers or the educated Northerners . . .[29]

In December, 1949, the same year the *Daily Comet* was transferred to the north, Dr. A. E. B. Dikko, the first medical practitioner in the North and Mallam Abubakar Iman Kagara, the influential editor of the *Gaskiya Ta Fi Kwabo*, organized a pan-northern cultural organization, the *Jam'iyyar Jeme'ar Arewa* (Northern Nigerian Congress) which was changed to *Jam'yyar Mutanen Arewa* (Northern Peoples Congress, [NPC] when it was declared a political party on 1 October, 1951 shortly before elections into the Northern House of Assembly. The influence of the press in this action (though rather in a negative sense), was considerable for the activities of the *West African Pilot* and the *Service* in the South and the *Daily Comet* in the North shocked the Northerners into organizing for greater participation in the elective process.

It can be seen from the foregoing that the emergence of political parties in Nigeria owed much to the mobilization and integration fostered by the newspapers within this period. These newspapers provided what Hodgkin called "a network of communication . . . through which ideas, information and directives can be diffused from the great towns to the bush".[30] In other words,

[29] *Nigerian Citizen*, 1 July, 1949.

[30] Thomas Hodgkin, *Nationalism in Colonial Africa* (London: Frederick Muller, 1956), p. 87.

the press was a vital link in the transfer and nurture of Nigerian political culture as, until 1960, Nigerians were mainly concerned with what would become of their fatherland in the face of the powers imposed upon them by colonialism.

Conclusion

In this study, an attempt has been made to pinpoint certain historical trends that dominated educational, social and political life of Nigerians from 1859 to 1960. Assertions were made attributing to newspapers of the period the important role of influencing the various facets of life mentioned above. Some vital questions remain to be answered about the effectiveness of the press in the role attributed to it. For example, given the very low rate of literacy in the country at that time, the low per capita income, poor telecommunications and road facilities, limited circulations of newspapers, can one confidently talk of the influence of the print media?

Perhaps it may never be possible to state categorically the extent of press influence on the masses. *The Lagos Times* in 1882 seemed to offer an apt answer when it drew attention to the creditable role it had played on public issues by saying:

> How much success has attended our feeble efforts it is not possible for us to know altogether. Since success in a cause like ours does not always imply the immediate attainment of an object aimed at, but also the creation of sentiment and the production of sympathy which may eventually result in cooperation to attain the desired end . . .[31]

Although the press influenced directly the opinions of the literate minority, it also affected the illiterate masses to an extent demonstrated by the common-place estimation that for every one literate who read an African nationalist newspapers, as many as ten to twenty illiterates possibly had its comments read or retold to them. Newspaper-reading was then so popular that illiterates were said to buy and pretend to be reading it if only to impress those around on their currency about the latest nationalist "victory".[32]

Helen Kitchen's assertion that "small circulations do not necessarily mean limited impact" and that "one copy of a paper will pass through a number of

[31] *The Lagos Times*, 1 January, 1882.

[32] Thomas Hodgkin, *African Political Parties* (London: Penguin, 1961), pp. 31–34.

hands and perhaps to be read aloud to a gathering of family and friends",[33] lends weight to the unreliability of using circulation figures in developing countries to measure the influence of the newspapers on the masses. When one recalls that the literate few were not only editors of newspapers but leaders within their communities, organizations and political parties, then it will be obvious how nationalist information got to the masses.

Another question is whether the media of information in Nigeria are today having the desired influence on the cultural advancement of Nigeria? Although this question does not fall strictly within the scope of this study, yet it is pertinent as each culture embraces those aspects of the past which, usually in altered form and with altered meanings, live on in the present. However, before attempting to answer the above question, we must first define clearly what influences can be called the desired ones.

Two view-points immediately suggest themselves. One is that the greatest thing that can happen to Nigerian culture is the recapture of those artifacts, activities, and ideas that formed the glorious golden era. To those who espouse this view, all alien cultures should be discarded. The other view recognizes both the place of communication in any cultural development and the tremendous explosion in the capability of the media to transmit information from one part of the world to the other. Those in this group are ready to tolerate some alien intrusion into the indigenous culture.

It is necessary to realise that mass media and improved transportation have literally turned the world into a global village. The contiguity these occasion not only leads to physical but, more importantly, to ideological perturbation. It is, therefore, extremely difficult to find a corpus of cultural values that can claim to be authentically African or Nigerian. It appears that what Nigeria needs is not the "pure" Nigeria of old nor the allienated Nigerian who has so imbibed the western or other cultures that he becomes a stranger in his country, but a synthesis of the old and the new. What is important is that what emerges fits the immediate situation in meeting the group needs for survival and/or promotes the psychological adjustment of individuals. However, attempts should be made to retain, as much as possible, those aspects of the two cultures which will make the end product desirable and healthy.

In this, the media have a responsibility. They must rise above acting only as conduits and reflectors of policies and activities of those in authority and assume the leadership role. They can perform this role successfully if they are

[33] Helen Kitchen, ed., *The Press in Africa* (Washington D. C.: Ruth Sloan Associate Inc., 1956), p. 78.

educated in the ways of the people, appreciate those ways and, in turn, bring to bear on the people's lives changes that enhance both the psychological and societal advancement.

Early Nigerian newspapers, starting with the *Iwe Irohin* seemed to have understood very well the society which they served and so dealt with and got involved in issues in a way that generated favourable reactions. This is why nostalgic statements on the roles of the early newspapers appear more often in print. For example, Echeruo thinks that

> the newspapers of today cannot claim to be organic successors to those of the 1860's, the 1890's, the 1920's or even the 1940's. For those decades were the high moments in the history of the Nigerian Press when newspapers and their editors staked out a place for themselves in the national life and acted as those who believed there was purpose in having a Fourth Estate.[34]

What has emerged so far in this discussion is that the history of early Nigerian newspapers shows their great potential in creating and sustaining Nigerian culture. This is no reason why this potential cannot be developed and improved as long as the performance of the media continues to be a conscious, continuing and persistent programme of information, education, explanation and guidance which, from day to day, will activate the people to an understanding of the dilemma in which they are and the opportunites the world offers. In this way, the process of cultural development will mean for Nigerians not only an awareness of the past but also an addition to their innate biological and physical capacities. It is in striving to help Nigerians achieve these goals that lie the noble roles the press can play in the development of their contemporary culture.

[34] M. J. C. Echeruo, "Developments in the Nigerian Press 1960–1971," in *Nigeria Magazine*, Nos. 110–112 (1974), p. 50.

PART IV:

Modern African Society

CHAPTER THIRTEEN

Commitment and the African Writer

Prof. C. Achebe
Department of English,
University of Nigeria, Nsukka

What is Commitment?

Commitment may be defined as a sense of obligation or a strong attachment to a cause. When we speak of a writer's commitment we mean his attachment to particular social aims and the use of his writing to advance those aims. This, of course, implies a belief that literature can and should be used as a force for social change, and that a writer has a responsibility to do so.

Not everybody shares this belief. There are some people who hold that the writer's only responsibility is to his art; they maintain that the writer's truest guide is his own "inner light" and not some "extraneous" social concern. This view of literature (and the arts in general) is sometimes referred to as *Art for Art's sake.* It is a peculiarly European view, and although not as popular today as in the past, it still exists.

The view of literature (and of writers) as socially responsible, on the other hand, has been gaining ground in recent times, especially in those parts of the world where rapid social changes are taking place or where social oppression in one form or another occurs. Africa fits both criteria: it is undergoing radical changes and its peoples are subjected to foreign and domestic oppression.

Since the days of the slave trade, Africa has suffered as a victim of Europe. But she has not always been a passive victim. She often fought back; she often protested and pleaded. But occasionally she has behaved like the lizard who ruined his own mother's funeral. She has, out of some incredible blindness, lent a hand to her own destruction.

Throughout this period of physical suffering, mental anguish and spiritual confusion, African writers have emerged and used the weapon of literary expression in defence of, and commitment to, their continent and people.

Olaudah Equiano

A remarkable 18th century writer of Nigerian origin, Olaudah Equiano, otherwise known as Gustavus Vassa, the African, was kidnapped from the Igbo village of Iseke (in Ihiala Local Government Area) and sold into slavery at the age of twelve. After many years of suffering the cruel fate of slaves in Europe and the New World he secured his freedom and settled down in London. In 1789 he published his autobiography in which he set out to do two things:

(a) to shock the conscience of Christian Europe with the detail and the enormity of the crime of the slave trade and slavery; and
(b) to show that Africa was not the land of bestiality and darkness which Europe said it was.

In the first part of the book Equiano paints a nostalgic and engaging picture of his life as a child in a happy, orderly African homeland. It was an attempt to counter the accusation of barbarity made by Europeans against Africa. "We are almost a nation of dancers musicians and poets," said Equiano. In other words, his people did not live in savagery as Europe needed to believe, but in orderly societies rich in culture and the lively arts.

Elsewhere in the book Equiano says: "Our women too were, in my eyes at least, uncommonly graceful." If his protest sounds a little mild and apologetic to our modern ear we must remember the temper of the Europe he wrote for. Equiano was a committed writer who sought to change the lot of the African slave literature.

L. S. Senghor (1906–)

One hundred and fifty years after the publication of Equiano's autobiography we find a great African poet, Senghor, writing these words:

> They call us cotton-heads and coffee men
>   and oily men
> They call us men of death
> But we are men of the dance whose feet only gain power
> When they beat the hard soil

Senghor did not experience slavery like Equiano. Indeed the slave trade had ended long before Senghor was born in 1906. Yet his words are not very different from the words of Equiano. Why? A new form of slavery had taken the place of the old. This new slavery was colonization. Senghor grew up in

French colonial Africa. As a French subject, he was taught that Africa had no culture and no history and that the aim of French colonization was to civilize Africans and *assimilate* them into French culture and citizenship.

As a student in Paris in the 1930's Senghor began to question the myth of the French "civilizing mission". With other black students he launched the intellectual and literary movement called *Negritude* which challenged the arrogance of Europe as the sole proprietor of culture and put forward counter-claims for the black man. If Europe excels in intellect and logic, they said, Africa is supreme in feeling and emotion. Senghor's movement was revolutionary. But his personal style has remained moderate and conciliatory. He sees himself as a "cultural mulato", a mediator between Europe and Africa. His commitment to Africa does not preclude the acceptance of certain specific European contributions. As a devout Christian, Senghor does not allow his feeling of grievance against Europe to overwhelm his sense of Christian forgiveness and universal brotherhood. Let us look at his words again in their wider context:

> Now While the Africa of despotism is dying – it
> is the agony of a pitiable princess
> Like that of Europe to whom she is connected
> through the navel –
> Now fix your immobile eyes upon your children
> who have been called
> And who sacrifice their lives like the poor man
> his last garment
> So that hereafter we may cry here at the rebirth
> of the world being the leaven that the
> white flour needs.
> For who else would teach rhythm to the world
> that has died of machines and cannons?
> For who else should ejaculate the cry of joy,
> that arouses the dead and the wise in a
> new dawn?
> Say, who else could return the memory of life to
> men with a torn hope?
> They call us cotton heads, and coffee men, and
> oily men,
> They call us men of death.
> But we are the men of the dance whose feet only
> gain power when they beat the hard soil.
>
> (from: "Prayer to Masks")

David Diop (1927–1960)

Senghor's younger countryman, David Diop, sees the matter differently. He rejects Christianity and the claims of European civilization quite unceremoniously as the opening lines of his poem "Vultures" clearly show:

> In those days
> When civilization kicked us in the face
> When holy water slapped our cringing brows . . .

Clearly Diop does not like either "civilization" or Christianity. But equally strong is his distaste for an Africa which cringes before its tormentor. Again and again in his poetry he takes issue with those who accept humiliation instead of striking back. His style is militant. Where Senghor's long sonorous lines may suggest the slow dignified pace of the Gregorian chant Diop's harsh lines sound like the blaring trumpet of martial music. His poem "Africa" is a capsule history in powerful poetic terms of Africa's victimization. The sense of despair generated in the young African by Africa's long-suffering docility in the face of humiliation is superseded by the triumphant image of the young tree growing slowly and stubbornly to the fruition of liberty, a liberty which will not be *offered* "on a platter of gold" but *achieved* in bitter struggle.

Africa

Africa my Africa
Africa of proud warriors in ancestral savannahs
Africa of whom my grandmother sings
Of the banks of the distant river
I have never known you
But your blood flows in my veins
Your beautiful black blood that irrigates the fields
The blood of your sweat
The sweat of your work
The work of your slavery
The slavery of your children
Africa tell me Africa
Is this you this back that is bent
This back that breaks under the weight of humiliation
This back trembling with red scars
And saying yes to the whip under the midday sun

But a grave voice answers me
Impetuous son that tree young and strong
That tree there
In splended loneliness amidst white and faded flowers
That is Africa your Africa
That grows again patiently obstinately
And its fruit gradually acquire
The bitter taste of liberty.

In another poem, "Nigger Tramp," Diop projects Africa in the image of a black beggar taken out of his natural home where he would have been entitled to human respect and abandoned to wander in disgrace through Europe. The poet blames himself for living so long in heedless ease in the face of such horrendous injustice and pledges henceforth to create chaos in the world to avenge this man and to restore the lost glory of Africa.

Have patience the Carnival is over
I sharpen the hurricane for the furrows of the future
For you we will remake Ghana and Timbuktu
And the guitars shuddering with a thousand strokes
Great mortars booming under the blows
Pestles
Pounding
From house to house
In the coming day.

(from "Nigger Tramp")

Diop did not live to see the revolution he prophesied. He perished in an air-crash off the coast of Dakar in 1960 with his wife and all his unpublished manuscripts.

Agostinho Neto (1922–)

A mild-mannered Angolan physician practising medicine in the black ghetto of Luanda, Neto was drawn irresistibly into political involvement and activism by the cruelty and obduracy of Portuguese colonial rule.

While David Diop prophesied militant action leading to freedom *in the future*, Neto accepts the inevitability of struggle *now*. In his poem, "Farewell at the Moment of Parting", the protagonist parts company with a mother who had taught him to wait and to hope and pronounces the famous clarion-call to immediate action: I wait no more, it is I who am awaited.

Farewell at the Moment of Parting

My mother
(oh black mothers whose children have departed)
You taught me to wait and to hope
As you have done through the disastrous hours.
But in me
life has killed that mysterious hope;
I wait no more
It is I who am awaited.
Hope is ourselves
Your children
Travelling towards a faith that feeds life.
We the naked children of the bush sanzalas,
Unschooled urchins who play with balls of rags
On the noonday plains ourselves
Hired to burn out our lives in coffee fields
Ignorant black men
Who must respect the whites
And fear the rich,
We are your children of the native quarters
Which the electricity never reaches;
Men dying drunk
Abandoned to the rhythm of death's tom-toms,
Your children
Who hunger
Who thirst
Who are ashamed to call you mother
Who are afraid to cross the streets
Who are afraid of men
It is ourselves
The hope of life recovered.

Neto's commitment to African freedom found concrete expression in the long war which his people waged under the banner of his MPLA against the Portuguese. It was reported that MPLA guerillas went into action against Portuguese forces chanting Neto's poems.

The Black Man As Victimiser: Commitment as Self-Criticism

The above discussion has been concerned about commitment of the African writer in the face of racial oppression by Europe. But there is another side to the matter. In the 1950's Mabel Imoukhuede Segun wrote a poem, entitled "Counterfeit Olympus", in which she satirized white colonizers who carried on as though they were olympian gods. She compared their senseless destructiveness to the havoc of an unguided bull-dozer. In the 1960's, after Nigeria had attained independence, John Ekwere (poet and broadcaster) wrote a "Rejoinder" to Mrs. Segun's poem and shifted the blame of victimization from white to black shoulders.

Rejoinder

"Now no more the palefaced strangers
With unhallowed feet
The heritage of our fathers profane;
Now no missioned benevolent despots
Bulldoze an unwilling race;
No more now the foreign hawks
On alien chickens prey –
But we on us."

It can be said from the large number of African works (novels, poems and plays) in the post-independence era which have adopted the attitude of Ekwere's poem, that commitment has taken on the face of disenchantment and self-criticism. The Gambian poet and surgeon, Lenrie Peters, confronts the matter squarely in the extract from his book of poems entitled *Satellites*. He portrays a black man (politician) who *preys* on his own people.

Meanwhile
The politicians came and went
Meteors about the sky –
It was necessary to seek loans
To beg in style
It will cost each of you
A meal a day.
The taxes rose
The Common Income fell
The death rate stayed alive.
But excuse me, sir;
We're free.
Why do we have to beg?
Industrial development
Dams, factories, the lot –
Change the face of the Continent.

'I see
But my children –
Beg pardon Sir,
Will they go to school?'
Later!
'Will they have food to eat and clothes to wear?'
Later I tell you!
'Beg pardon Sir;
A house like yours?'
Put this man in jail.

(from *Satellites*)

In this quick and over-simplified account of the various ways in which African writers have shown their commitment to their people in the last two hundred years the main examples have been taken from poetry. It must not be assumed from this that poetry is the only literary form in which commitment can be demonstrated. The same case could be made from a study of African fiction and drama. But poetry does have one advantage in this kind of quick survey on account of its brevity.

CHAPTER FOURTEEN

Drama and Conscientization

Kalu Uka

Department of English,

University of Nigeria, Nsukka

Every society constantly faces challenges to its immediate political, social, moral and aesthetic ideals. Many methods are adopted for combating each challenge. Many failures, many successes do result. In the process the human persons in that society change or modify their thinking, adopt new ideals, discover other ways of meeting challenges.

No method, however, in whatever society, has yet been invented, to replace planning and projection in a carefully programmed procedure. Indeed, so central is planning now that it has become an important science for study, requiring a deft art for its execution and application. And, nowhere else in the modern world is the need for planning and guidance for a society more urgent than in Africa and other "Third World" countries, Nigeria included. In these countries, both because of their peculiar local developments, and, also, because of the phenomenon known as colonialism, the urgent need to plan and programme activities inevitably leads one to the question of *priorities* and *end-results*. Because of seeming new-found wealth, economics or the basic question of decent living standards and survival for the present and future generations becomes a vital matter of material, concrete results, visible on the persons of the people in the society, visible in their living houses, visible in their children's wear and food, visible in the changing faces of villages, towns, and urban centres.

In such circumstances, society tends to measure usefulness in terms of immediate utility; it tends to measure value in terms of the concrete and visible. The engineer can build a bridge or a house, no matter if it collapses a day after; the Doctor brings dead people back to life; the Agriculturist doesn't buy food, etc.

Our subject today, "Drama and Conscientization", requires us, at least in part, to, somehow, fit drama and theatre into this pattern of social utility.

This may not be too easy, not because it cannot be done, but because drama and literature in general (which are obvious kindred), are often rated very low on the utility scale. Indeed, most subject areas in the humanities tend to suffer this low-rating because of the very nature of their intangible, spiritual, non-material, but still vital, being. People who pursue interests in the humanities are either loafers, drop-outs, or dreamy aesthetes, impractical, lacking a mathematical orientation, etc., according to a certain kind of *popular* weighing of values and categorization within the scale.

The situation is not much improved by the truth that ours is a society faced with a long period of transition from rediscovering its true original roots after the colonial impact to achieving true selfhood based on its own contextual definitions.

To straighten the picture somewhat, before plunging into the heart of the matter, it is necessary to examine a few simple preliminary facts, which sound like propositions. Examined closely, each quickly yields a strong inter-relatedness to the issues raised in the other. When these links are understood, there is a better chance of achieving greater understanding of the subject.

First: *Literature* — dramatic, poetic, or fictional — precedes discussion of its nature and value. This fact is amply examplified by the African's traditional enjoyment of oral literature, its performance, its modes, and its ways of teaching young and old in the days of our forefathers. Where is that folksy or folklore tradition today, as one begins to examine and ask for utility in the arts? Yet, folklore *did* do something for the African people.

Second: *Modern* (or, civilized) man must today justify all his *significant* activities. Is drama significant, or must it be asserted that life is too short and transitory to be spent on such an unnecessary activity, an activity better reserved for childish minds? One should remind everyone of the old adage that the difference between a man's and a boy's toy is the price.

Third: The "justification" which civilized man seeks for his major activities usually rests on the prejudicial claims of morality, science, and efficiency. We call the claims prejudicial because neither morality nor science, nor efficiency makes concessions to others. Their demand is absolute.

Fourth: *Man*, however, is essentially a *political* animal. Hence he will reduce "value" to slogans. For example, Nigerian mass media, newspapers, radio, television, today fill one's ears with slogans about the impending 1979 elections (recall Mike Ejeagha and his music); about OFN (again musician Ejeagha and co.); about community development projects; about National

UPE; about *freedom* of the Press; about a new constitution for Nigeria; about price control; about Police efforts to curb armed robbery, etc., etc. When the politician has reduced ideas or intentions to slogans, he usually gets away with the impression that he has made concrete contributions of great value. The interesting question is not just, "has he really?", but how could he, without the skills, presentation and talent of the artist? In this case, the musician, or, as we will all see elsewhere, the dramatist. After all a good lyric needs a good tune to bring it to life.

Fifth: The position of man as a political being links with that of him as a *moral* being. Morality exists in *fixed* systems. Everything happening within "the system" is right and commendable but outside it, the "offence" is variously, punishable with ostracism, imprisonment, or even death.

Sixth: In fact, to defend the kind of subtle "values" which are less easy indeed to define than are the claims of politics and science, as the "values" of drama, it is necessary to have an *epistemology*, a system of knowledge, within which one can talk, *not* at cross purposes, but cooperatively, in a strategically viable manner, so that problems are attacked on various fronts. In western philosophy, for instance, Aristotle *displaced* Plato in the development of western intellectual tradition of knowledge systems for this very reason.[1]

Seventh: Imaginative literature, which is what drama is, is a *formal* presentation in *language* of what may or may not be *literally* true. Hence, we need an epistemology to grasp it, or

Eighth: *Confusion* will arise and continue because oral literature which also, in Nigeria and Africa, includes drama, depends on, and has encouraged in those who grew up in it, the ear for listening to the memorable and has induced a *taste* for figures of speech in the participators, as witness the centrality of proverbial communication in Igbo philosophy, life, and extrapolation about experimental conclusions.

Ninth: The modern issue, and the *crux* of conscientization is *how to communicate* in both "intellectual" and "non-intellectual" ways, the pleasure(s) derived through the reading, study and performing of drama. This is a very crucial *how*.

Tenth: Finally, drama is always and ever, a document of history or phases of history. To put great alongside not-so great, in *Veronica, My Daughter*, for instance, we see the effects of the brideprice law of Eastern Nigeria, 1955,

[1] cf. J. Bronowski and Bruce Mazlish, *The Western Intellectual Tradition* (Gt. Britain: Penguin Books, 1963) and David Daiches, *Literature and Society* (N.Y., 1968).

while in Shakespeare's *King Lear* we have a glimpse of conflicts that could be generated by inheritance laws in Renaissance England, and in *Macbeth* we intuit a little bit of child care at *some* time in the history of a certain people, possibly, the Scottish or another.

To summarize then, this discussion has attempted to assert that for drama to become an instrument for conscientization, one needs to understand a whole gamut of factors, namely, that drama, properly understood, has always been present in the political, social, economic, intellectual, moral, scientific, and cultural living of Africa; that (as was asserted very early in this discussion) many methods are adopted in any given society for tackling the challenges of each phase of significant activity; that, by understanding the: (a) history of theatre and drama in Nigeria; (b) critical nature of drama, and how it imparts *consciousness*; and (c) the excellent professional opportunities in theatre today, one can place drama in its proper "division", even in a computer-planned programme for development in Nigeria in the 20th century.[2]

History of Theatre and Drama in Nigeria

By many accounts[3] the history of drama in Nigeria, as in any other predominantly non-literate society, is as long almost, as the people's memory. In those pristine societies the "performances" which seem to us "dramatic" were dances, minstrelsy, initiation rites, secular ceremonies. Indeed, according to E. T. Kirby, traditional performances in Africa fall into the seven categories of "*simple enactments, ritual and ritualized enactments, storytelling performances, spirit-cut enactments, masquerade and masquerade enactments, ceremonial performances* and *comedies*".[4] (Emphasis mine).

In Nigeria, the *bori* performances of Hausa-speaking communities of Northern Nigeria,[5] the Yoruba *orisha*, the Igbo *mmuo*, the Ijo *owu* are a few examples of the many interlocked varieties of African "performances". Many of these combine religion, magic, and art, and eventuate in *spectacle*.

[2] cf. Osita Nwoka on the Think Tank, *Daily Times*, 18 February, 1978, p. 14.

[3] cf. Ola Rotimi, M. J. C. Echeruo, D. I. Nwoga, and many other Nigerian writers, critics and directors in various reference books.

[4] E. T. Kirby, "Indigenous African Theatre," *The Drama Review* XVIII/4 (December, 1974), p. 22.

[5] Andrew Horn, "Ritual, Drama and the Theatrical: The Case of Bori Spirit Mediumship," a paper presented at the seminar on the Interrelationship of the Arts in Nigeria, Unilag, February, 1978.

Loosely, they are, and have been called, drama. It is best to say they have been called drama because this is not the place to show that the "analysis of these various kinds of performances may begin with what they are *not*, that is, drama formally conceived", while we note that they "preceded and engendered"[6] drama, and yet remain their own viable entities, as performance. Historically speaking, they are still evolving accordingly as society changes.

Drama and theatre, in the broadest possible sense, subsume these elements and those of most *structured* performances presented before *an audience* (in an envelope of stage-house or arena, lights, etc., in modern times).

The history of *this* formal kind of presentation in Nigeria is as old as the country itself. It began,-in earnest, in 1960, emanating from both Mbari centres and the former University College. Ibadan's Travelling Theatre, whose rendition of Soni Oti's *Danda* (1963) – an adaptation of Nkem Nwankwo's novel of the same name, followed from the UCI Dramatic Society's earlier tour of *The Scoundrel, Suberu* (1959) and adaptation of Moliere's *The Scoundrel, Scapin* – set off a tradition of theatre tours which has grown and flowered in the popular, even if more sectional, tours of the Yoruba folk operas of Hubert Ogunde, Duro Ladipo, and Ogunmola[7] Theatres. They have flowed over into the postwar tours of Nsukka's "Anaedo – Four-D Theatre" productions from the Institute of African Studies (of *A Drop of Honey*, 1972–1973; *The Lost Finger*, 1972) and the Department of English, Drama Section's tours to Calabar, Enugu, Ife, and Lagos with *A Harvest for Ants* (1975–1977), *The Wedlock of the Gods* (1974), *The Rhythm of Violence* (1972), and *Edufa* (1972).

These contemporary theatre performances have also bloomed in the new State Cultural Centres at Port Harcourt, Calabar, Benin and Kaduna, and within the activities of various State and national festivals of the arts, culminating in the controversial FESTAC '77. The major names of directors, actors, designers, and technologists have varied from John D. Ekwerre, Meki Nzewi, Ola Rotimi, Paul U. A. Worika, to Kalu Uka, Dapo Adelugba, Jimi Solanke, Sunbo Marinho, Ralph Opara, and many others to whom credit for conscientious work must be given. It is a history of expanding and lively theatrical activity, inspired from various sources, not least, the

[6] *Ibid.*

[7] See a typical tour schedule: *Daily Times*, February, 1978. Note the "Eastern" areas, as always, *are* excluded. Politics?

earlier, even if now defunct 1960 Masks and Orisun Theatre companies of Wole Soyinka.

Theatre Arts in Nigeria: Acting, Productions, Trends in Development

In the work of these many newcomers, and in the pioneering work of Professor-Playwright Wole Soyinka, director Yemi Lijadu, and the recent addition of the feminine touch of Dr. (Mrs.) Zulu Sofola, the theatre arts in Nigeria have assumed wider dimensions. As in writing, so in production, *experimentation* has dominated; western style proscenium has been blended into, or been juxtaposed with, or modified into, various forms of African open-air, arena, or theatre-in-the-round styles. Themes, scenery, views, and space have been more panoramic in an attempt to match the epic dimensions of original indigenous material; the audiences have been wheeled closer and closer to the performers. New theories of aesthetic distance and concepts of dramatic appeal have been tried out, the propaganda values of drama, such as any politician would wish, have been attempted and the socially corrective and instructive possibilities of drama have been incorporated from the nuances of James Iroha's Zebrudaism to the petulant satires of Soyinka's *The Road*. On television, though production styles have remained primarily at basic levels, yet the *potential* impact of a "hot" medium art, from the mannerisms of Joe Molokwu's defunct *Na So You Be*, to the half-throbs of Mrs. Elizabeth Okaro's *Tom-tom*, has been tasted. What remains is actually focussing the central issues into "conscious relevance" within the society, atomized and heterogeneous as it seems.

One obviously important way to focus into conscious relevance is to see what our more gifted actors and actresses, people such as Miss Elizabeth Osisioma, now of the Department of Theatre Arts, University of Calabar, Miss Ori Enyi-Okoro, Miss Nwamaka Ume, Mr. Jimmy Johnson, Mr. Ralph Opara, Mr. Azubuike Ikemefuna, are doing with their histrionic talents. In and around Lagos today, others such as John Chukwu, Taiwo Ajai, Jimi Solanke are more or less scrounging around, waiting for the great opportunity either in or outside the National Theatre, to make an imprint on acting careers in this country, such as Sir Laurence Olivier, Yul Brynner, Anthony Quinn, Richard Burton, Elizabeth Taylor, and other immortal Hollywood masters have indelibly left in the minds of countless millions of theatre, film, and television viewers.

Trends in theatre arts development in Nigeria today show a running battle between forces that would impede progress such as economic and commercial priorities and anti-art philistinism where the large money-holders never patronise the performing arts, and the forces that encourage continued development, such as the training schemes of state cultural centres, Federal Government's Arts Council, universities' teaching programmes, and the needs of primary and post-primary institutions to build characters of the young by examples in practical team work and practical leadership exercises, such as sporting activities, also complementarily provide.

Theatre as Art Form

"Conscientization" in drama can also be realized by a thorough grasp of the manner in which theatre is conceived of as an art form. Earlier, it was mentioned that theatre and film, and television and radio have common bonds. The theatre, which, since the days of our forefathers, had always had a monopoly on dramatic performance as entertainment, communal ritual, or festival, has now lost that commanding position. Today, more people, even in technologically backward Nigeria, can see a televised or filmed show, on any one evening, than could ever attend the live theatre in one year. Professor O. G. Brockett, pondering this fact, has asserted, that

> ... theatre may be likened to a hand-crafted product in an age of mass production ... Thousands of copies of a film may be printed and shown throughout the world SIMULTANEOUSLY and year after year, and each showing can be almost identical with the others ... Similarly, a televised program is normally viewed by millions of people SIMULTANEOUSLY, and most often it is taped so that it may be reshown at will. In contrast, a theatrical production can be seen by only a small group of people at one time — usually not more than two thousand and more often a few hundred — and at each performance it differs, for, not being fixed on film or tape, it necessarily changes.[8] (Emphasis mine)

Here then are some of the reasons why, even in highly advanced societies, the theatre compares unfavourably with film and television. Theatre seems, even in Nigeria, to slide into a minority art because powerful factors tend to limit its audience and to make it expensive; by limiting the potential financial returns, its artists tend to be less limelight personalities.

[8] O.G. Brockett, *Theatre, an Introduction*, (New York's Holt, Rinehart and Winston, 1974), p. 9.

However, it is in these very negative factors, ironically, that the powers of theatre for rousing consciousness in our society lie. We will dig into that consciousness when we return theatre to its artistic base, to the skill which characterized it from its origin, and which our forefathers called, *nka*.

The *nka*, the *art*, in theatre, inheres on its three-dimensionality by comparison with film, television, or radio. This three-dimensional trait gives theatre a psychological advantage by bringing performer and spectator as close as three or even fewer feet apart, or even obliterating space, a distance which television, radio, or film can never match. Properly used, theatre can uniquely revolutionize society for it can hereby evolve an artistic application and translation of theory into practice which will answer to that need for an epistemology which was underlined earlier. Art then becomes a "systematic application of knowledge or skill to achieving some predetermined result",[9] thus making drama as crucial as the craft of medicine, politics, or science. So that, without losing our heads or bearings in the continuing debates as to which are "useful" of "fine" arts, we can use drama for the following "fine" but very "useful" ends:

1. A means whereby man seeks to understand the world around and in him, discovering as science does, hidden truths, recording the discovery as fact in the way history does, or exploring the discovery as idea, in the manner philosophy does. Indeed a play, then, like some aspects of the social sciences, psychology, and sociology, may become another means for questing after underlying principles and truths, and relating them to human existence. However, the difference will remain that where the historian, the philosopher, the scientist perceives patterns and marshals proof in logical exposition which the intellect absorbs, the dramatic artist directly involves the audience's feelings, imagination, and intellect in order to evoke a direct response, since the "events" of a play seem to "occur" right before the viewers' eyes. Such "events" are not life, as we said earlier, but are "real" to the extent still, that they are life-like, stripped of irrelevant detail and organized into a significant connected pattern, causally illuminating and commenting on the human experience it presumes to create.

2. As a manipulator of imagination which then receives the invented characters, their motivations, actions, and dialogue, at some aesthetic or psychic distance, as vicarious experience, as entertainment which throws off impressions, bits of knowledge about sharing sympathy (empathy), "disinterested contemplation"[10] of everyday frays of human life, or about

[9] *Ibid.*

[10] *Ibid.*, p. 12.

committed involvement in the solution of the manifold human problems that beset man daily.

In such an art, drama becomes all-embracing, and so will the kind of entertainment which it produces. With Professor Harold Clurman, we can assert that the source of satisfaction is

> . . . When my interest has been aroused, when my detached capacity for feeling, thought, sentiment, laughter and passion are brought into play. I am entertained when my senses are quickened, my soul touched, my mind alerted. Being healthy, I cannot be fed adulterated stimulants or strong sedatives; nor am I gratified by timed stabs at my sensibilities. I want my entertainment to exercise my faculties as vigorously and as completely as possible.[11]

Dramatic art, then, is one way of ordering, clarifying, understanding, and enjoying experience.

Theatrical Form, Structure, Style, Audience and Criticism

If drama, then, is an art form, functional in educating our sensibilities and functional in the manner in which it offers us complex entertainment, we need to know in detail how its *form*, *structure* and *style* possess characteristic qualities which benefit an audience, an entire populace, through criticism, that other art of explication which, together with performance, can open the eyes of the general citizenry to the merits of drama as a vehicle for conscientization.

Given our semi-literate society in modern Nigeria, it is clear that any discussion of how theatrical form, structure, and style work on an audience through helpful guidance criticism, must first delineate what place audience and critic occupy.

As has been mentioned before, the primary motive for any group to go to the theatre is for entertainment. Entertainment truly understood is not a simple desire to relax from the cares, tensions, and worries of a challenging world. Entertainment is a desire to be renewed through the exciting insights and provocative perceptions of significant topics, advocacies for action in political, social and moral issues, and a heightening of our awareness of our immediate surroundings.

Somewhere in the subconsciousness of audiences these two contrary views

[11] Quoted in Hatlen, *Orientation to the Theatre* (New York's Appleton-Century-Crafts, 1962), p. 16.

of entertainment as a value produce a "fright" in the minds of theatre-goers which adds to the problems of getting theatre to live for its people. This "fright" takes the form of a nonchalant attitude to theatre by audiences. They are not aware that they do, and can exert, collectively and individually, a significant influence on the fate of theatre. The average spectator becomes like the average voter in the country. He cannot see how his one tiny vote can influence the choice of a representative; he cannot see how his actions can influence government policy. But voter power is immense, as the current slogans urging people to register for 1979 suggest. So too, the lethargic theatre-goer must recognize and use his right and power as audience-member and critic.

In a true sense, every member of the audience is a critic. When one sees a play, be it *Zebrudaya*, or *The Lost Finger*, one passes judgement. One example here might suffice. In 1973, here in the Arts Theatre, a play, *A Drop of Honey* was showing. The play shows some of the human aberrations of war-time life bringing together refugees, doctor's clinics, reverend father's confession and relief distribution houses, lawyers' clubs, etc. A young vivacious and buxom refugee girl is attracted to a quiet, devoted Rev. Father. She tries to seduce the priest. At the point where her tempting fingers begin to caress and touch a chord in the priest's man's heart, the priest is about to stop resisting. One of the student reverend sisters here, at that juncture, tore up the programme, objecting to that "silly mis-representation" of the "priesthood", and started walking out. It took another student reverend sister to recall her and remind her that what she saw was "only a play".

However fleeting, ridiculous, or inaccurate a judgement upon what is seen is, it is still a criticism. Criticism, of a more reasoned, structured kind, is required from a trained mind, not only to assess the play, but also to guide such a member of the audience as our student reverend sister. The critic then, is the person who can *formulate* judgements from his initial impressions during and after the performance, to a thorough analysis, showing him to be able to understand plays, theatrical practice, and audience well enough to assess them effectively.

The meaning and purpose of criticism then would be to illuminate the theatrical piece both for the creators of it on stage and for its consumers in the audience. Such criticism would refer to specific portions of a play, characterization, structure, form, styles of acting and staging. Such criticism whether adverse or favourable, should normally serve the three basic functions of exposition, appreciation or denunciation, *and* evaluation.

In Nigeria, as elsewhere in the literary and theatrical world, the standard-bearer critics who have done this kind of work base their judgements on extrapolations from the qualities of landmark plays and playwrights. Such landmark plays, wherever and whenever they have been written, yield both unique and common characteristics upon which conclusions can be based as to the nature of effective, meaningful, dramatic action.

On dramatic *form*, for instance, we now accept, from Aristotle to M. J. C. Echeruo and Wole Soyinka, that a play must have a "beginning, middle, and end" in principle. Thus, since a play is a representation of man in action, physical and mental, its form must be *complete* and *self-contained*, embodying within its framework all that is necessary for understanding it in its cultural context and beyond, in its universal implications. For this reason, dramatic action must be:

1. *Organized purposefully*, so as to arouse "a specific response, such as pity and fear, joy, ridicule, or indignation, thoughtful contemplation, or laughter, simply or in a complex manner, and the events, characters, the mood and other elements similarly controlled."

2. *Varied*, in "plot, characterization, ideas, mood, or spectacle", to avoid monotony and predictability.

3. *Engaging and sustaining in interest*, so that characters command audience's attention, situations are compelling, the issues are vital enough to warrant concern, and the aural and visual devices are novel enough to excite and hold interest.

4. *Probable*, by which "all its elements are logically consistent, so that, according to Kenneth Burke, the play's form "is created through arousal and fulfilment of expectation".[12] (Recall here too, the *Drop of Honey* example).

When these general principles have been followed, in a strictly disciplined, even if experimentalist mode, landmark dramas result. Landmark plays are those which have been "tasted, chewed and swallowed" by their audiences and have been repeatedly received for a long enough period of time to merit the title of "classic", to yield upon analysis, the principles that spell out what may be called "the idea of the theatre". In these classic plays, organization or structure, and style have been used to "*direct* people's attention to relationships which create meaningful patterns" in the culture of man.

Three of these structural and stylistic patterns of unifying experience are outstanding. They are the principles of *thought character*, and *cause-to-effect arrangement of events*.[13] Through the use of these three principles, the

[12] Brockett, pp. 31–32.

[13] *Ibid.*

theatrical form, structure, and style of plays can conscientize a community over a period of time.

Conscientization in Nigerian Theatre and Theatrical Practice

Traditionally, the dominant organizational principle in dramatic action to arouse the consciousness of the people has been the *cause-to-effect* arrangement of incidents. This principle is amply illustrated in one of the oral traditional accounts of the early migration and settlement of the Ohafia people of southeastern Nigeria, from Ibeku through Abam to the present site when they popularly explain, on being asked *how* and *why* they moved, "Ife mee ngu, ngu mee ọba, ọba mee kpogoro",[14] which is an idiomatically symbolic cause-to-effect, mechanistic language.

In the drama of the "Western World", Sophocles used this method in *Oedipus Rex*, just as in Nigerian drama, Wole Soyinka uses it in *The Road*. In both these tragic plays, the playwrights first set out in the opening scenes all the necessary conditions out of which later events develop.

In the drama of the "Western World," Sophocles used this method in *Oedipus Rex*, just as in Nigeria drama, Wole Soyinka uses it in *The Road*. In both these tragic plays, the playwrights first set out in the opening scenes all the necessary conditions out of which later events develop.

In both plays, the situation, the desires, and the motivations of the characters are so stark that the quest which Oedipus and the Professor embark upon, the helplessness and miserable ends of both protagonists, is derived from the original causes of their mitigating conflicts, inner and outer, leading to crises within and without. Each play's substance is the efforts which the characters make in order to overcome the obstacles on their road to apprehending life. In fact, it is the skilful construction of *Oedipus Rex* (as a play with a prologue and five episodes, typical of Greek tragedy, but delaying the "point of attack" in the initial exposition) which piles up a number of important themes – happiness man's fate and destiny, the relation of man to the gods, man as scapegoat, blindness, and sight – and in the end affects the audience's psyche in that peculiar rousing of consciousness which Aristotle very early named "catharsis." With Wole Soyinka, it is

[14] cf. Ohafia heroic poetry traditions, e.g. a record by Udumeze Kalu, and further studies by Mrs. Grace Kalu Agwu (1974) and, currently an unpublished doctoral thesis by Chukwuma Azuonye, University of London (1977).

the schematically skilful division of *The Road* into two parts (a new departure, but which delays the revelation of Kotonou's motivation) which, through suspense, irony, satire and topical allusion, forces the audience to see that man may not challenge the gods, least of all, try to imprison a spirit in masquerade as the Professor imprisons Murano, without paying the highest price.

Each play, then, through a plot structured to reveal a cause-to-effect order of events, shows a balance of relevancies in which man intuits but never solves the mystery of his relationship with the supernatural movers of his world.

That the passage of nearly three thousand years has not reduced the theatrical effectiveness and appealing fascination of *Oedipus Rex*, and that *The Road* has enjoyed popular acclaim in International and Commonwealth arts festivals since 1965, attest to the enduring power and meaning with which any landmark play moves the consciousness of a people.

The second, and less often used principle of organizing theatrical action to arouse consciousness, is *character*. The incidents may be loosely joined, but they will always be held together primarily because they centre around one main person. Such plays may be historical dramas, such as John Drinkwater's *Abraham Lincoln*, or the play may show an individual character's responses to a series of experiences. Such plays include Christopher Marlowe's *Doctor Faustus* or *Tamburlaine* and Eugene O'Neill's *Emperor Jones*. In Nigerian drama, Wentu, the accursed witch of Eroboland in Meki Nzewi's *The Lost Finger*, is a good example. As in Marlowe's *Faustus* where the learned doctor makes a pact with the arch-devil, Mephistopheles, so in the "cinematic-epic", Wentu the witch is cursed to return from the dead to Eroboland every seven years, bringing in her wake a flood of disasters, intrigues, and war. In *Doctor Faustus*, Mephistopheles makes the young theologian commit a sacrilegious carnality by asking to make love to the ghost of Helen of Troy, the most devastatingly beautiful woman of mythical antiquity, who "launched a thousand ships", and brought to ruin all of Ilion (Troy).

It is relevant to compare also another Nigerian play which spawns characters like ghosts from the past, and throws them into the midst of the living present so that past, present, and future may confront each other by juxtaposition, comparison, and projection, and together answer the question, "what is man's nature?" The play is Wole Soyinka's *A Dance of the Forests*, a play which, by loose construction, mythic implication, and ritual proverbializing, centres around the *one* character called Adenebi, or Forest Head, the warrior, man and wife returned from the dead, the Carver-artist Demoke, the portent evil Eshuoro, and the wily monster-woman Madam Tortoise (Rola). Each revolves around Forest Head, each acting out his or her previous existence, and reincarnating an identical humour in the present as in the past he or she possessed.

Again, in the end, both Marlowe and Soyinka underline an important aspect of human life which goes back, so to speak, to what Professor Francis Fergusson calls the "pre-rational basis"[15] of true drama, the basis upon which landmark plays become

> . . . the sphinxes of literature, with the disconcerting property of showing up those who would interpret them . . . [because] . . . mysterious they are and will remain, [though] we can see that they mirror human life and action, both with extraordinary directness, and from many angles at once, catching the creature in the very act of inventing those partial rationalizations which . . . underlie the structure of incident and character, . . . in the performable rhythm of life and action which may still touch us though originally realized in the customs, beliefs, and ritual forms of antiquity . . . [16]

The third principle on which organization of dramatic action for rousing consciousness can be based is that of *basic idea* or *thought*. This kind of organization embodies the ideas in scenes which inter-link largely because they illustrate aspects of a larger theme or argument. In western literary drama Bertolt Brecht has employed this method in the play, *The Private Life of the Master Race*. The play depicts the rise of Adolf Hitler's Nazi party by using a *series of scenes* which illustrate the inhumanity of the ideology. Many absurdist European playwrights, notably, Samuel Beckett, also write plays not to develop a story, but to circle round, exploit, embroider, and peck at a concept, a mood, or an apprehension. Plays such as *Waiting for Godot*, and Luigi Pirandello's *Six Characters In Search of an Author* examine levels of reality and illusion. In Nigerian and African drama, Ola Rotimi's *Holdin' Talks*, Tewfik Al Hakim's *The Tree Climber*, or *The Fate of a Cockroach* are examples of absurdist *ideational plays*. The idea is loosely set forth, and an approach, much like that of music improvisation, is encouraged so that themes are then elaborated and extended into a "collection of moments", sometimes *ad nauseam*. Through the scenes, anxieties, aspirations,

[15] Francis Fergusson, *The Idea of a Theater* (New York: Doubleday Anchor Books Inc., 1949), p. 16.
[16] F. Fergusson, pp. 16f., *passim*.

ideals of youth such as opposition to war and to social conventions, etc., are shown. The play "develops", if it does, not linearly, but "spirally" or "vertically" through a set of motifs.

Again, as in the other two cases, the playwright aims to arouse the people's involvement; his goal is to urge them into action, especially in the modern period when imitativeness abounds, motives are confused, feelings are politicised, respectability is lost, causes are fought and lost, young people have no bearings in the mazes of transition, examinations leak, the word "discipline" loses significance in much loose usage. "Isms" arise as playwrights seek new ways of penetrating people's awareness. Wole Soyinka gives us the country of "Isma" in *Kongi's Harvest* whose prologue reads:

> Ism to ism for ism is ism
> Of isms and isms on absolute-ism
> To demonstrate the tree of life
> Is sprung from broken peat
> And we the rotted bark, spurned
> When the tree swells its pot
> The mucus that is snorted out
> When Kongi's new race blows
> And more, oh there's harvest of words
> In a penny newspaper
>
> They say, oh how
> They say it all on silent skulls
> But who cares? Who but a lunatic
> Will bandy words with boxes
> With government rediffusion sets
> Which talk and talk and never
> Take a lone word in reply.[17]

In *Madmen and Specialists*, we hear the Old Man, in a frenzied effort to remove, by surgical incision, "the cyst" from the "system," castigate one of the mendicants:

> . . . you cyst, you cyst, you sprint in the arrow of arrogance, the dog in dogma, tick of a heretic, the tick in politics, the mock of democracy, the mar of marxism, a tic of the fanatic, the boo in buddhism, the ham in Mohammed, the dash in the criss-cross of Christ, a dot on the i of ego, an ass in the mass, the ash in ashram, a boot in kibbutz, the pee of priesthood, oh how dare you

[17] Soyinka, *Kongi's Harvest* (London: Oxford University Press, 1967), pp. 1—2.

raise your hindquarters, you dog of dogma, and cast the scent of your existence on the lamp-post of Destiny you HOLE IN THE ZERO of NOTHING![18]

So, loosely constructed or tightly economised, the theatrical form, structure and style of the dramatist, however organized, is ever purposefully directed, calculatedly channelled to evoke people's responses.

Opportunities in the Theatre Today: Core of Conscientization

Some of the problems any theatre encounters anywhere, as well as some of those practical problems peculiar to Nigeria have been discussed. The growth, in spite of the draw-back, of theatrical activity in Nigeria has been traced. The work of actors, designers, playwrights and technicians has been examined.

Obviously such a large-scale activity involving, either in creativity or in criticism and direction, such names as we have mentioned, is intended to fill the gap in the cultural life of the community. Therefore it cannot be the activity of the idle loafer; dropout, romantic dreamer or the unscientifically-minded. Drama and dramatic activity, especially in the way they have tried to reach out to the population through popular tours, specialized production and arts festivals, are an essentially vital aspect of the life of this country. By now, extending such life by the uses of modern technology, the foundations for this and future generations to have a basis for grasping and understanding the kind of consciousness and awareness we possess, is being laid. The formal introduction and existence of dramatic activity in our curricula calls for an even greater involvement by all sectors and divisions of the country in the theatre arts. Some means by which this can be achieved are discussed below.

(a) *The Theatre as a profession*

The best way to ensure the permanent contribution of drama and theatre to the societal values may be to tie it to our bellies. Theatrical talent, as well as literary talent, abounds in the country, but almost all our performers are part-timers. The prospects of a viable living wage exist only for a few as yet. This is a sickness which must be cured through, if necessary, paid governmental jobs in the numerous cultural centres in the states and federal centres such as the National Theatre.

[18] Soyinka, *Madmen and Specialists* (London: Oxford University Press, 1970), p. 76.

Indeed, one of the more blatant contradictions of the education received in Nigerian schools, colleges and universities is that for the prospective theatre worker, in spite of radio, television and theatre houses, opportunities for a direct job in the area of training seem non-existent, maybe because our education has neither goal nor relevant content which should shape the end.

(b) *Theatre as avocation*

So, they begin to regard theatre as merely an avocation. They have acquired all undergraduate liberal arts education; they have been officially certified as "suitable in character and learning", but it makes no difference whether that learning was in history, philosophy or even English, theatre is a sideline. A serious-minded classicist or historian, or biologist, could justifiably turn to theatre as critic, producer, or actor; a home science teacher could become a costume or scenery expert.

(c) *Theatre in education*

Where theatre and drama, for a variety of reasons, still suffer as they do in Nigeria, conscientization may best be achieved through outlets in various educational situations. Here, in fact, we find largest number of paying jobs, to teach and produce plays. Teaching and production could go on in the post-primary levels, whereas specialization in directing, lighting, costuming, administration, and special areas such as children's and handicapped people's theatres, etc., can go at university level. Demonstrations, projects, and lectures in the history of theatre, dramatic literature in general, and the theatre arts could also be given by a gifted and devoted teacher. Here, in educational theatre, achievement should be measured by the students' development, problems encountered and mastered, handicaps overcome. The distinction between the high standards and excellence of the professional and those of the learner must be insisted upon.

(d) *Children's theatre*

Conscientization, like any other evangelizing campaign to convert should work best and easiest with children. If, according to some philosophers, the mind is a kind of "tabula rasa" on which one may print anything, the child's mind, as it grows into society and its values, is one of the most malleable "tabulae". Children exhibit their *histrionic* sensibilities unabashedly (unlike restricted adults) as is seen in childhood games. Based on such potential, the theatre worker can take children's theatre into the professional, the community, or into the educational fields.

In these fields, it will be possible to conscientize adults about children, in which case adults are the audience. It will also be possible to use children to perform for other children, in which case children are the audience. It will also be possible to have adults perform for children; in this case audiences may be mixed – children and adults. There is also what Professor Brockett calls "creative dramatics" in which children are stimulated to improvise dramatic situations based on classroom discussion or study of stories, folktales, historical events, common social situations, manners and customs of people in various periods and countries, and even mathematical problems. Knowledge in child development psychology and specific techniques for teaching children should then be complemented to knowledge in other areas of child care in our social programme. After all, in army barracks, etc., children are often seen parading while at work and eventually became good officers as their fathers, uncles, and mentors have in real life.

(e) *Secondary, T.T.C. and diploma college theatre*

From childhood, one goes into the problematic period of adolescence. In Nigeria today, to judge from population figures, a large majority of young people are in secondary, teacher training, and technical colleges. Now that voting age has been reduced to eighteen, the crucial importance of this age group increases. Many more are employed in lower ranges of the ministries, in motor parks, etc. Theatrical activity among them can be a healthy channel for programming them into national obectives. Their activity can be extended into vacation time, cultural centres, or even extra-mural theatres, for if they can use extra-mural for G.C.E. O/L and A/L preparations, why not use it to gear themselves into theatrical?

(f) *University and community theatre*

At the university, as well as in the community theatre, performance becomes a mature application of theory to practice, a matter of distinguishing between the toy of the boy and the toy of the man. Conscientization through drama has the greatest potential at the university level because there is a wide variety of teachers goals extra-curricular work which then naturally overflows into the community and post-schooling work in theatre. Directing, designing, and costuming become at least semi-professions.

(g) *Professional campaigns and employment opportunities*

From detailed involvement in university and extra-curricular community theatre work, a person could, given the right atmosphere, then be considered fully equipped to launch out into professional acting in a company. Conscientization of Nigerian aspirations through drama could then flower when our gifted performers can benefit from permanent companies which pay hire sensibly, pay well, and organize activity in some way such as New York's L.O.R.T. (League of Resident Theatre), draining financial subvention from philanthropic and research foundation organizations. In Nigeria, the old and worn-out threads of the 1960 Masks, the Orisun Players, the Hill-top Arts Theatre, the Cross River Theatre Group, the Oak Theatre, Anaedo 4—D Production, the Soni Ensemble, the Unibadan Masques, the Ife University Players, the Paul-Worika Players, the Demers Nwoko New Culture Productions, the Ayorinde Performers, could be built into a mammoth National Players Ensemble (N.A.P.E) which, under a two-year term Director, could mount productions in the National Theatre, Lagos and at every State Capital every month throughout the year, thus demonstrating in concrete terms, how drama could harness the turbulent creative talents of Nigerians and channel them meaningfully into a programme for education, enlightenment, entertainment and even propaganda, which will reach back to the roots of our pristine culture.

Conclusion

Theatre today, then, is the inheritor of a tradition that can be traced back to the beginning of any people's oral or recorded history. Between its origins in primitive times and the present, many and complex changes have taken place, the most important of which have been surveyed in their various rousings of communal spirits and participation. From this survey a number of conclusions may be drawn.

First, the theatre is a vital and organic part of society. The forms it takes and the value placed upon it vary as historical and social conditions change. The theatre can remain a healthy institution only when it changes along with altering social conditions. When responsive to its age, the theatre fills a basic need in men's lives, but when it becomes static or too restricted in scope, it ceases to be important to its time.

Second, the theatre always reflects the *ideas* of its age. Each theatrical style has resulted from the attempt to find means adequate for expressing a view of reality and man's place in it. As man's conceptions about himself and his world change, his dramatic expression changes.

Third, there is always a close relationship between the drama and theatrical conventions of any age. The dramatist's conception of the theatre and its possibilities dictates to a large extent what demands his work make on the theatre. The plays of any period, therefore, have many common features because they use the same conventions. Consequently, in seeking to understand a play it is important to know the theatrical conditions under which it was written.

Fourth, while historical and social conditions, ideas, and theatrical conditions are important determinants of dramatic expression, the playwright's vision is the ultimate source of greatness. A study of the Elizabethan period, for example, helps to clarify many characteristics of Shakespeare's work, but it does not explain why only one writer of Shakespeare's stature appeared.

Fifth, although every play is clearly a product of its age, the great plays are timeless. Great drama provides a means by which the present can feel its way into the past, comprehend it, and perceive the continuity of human experience.

Sixth, theatre and drama are important means through which one may learn of man's ideas and feelings. Like history, science, or philosophy, theatre is a form of knowledge, but one that functions through feelings as much as through thought.

Seventh, the theatre should be studied in its total context, the scope of which is suggested in the preceding six points. A combination of the approaches outlined above yields a fuller understanding of the complex art of the theatre.

Eight, the dramatic impulse is natural to man and cannot be eradicated. The theatre may fluctuate in popularity, and the pleasures it offers may be fulfilled at times by other activities, but the theatre in one form or another will always be a part of human society.

Drama, then, matters, because it is to human beings, a *source of consciousness*. Such consciousness is revealed in landmark plays; such plays are not, however, "discreet objects" which we capture in a theatre, but rather the plays are "analogues of our human lives which we encounter . . ."[19]

[19] Richard Gilman, *The Making of Modern Drama* (New York: Farrar, Straus and Giroux, 1972), Foreword, p. x.

CHAPTER FIFTEEN

Mass Media and National Development

Dr. S. A. Ekwelie
Department of Mass Communication,
University of Nigeria, Nsukka

For the Third Development Plan, 1975—1980, Nigeria has proposed an outlay of ₦ 380,225,000 on public information.[1] Of this amount, a total of ₦ 234, 341,000 will go for federal information services while state governments shall have spent a sum of ₦145,884,000 by the end of the plan period. As stated in the plan, the objectives of government information policy is the creation and maintenance of an efficient information media system that would promote the ideals of unity and progress, in addition to presenting to the rest of the world balanced and up-to-date information about the country. To achieve this dual objective, the statement continues, policies will be articulated and programmes executed in the following areas: broadcasting, newspaper, news distribution in the form of a national news agency service, continued subscription to leading world news agencies, if only as a temporary measure, and the development of adequate man-power.

For good measure, the plan has promised the procurement of more broadcast equipment and the acquisition of production techniques. Taking cognisance of existing stage government newspapers, the planners have held up the promise of consolidating and rearranging such newspapers in an attempt to make them viable. The climax of this aspect of the plan will be the organisation of a federal government newspaper corporation that is meant to ensure objectivity, efficiency and reliability of the whole newspaper sector. Such a corporation would be encouraged to maintain a string of efficient staff correspondents in selected zones of the world, starting with Africa.

By establishing a national news agency, the government wishes to ensure that the outside world receives factual information on Nigeria. Appropriate emphasis was put on the need for staff training. Predictably, the planners

[1] This amount covers items which media people do not cover in their regular assignments. Some of the money will, for instance, go for library services.

have promised to use Nigerian and overseas institutions for man-power development for this sector. In pursuance of greater man-power development, bursaries will be made available.

Role of Communication

Every government, no matter what its ideological stripe, recognizes some role for the communication media in national development. Some ideologues and planners have, on occasion, overstated the importance of the media by implying, as McLuhan has proclaimed, that the *medium* is the message.[2] They seem to be saying that once the structure – an impressive printing plant or a powerful broadcast equipment – is there, the country of possession is on a threshold of social progress. In reality, this approach is nothing more than a celebration of structural formalism, an index approach, that does not begin to tell the story of how the media are being deployed. This approach seems to confuse what the media *can* do with what they *actually* do. It ignores the non-subtle point that installing a media system and promising to use it for a particular purpose is not in itself a proof of fulfilment of the objective.

Different studies in different countries have found that developing countries need the media for the evolution of a new psychological personality. Lerner, in a well known, if now controversial, study of the Middle-East has credited the media with the potential for creating empathy – the ability to project onself into the role of another, "a high capacity for rearranging the self-system on short notice".[3] The South African government, in a back-handed tribute to the mass media, had until quite recently resisted the introduction of television into that country. The reason given was the fear that introducing television would mean importing films from the United States, a development that was bound to expose black South Africans to racial struggles in the United States. The worry in Pretoria was that such an exposure was most likely to crystallize a new set of aspirations among the down-trodden black majority and evoke among them a vision of violence as well as eventual success, all on the North American model.

Pool, in his study of the media in the modernizing process, has asserted that the media do produce "characterological change", a terminal feature,

[2] His avant-garde ideas are contained in Marshall McLuhan, *Understanding Media* (New York: McGraw-Hill Book Company 1965). See especially pages 7–21.

[3] Daniel Lerner, *The Passing of Traditional Society* (New York: The Free Press, 1958) pp. 43–75.

it would appear, of the communist media. He however cherishes the ability of the media to instil empathy in the new nations of Africa, Asia and Latin America.[4]

In his studies of diffusion of innovation among peasants, Rogers has found correlation among literacy, education, cosmo-politeness and innovativeness, along with empathy. His studies have shown that media exposure (which must be defined as exposure to the media without necessarily worrying about what the exposure was to) is an intervening variable. In common parlance, he is saying that the presence of the media makes a difference as to what impact modernization or literacy, for instance, would have on individual empathy. In short, he is saying that the mass media can aid development in traditional society.[5]

Schramm, in his remarkable work on media role in national development, concludes that "communication is always at the very centre of existence, for any society, developing or not". The need for information sharing, he says, is especially urgent in the new nations in which "the tasks assigned to the communication media are vastly greater than before the time for development". In a graphic passage, he asserts that countries in a hurry cannot afford the luxury of an inert mass. They require the informed co-operation of all the people. Therefore, "they are going to have to speed the flow of information, offer education where it has never been offered before, teach literacy and technical skills very widely. This is the only way they can rouse and prepare their populace to climb the economic mountains".[6]

These research findings, and the pronouncements which have flowed from them, have propelled governments toward impressive investments in media development. They explain, at least in part, the tantalizing hope which was raised in Nigeria's Second National Development Plan, 1970–1974. "An important function of Government information services in a developing country like Nigeria should be to mobilize support for national development measures and programmes . . . A serious attempt will, therefore, be made during the 1970–1974 period to utilize the improved media to generate

[4] See Ithiel de Sola Pool "The Mass Media and Politics in the Modernization Process," in Lucian Pye, ed. *Communications and Political Development* (Princeton, New Jersey: Princeton University Press, 1963), pp. 234–253.

[5] Peter Godling, "Media Role in National Development," *Journal of Communication* XXIV/3 (Summer, 1974), pp. 39–53.

[6] Wilbur Schramm, *Mass Media and National Development* (Stanford, Cal.: Stanford University Press, 1964), p. 19.

general and popular support for the implementation of measures and programmes for economic and social development at all levels — federal, state and local." They have raised hopes, sometimes to the level of fantasy, but seem to have ignored a central fact: that media content and the use to which it is put is the real index of media utilization. This functional approach helps one explain why the same media system would produce different results in two different environments if all the other variables are held constant. On a global level, it would help explain why a vast majority of people would scramble for the BBC in a period of national crises in a rush for reliable information.[7]

The Possibilities

Theories and aspirations apart, the mass media have valid credentials for contributions toward improvement in every facet of societal life. The media are known channels for news, information, education, entertainment, leadership, conferring status and creating symbolism, among other things. These represent the general functions of the media, no matter what the locale. It is the way the media perform each of these functions that would go to support or undermine the claim that they are contributing to national development. In other words, the question of media use revolves around national policy, media policy, reconciliation of what the government directs and what media managers actually offer and the reaction of media consumers — readers in the case of the print media and listeners and viewers in the case of the broadcast media. The news function, although generally important, may come to very little if the media have a policy of publishing foreign items of news to the neglect of local events. Nor is the function of opinion leadership of much influence if the only opinions offered are on distant events from other countries. The education function may be all important and promising but if the content of media education is the space age for a peasant culture, its utility becomes at best doubtful. This point is well made by Dizard when he observes that television in some countries has proven a mere boondoggle.[8]

[7] "It has been said in Saigon that if the BBC were to announce the death of the Prime Minister of South Vietnam, and he were to appear next day in the streets of Saigon, no one would recognize him." Julian Hale, *Radio Power: Propaganda and International Broadcasting* (London: Paul Elek, 1975), p. 48.

[8] Wilson P. Dizard, *Television: A World View* (Syracuse, New York: Syracuse University Press), p. 18.

On the basis of the foregoing discussions, each country should develop its own media-use strategies, creating a balance between a serious-content orientation and pervading frivolity. The following review of the situation in Nigeria, together with recommendations, may help make the points more clearly. Both the review and the recommendations proceed from the assumption that Nigeria is fairly typical of the developing countries of Africa.

The News Function

Newspapers, magazines, radio and television offer news items on a regular basis. From radio, Nigerians receive an approximation of instant news since there is a news summary on the hour. From newspapers and magazines, they receive in some progression detailed accounts of news events. Television has, since 1959, joined the other three in keeping Nigerians informed on events of the day, on events inside and outside the country. One objective of this news function, one must assume, is an attempt to help develop an informed citizenry. The idea is to bring more and more Nigerians into a participant political culture. So, when newspapers and magazines devote their columns to what the leaders are doing and saying, the idea is that readers should follow the activities of their leaders so as to be equipped to pass informed judgement on them whenever there is a chance to pass a verdict. When radio and television bring to listeners and viewers not only the voice of the minister but also his visage, there is an attempt to authenticate beyond doubt what he actually said and did. News output from both the print and broadcast media is an attempt at political development since news dissemination is meant to instil awareness among the masses and thereby kill lethargy among them.

But the real question is: What kinds of news do Nigerians receive from their news media? As of 1977, Nigeria had some 32 newspapers of varying descriptions and frequencies. Of these, eight, and the most buoyant at that, belonged to state governments. They ranged in respectability from the raunchy *Nigerian Tide* of Port Harcourt to the glittering *New Nigerian* of Kaduna. Among non-government newspapers, the *Daily Times* led in popularity with the up-start *Punch* in the second place. Some of the newspapers were fledgling and very local in both their appeal and emphasis. Among these were *The Nigerian Mirror* of Onitsha and the *Nigerian People* of Calabar. All of the newspapers suffered not only from a general lack of news-gathering facilities and techniques but also from the general lack of access to those who made the news. By default, they had to depend on public relations handouts based on bland ministerial speeches and platitudes.

The effect has been that Nigerians now read between the lines. In Lagos, a city noted for cynicism, the people have learnt to place more credence to what has come to be known as Radio Rumour than in news from the regular media. In the provinces, government announcements are frequently greeted with yawns and deserved skepticism. News in government newspapers is just that — *news in government newspapers*. On occasion, attempts have been made at meaningful reporting but because of legal restrictions, an unhealthy fear of possible consequences or outright laziness on the part of reporters, a news item would normally raise more questions on the mind of the reader than actually get answered in the news column. In one bewildering report in 1976, a national daily came up with the report that some insurance companies had been blacklisted by the federal government. Reading the news outside the newsroom of the newspaper concerned created only anxieties since the reader could not then tell whether his own insurance company was among those in trouble. The news function had thus turned into a dysfunction. But the high mark for news without information must go to an attempt by the second Nigerian head of state, J. T. U. Aguiyi-Ironsi, who excited the nation one day in 1966 by indicating an intention to give a radio address. At appropriate intervals, the Nigerian Broadcasting Corporation had promoted the up-coming event. Naturally, the nation was awash in rumours as to what his intensions might be. The time for the broadcast at last arrived. Listeners glued themselves to their sets. There was a drum roll followed by the national anthem. Then came the broadcast which sounded something like this: "There is no truth to the rumours currently circulating about me in the north. Good night."

Ordinarily, people get their first intimation with a news event from radio. Out of necessity, radio news is normally skimpy and people try their newspapers for details and more information. The scenario is universal but in Nigeria, the attempt is not very rewarding. It is easy to prove that news as it is reported in Nigeria leaves much to be desired. Some news magazines such as *Newsbreed* and *Afriscope* have done a fine job but their in-roads into news interpretation are not yet remarkable. The menu is rather overflavoured with windy, long political essays with only limited flashes of interpretation.

One would like to see news interpretation in news columns. As a young country, Nigeria can use a lot more news background and perspective than are presently available. The *Daily Times* has enough facilities to do a better job of reporting than is presently the case. Government newspapers are in an unenviable bind. All the talk about press freedom amounts to nothing when a reporter knows that the chances of keeping his job turns upon his ability and willingness not to ruffle any feathers. Radio and television news has been not much more than a focus on the government and government ministers. News evaluation is based on a survival sense of what would please one's superiors. The net effect of all this has been that Nigerians have learnt to fend for themselves. Where the media cannot provide news linkages, the citizen fills the gap by speculating and spreading rumours. In the process nobody is informed. The difference between the quality of news offered now and what is possible undermines all the discussion about utilizing the news media for informing the people about government activities.

The Education-Information Function

The media of mass communication have a significant assignment in spreading general information as well as formal education. Britain now has the "University of the Air" on which some citizens depend for their formal education. The Chinese have been using a similar system to spread education to distant places in their vast country. In some South American countries, formal lessons are broadcast and beamed to places otherwise unreachable with the usual machinery for normal school education. An experiment initiated in Colombia in 1961 matured into a full range of primary-school subjects that were relayed to schools *during* school hours. The United States government aided the projects by supplying television receivers for placement in rural schools. In 1963, Argentina started a television series that broadcast high school subjects from the capital. The idea was to broadcast instructions to students who lived in remote areas. The Guatemalans went even further by incorporating for telecasting a schedule of educational programmes that ranged from anti-literacy campaigns to university-level lectures.[9] The mass media have been particularly helpful in adult education and studies have shown that classes taught through some mass media are no less effective than those conducted by conventional methods. The following report is illuminating: "Now the evidence comes in on the newer devices. For example, out of 393 experimental comparisons of classes taught chiefly by television with classes taught by conventional classroom methods, there was no difference (in what the pupils could do in the final examination) in the case

[9] *Ibid.* pp. 233–234.

of 65 per cent of all the comparisons; in 21 per cent of the cases, the television class wrote significantly better examinations than the conventional class, and in only 14 per cent was the conventional class superior."[10]

That the mass media can and do supplement existing educational facilities is no longer in doubt if ever it was. That the media can at times supplant these facilities is not in doubt either. In fact, the realization of this possibility has spawned all sorts of ambition for the media, some of them not demonstrably anchored in either reality or logic. In the case of Nigeria, the attempt to teach by radio has spanned the whole period of hunger for mass education. In a 1951 report, a British official, then working for the fledgling Nigerian Broadcasting Service, the precursor of Radio Nigeria, had described radio as the most powerful medium for influencing and educating the people and further described it as the "most potent mass disseminator of culture and information" the world had possessed. He believed that radio could help Nigeria in its journey toward what he called "an enlightened democracy".[11] At the time of his report, the number of trained teachers in Nigerian schools was abysmally low. According to the Ashby report, which post-dated the 1951 report, 82,000 teachers in primary schools throughout the country were unprepared for their jobs. Nearly 75 per cent of those teachers were uncertificated, 66 per cent had had no more than primary-school education themselves. In short, according to this report, 90 per cent of the teachers were not properly trained for the task of imparting knowledge.[12]

Planners, therefore, saw a role for radio in Nigerian education. When television was finally introduced, imagination as to its utilization ran wild. When the governments of Western and Eastern Nigeria introduced this visual medium, the former in 1959 and the latter the following year, they declared the intention of devoting 50 per cent of all programme time to news, educational and public-service programmes. Before and since then, mobile cinema has been used by governments, regional and federal, to spread information to both city and village people. Cinema vans snake up and down country roads with the celluloid wonder and villagers turn out in large numbers to view and perhaps learn. Information ministries also employ the medium of pamphlets in publicizing government plans and activities. One

[10] Schramm, p 141.

[11] Nigerian Broadcasting Corporation, *Five Years of Broadcasting 1951–56* (Lagos: Federal Information, undated), pp. 8–9.

[12] Anonymous, "Television in Nigeria," *Nigeria Trade Journal*, 7:4 (October–December, 1959), p. 165.

of the most pervasive of such outfits has been the Gaskiya Corporation which was meant to serve the whole of what was politically known as the north which encompassed the present Bauchi, Gongola, Kaduna, Kano, Niger, Kwara, Plateau and Sokoto states.

In short, the Nigerian people have various avenues of keeping informed: by radio, television, the cinema, newspapers, magazines, other pamphlets, including government gazettes, and bill-boards. Through these media, Nigerians have a chance of learning about the need for, say, inoculation against cholera or whooping cough, about the necessary steps against other diseases, about their legal and constitutional rights, civic duties, including the need to pay tax, register to vote and actually vote at election time, and about deadlines for other contributions toward national development. The central point in all this is the dissemination of information throughout the country. According to the Third National Development Plan, the major information emphasis is on the development of radio and television "as the most important media through which the larger section of the population could easily be reached". In pursuit of this objective, 62.76 per cent of the capital outlay (₦380,225,000) will be spent on the expansion and consolidation of radio-television services.

Through some of these media, citizens would have a chance to put in a word of criticism or praise with regard to government activities and the state of the country in general. For obvious reasons, only newspapers (along with the other print media), radio and television offer these opportunities. Those who employ the book medium are engaged in long-term plans and normally end up with post-mortems on plans already executed or abandoned in the face of difficulties or in the light of other priorities.

Conceptually, the structure looks impressive and promises great rewards. But the real problem revolves around the will and ability to employ the mass media for the purposes described. As is obvious to many media consumers, a gap exists between what is projected and what actually takes place. The idea of employing radio as a multiplier of existing educational facilities has not really gone much beyond what it was: a dream. Although times have been set aside for broadcasting lessons, the medium is defective without the provision of receiver sets for schools which are supposed to be the beneficiaries of those broadcasts. A lot of schools are yet to see radio sets. The other dream, that of deploying television for the same purpose, has proved something of a nightmare. Part of the problem, admittedly, is infrastructural in the sense that television signals can be received only in predefined places. In both Anambra and Imo states, for instance, only Enugu, Nsukka, Abakaliki,

Awka, Onitsha, Aba, Owerri, Umuahia and a handful of other places are endowed with the basic infrastructure for television reception on which revolves, in part, the success of the scheme.

It is significant that primary schools have yet to be given television sets for pupils to follow the programmes ostensibly beamed at them. So, when an educational programme is on the air, the studio people are more or less talking to themselves in a dialogue of the optimistic. Even the timing of these programmes is not very helpful.

The country has been more fortunate with the use of these media for general information sharing. With the constancy of the broadcasts and the diversity of the language medium, a lot of Nigerians have a chance to eavesdrop on announcements. It is tempting to infer that a majority of Nigerians have this opportunity but the statistics point in the opposite direction. Although the number of sets in the country is still not determined, it is still safe to say that a vast majority of the people have no chance of getting their information direct from radio, not to talk of television. Again, there is the problem of illiteracy. The literacy rate is not anything much higher than 30 per cent. So, information sharing by the print media is that much restricted. Again, it is clear that it is the same group which can read that comprises the bulk of consumers of both radio and television messages. The opportunity for an average Nigerian to share in information without an intervening factor is very limited indeed. It occurs, for instance, when the message is conveyed in his mother tongue and is brought pictorially by a mobile cinema van, as happened in 1953, when the government of the then Eastern Nigeria put together a documentary that portrayed the people of Nsukka as resistent to the census idea.

In spite of these limitations, much information comes through the mass media. In that sense, the communication industry is doing well on a quantitative basis. But the facade crumbles when subjected to a critical analysis. What, for instance, is the point in teaching pupils how to speak a foreign language through a medium like television to which they have no access? What are the chances of success for a campaign that is conducted in an esoteric language? What is the implication of producing newspapers whose circulation is impeded by bad roads, lack of fuel or political considerations?

In the light of these limitations, it will be rewarding to dovetail the communication media into traditional communication patterns. From all indications, high media consumption, together with literacy and other assets for effective communication, is co-existensive with the city. In other words the media have the highest audience in the cities where the educated and literate urban middle-class people are mostly found. In the rural areas, members of the middle-class are scattered. These include some chiefs who worked in the city but are now in retirement, school teachers, who conduct the intricate business of letter-writing and hooking up as best as they can villagers with trappings of modernity.

It will be advantageous to come up with communication policies that are capable of exploiting such relationships. The print media may help by printing not only in English but also in vernaculars. The introduction of the *Ogene* by the *Daily Star* newspaper is a step in this direction. On the whole, it will be useful to do an occasional study of how best to get information to the people, realizing that in communication it takes much more than purity of doctrine to produce the desired result. Moreover, a lot of planning must precede publicity campaigns. As Schramm has advised, "if a developing country is to make best use of its facilities in the great campaigns of development, early in any given campaign someone will have to look at the problem broadly – move broadly, that is then from the viewpoint of radio, or the extension service, or schools, or newspapers, or films. Someone must look at the needs for change, at the likely dynamics of change, and at the resources available, and then design the system of messages, channels, and events that promises to be most efficient at bringing about the change desired".[13]

The Economic Function

Before the emergence of cities and that of the mass media as a coupling link among the people, villages and little neighbourhoods had ways of advertising their ware. In some communities, children would sing recognizable ditties to announce availability of goods. Even today in the cities, one can still hear the matin song of pap sellers. But this clinging to tradition has become only part of the story of advertising. The mass media have taken over the announcement and seem to be doing a remarkable job. Today, newspapers are full of advertisements, ranging from non-productive obituaries to full pages of supplements on whole economies. As a country develops economically, the appetite for advertising becomes whetted and since newspapers depend very much on advertising revenue for their own solvency, no convincing is needed to get them to devote a large measure of their space to economic announcements. By 1964, the *Daily Times* was devoting about 49 per cent of its total space to non-advertising matter, that is, to what journalists call

[13] Schramm, p. 148.

news-editorial matter, and 51 per cent to advertisements. Today, the proportion has changed in favour of advertising.

In 1961, the then Eastern Nigeria Broadcasting Service launched into the commercial age by extolling *Mentholatum*. Nigeria had by then begun to witness the beginning of air-wave commercializm. Today, every station carries advertisements and the rate ranges from ₦16 for radio spots to ₦120 for 30 seconds on television. The *Daily Star* charges ₦600 for one full page. By advertising goods and services, the mass media contribute to the growth of the economy. Companies need to sell heavily to profit heavily and the most painless way to get the public to buy is by advertising. The link between advertising and national development is obvious. The media devote space and time to announce the availability of goods and services. Consumers get attracted and then decide to buy such goods and services. The selling companies receive more revenue for growth and expansion and thus find themselves in a position to employ more persons and thus contribute directly toward economic development.

It must be remembered that the communication industry is a fast growing one. Every state capital plans to have a newspaper of its own, together with at least one radio station and television station. The media in the private sector are also growing. The number of newspapers in the private sector is on the increase. The *Daily Times* has come up with a lot of sister publications—*Lagos Weekend*, a scandalous weekly, *Sporting Record*, *Evening Times*, *Times International* and *Business Times*. At independence, there were relatively few broadcast stations, the NBC and its limited network of stations; today, there is an escalation. By 1962, Nigeria had only three television stations; today it has eight. By 1961, there were only four government newspapers in the whole country; today, eight government newspapers are published and more are on the drawing board. By 1960, the only African magazine of note was *Drum*, then published outside the country; today, a lot of new magazines are on the market.

The Opinion Function

Toward the end of his regime, General Yakubu Gowon was asked by a news reporter, while on a visit to Sokoto, if his government was planning on introducing universal free primary education. Without much thought on the subject, the general gave a resounding yes for an answer. Back in Lagos, officials were aghast at that announcement which reflected, at best, an idea that probably had not even reached a drawing board stage. In any case, the nation was thus thrown into the hysteria and confusion with the rubric of Universal Primary Education. In 1976, the *Daily Times* lamented in an editorial that a nation as rich as Nigeria had not evolved a crime-control policy. Within 72 hours or so, the federal government came up with what must be regarded as a hastily thought-out ₦100,000,000 anti-crime programme. About 1974, the *Renaissance*, the Enugu government newspaper which preceded the *Daily Star*, wondered in an editorial why the Niger bridge had remained a toll bridge while other bridges in the country were toll-free. A few weeks after, the toll was lifted. Also in 1974, the University of Nigeria newspaper, *The Record*, wrote an editorial on how to keep the Nsukka campus clean and ecologically attractive. Far into the planting season, the vice-chancellor ordered the cutting-off of all yam shoots, an abomination among the Igbo people, and the pulling-down of all intruding kiosks. In 1977, after the federal government announced the incredible policy of deploying soldiers to help secondary-school principals maintain discipline in schools, newspapers and the general public reacted violently to the idea and asked the government to reconsider. But, the latter bull-headedly moved ahead with the policy which nobody wanted.

These examples point to what the media are capable of doing: moving, or failing to move, a nation in a particular direction. The first was only a leading question that enlisted a reckless answer. The others were arguments which represented the corporate thinking within each newspaper organization and all point up a fact that the news media do not always carry policy makers with them but not for lack of trying. And yet, opinion leadership remains an important feature of the mass media throughout the world. In Nigeria, it started with anti-colonial, nationalist newspapers most of which earned a halo of bravery for brazenly attacking the colonial administration. The tradition was carried over into post-independence Nigeria but the fire seems to have lost much of the heat.

In any case, newspapers, magazines, radio and television stations have developed vehicles for expressing their own opinions on issues and giving the general public a forum through which the rulers can get a feed-back on their policies. Editorial leadership is most common with newspapers, if only because of their frequency. On a regular basis Nigerian newspapers comment on different issues, some of them foreign but a lot of them local. The past decade has seen the country under military rule, a situation that is not very conducive to critical editorializing. Surprisingly though, Nigerian newspapers have carried on with the tradition of straddling the fence most of the time but going on the offensive once in a while. Part of the problem is the pattern of ownership. Most of the viable newspapers are government-owned. Even the most popular newspaper, the *Daily Times* is in government hands to the tune of a 60 per cent equity share ownership. With the exception of the *Punch*, all the newspapers outside the uncomfortable embrace of government are fledgling, insignificant and are largely ignored no matter what the cacophony of their crusade.

Early in its development, radio developed a policy of occasionally stepping into public policy debates with opinionated presentations in the form of news talks and commentaries. Generally, these commentaries do not reflect the opinion of the stations. In a sense, what the stations have been doing is to create a platform for those who have opinions. In other words, they are common-carriers of personal opinions. That tradition has been extended to television. The latter has become a medium for heated debates on public issues. The National Television service in Lagos has its *Public Opinion*, a programme that brings into focus the ever-willing and talkative Nigerians to pontificate on public policy. Television in Enugu has got the *Guest Speaker* and other public affairs programmes. All are designed to elicit commentaries from rather enthusiastic and vociferous citizens.

An ingenious way of criticising public policy in Nigeria is the practice of roaring at distant events and persons. Since the most effective sectors of the mass media are government-owned – all radio and television stations as well as the most viable newspapers – one does not get a chance to read much of criticism in government newspapers or hear much of this on the airwave. It is a very inhibiting arrangement and editors have to find ways of appearing brave and still keep their jobs. One of these is for the editor to criticise, say the Rivers state government, if his own newspaper is safely away in Jos, capital of Plateau State. The real test of bravery, needless to say, would come in the form of a rigorous criticism of the government which pays the editor.

In addition to worrying about job security, Nigerian journalists have got to worry also about several legal restrictions. There is a punishment for spreading rumours, there is the danger of committing sedition, a loosely defined political offence; there is the military rule, something of an antithesis to freedom. All these restrictions make editors think twice before writing, or accepting for publication, very critical articles. People have been gaoled for saying things they believed to be ordinarilly innocuous. In 1975, the editor of the *Sunday Star*, Henry Onyedike, and his features editor, Agwu Okpanku, were detained for an article that seemed to the government to be revivalist of the Biafran idea.

The problem about all these restrictions is that the government does not get a chance to learn of other options for a given policy. A lot of money has gone down the drain partly because people had not been alerted to the impending waste and because the press could not comment on commitments. At other times, the government had taken the approach that public opinion does not really matter to a military government. But it will be advantageous for the country to have a media system that cannot only inform the people about government activities but is also given the opportunity to examine these activities. A number of confrontations have taken place because the men in power have come to believe that any critical analysis of their programmes can only spring from a fountain of mistrust on the part of the press. And yet, the country can gain much when the press is allowed to subject public policies to public discussion. It would appear that the Nigerian media have on the whole tried to offer leadership in circumstances that do not encourage such practices. It must also be said that the will on the part of the Nigerian journalist to suffer personal privations for what he believes in can only lead to an enlargement of freedom. Judging from the level of literacy across the country and from the limited amount of information the ordinary Nigerian possesses, those Nigerians in the media have indeed a special calling. They are in a leadership position and, given the chance, can contribute tremendously to the good of all.

Entertainment and Other Functions

On a ferry boat from Onitsha to Asaba early in the 1960's, a young farmer bought himself a newspaper, promptly turned it upside down and began to exhibit the emotions of a person in the process of absorbing entertaining information. Another passenger, according to the story, seized the newspaper and cast it angrily overboard in a rabid campaign against all false claims to literacy. During the high-noon of Nigerian nationalism, some illiterates at Onitsha would pick up copies of the local newspaper and make the rounds of the market place, advertising before unsuspecting buyers and sellers the class to which they belonged. There is a suspicion these days that not all the roofs which sport television antennae actually have the real thing under them. Throughout history, the mass media have been known to confer status. People like to be identified with the so-called high-brow communication no matter what their real preferences. Those who take a liking to pornography make the party circuit with stories about their exposure to the *Economist*, the *New Yorker* or *Peking*

Review. But as party jokes get more indelicate, their sources appear more incriminating than the original posturing.

The mass media of information have acquired a lot more functions than one can readily suspect. In addition to the other functions already discussed, the media are known to be sources of entertainment and in that sense are therapeutic in application. Newspaper readers are exposed to cartoons and well written entertainment pieces. Magazines readers have a similar advantage and come off richer in their own stock of party jokes.

But the bulk of media entertainment comes from radio, television and the cinema. As is widely known, entertainment is the selling point of all three. A study of broadcasting in Nigeria found that during the period in review, the Eastern Nigerian Television devoted 62.49 per cent of the broadcast time to entertainment, as against 73 and 60.75 per cent on the Western Nigerian Television and Radio Nigeria.[14]

Cross-cultural comparisons show that these figures are not remarkable. What is remarkable is how Nigeria hopes to develop and popularize its cultures by, for instance, showing what it has been showing on television. Children in Lagos and other television cities are exposed to such Americana as *I Love Lucy*, *Dr. DoLittle*, *The Mary Tyler Moore Show*, *Mannix*, among others. From entertainment viewpoint, none of these can be faulted as originally conceived. The problem lies in the cultural transfer and their displacement value. Again, their importation is symptomatic of Nigeria's unreadiness to join the electronic age. Television is about the most ravenous consumer of culture. It puts entertainers on their toes in its constant quest for more and the unusual. Unable to satisfy this demand, countries like Nigeria take resort to importing packaged entertainments from North America, Western Europe and elsewhere. The net effect is that Nigerians and their children have to find escape in cultures they do not understand and could never live.

The dependence on foreign films is, however, more true of the past than of the present. A crop of good indigenous television shows has been introduced. Nigerians now have a chance to watch such plays as the *Village Headmaster* and *Masquerade*. Viewers have always had a chance to watch such raucous shows as the *Ukonu Club*, originally introduced for television in Enugu before the creation of Imo state but now with television in Aba.

[14] Sylvanius A. Ekwelie, "*The Content of Broadcasting in Nigeria*," unpublished M. A. thesis, University of Wisconsin, 1968), p. 76.

Teenagers have something to watch in *Sound City*, a poorly produced package of no indigenous cultural base.

Radio has always been more successful. As early as the mid-1950's, radio audiences were treated to such successful plays as *Ugbana Elege*, Shaki-*Shaki and Alao* and a series of take-offs from these originals. The idea of entertaining by printing foreign cartoons is questionable. But *Garth* has remained a regular feature of the Nigerian press and some readers seem to follow his adventures with surprising ease.

For the Nigerian mass media to contribute to cultural development, a new vista for television entertainment must be created. By implication, this will mean more investment in the entertainment industry, both in money and human resources. The country has enough cultural diversity to keep playwrights and gag-writers as busy as they could get anywhere else. The picture looks even more encouraging when one recalls that a lot of the skits are bound to come from new frontiers.

With patience and compassion, Nigerians can portray their numerous cultures on television and get other Nigerians to watch in amazement and appreciation. One motivation for the investment advocated is the need for total development. The Nigerian is not likely to compete the Western man in technological innovativeness. He is most likely to remain a few decades behind for some time to come. But in cultural traffic, he can march along inexorably toward the enlargement of the African personality, remembering as all should, that in McLuhan's "global village", nobody can really be left alone in cultural isolation.

The establishment of an indigenous film industry will prove contributory to the general theme of cultural development. A few films such as Balogun's "Amadi" have attracted good reviews and one can only hope that the country is ready for more. Nothing in our experience will make us believe that our films can compete in technical quality with bug-budget Hollywood extravaganzas like "The Sound of Music" or "Caesar and Cleopatra." But one suspects that the force of nationalism will compensate for whatever local films may lack in special effects and other attractive features of foreign films. The Indians have developed a genre of highly predictable films that have quite a market in West Africa. Nigerians have the resources to produce their own films. They have also compelling cultural reasons to make a start in this sector.

This chapter has attempted to point out the contributions the media of mass communication can make toward national development. It has pointed, hopefully, to areas of strength and weakness in order to impress upon the reader that the success or failure of the media is a human dimension. Furthermore, it has been argued that the media in the developing countries show more potential than real achievements. In some respects, the gap between the two is attributable to both infrastructural difficulties and media personnel. A trained newsman, for instance, needs a healthy atmosphere in which to operate. A liberal legal climate is certain to contribute to such an atmosphere. The level of development in the other sectors of the national economy is generally a reliable barometer to media opportunities.

The chapter will be incomplete without reference to the dysfunctional aspect of the mass media. Media contents have proven sources of distress to millions. Some critics blame television for all sorts of crime and condemn newspapers for negativism in news presentation. The superficiality of news in general has been the source of numerous anxieties. The tragedy is that nobody has found an alternative to this media approach to human problems.

Some years ago, an American, in pain over all the crime and distressing news in American newspapers, decided to start a good news newspaper. The idea was to forget all the killings, kidnappings, divorces and anything that could detract from human comfort. His newspaper died in a matter of months.

The media in the developing world may wish to be good or bad news oriented or may wish to carry a realistic mix of both. But, the real criterion by which they will eventually be judged promises to be their contributions to national development.

CHAPTER SIXTEEN

Nigerian Music — Then and Now

Dr. W. W. C. Echezona
Department of Music,
University of Nigeria, Nsukka

Introduction

Nigerian music can be broadly divided into two categories: (1) Hausa or Northern music and (2) Southern music. If the Northerners are brilliant string and wind players and the Westerners masters of drumming, the Easterners are keyboard virtuosi, an ability they combine with no less enviable dexterity at drumming. The Igbos are wonderful players of xylophones and thumb pianos.

Northern music shows Arabic influences due partly to the proximity of the North to the Arab world and partly to the influence of Islam in both countries. Thus an instrument called *goge* known to have originated from Arabia is found in the North.

The Hausa kings rule Moslems who participate in the traditional rites and ceremonies and involved in the traditional music such as *waka* in which choruses are rendered by the *janmoos* while the chief priests, *lemomu*, or *ladanni* are the soloists.

The Moslem Yoruba developed Islamic culture that uses music the way traditional western society does. The most spectacular feature of this musical history is the co-existence of old and new forms and their corresponding musical practices as living arts in Nigeria. This confirms one of the basic tenets of African philosophy: that the past is always here with us and the future is not remote from us.

The spreading of Islam throughout Northern Nigeria accounts for the fact that the majority of Yoruba traditional musicians are mostly Muslims. At least three forms of neo-traditional music have developed as a result of the incidence of Islamic culture among the Yorubas. They are the *Waka*, *Sakara*, and *Apala*. The first two are concerned directly with the practice of Islam while the third one is used merely for social entertainment.

The topic of this study can be divided into two broad divisions: THEN, which discusses Nigerian music in the time past; and NOW, the situation from the advent of colonialism to the present.

Nigeria is a country with about 80 million people belonging to different ethnic groups, each with a unique cultural background. Nigerian music includes folk, traditional, modern, historical, contemporary and popular forms. It is an art form whose spiritual qualities and moods are shared by all. Many Nigerian songs embody statements which are nothing but pronouncements of the basic philosophy of Nigerian minstrels such as the *Obiligbo* in Igbo and their counterparts in the North and West who sing virtually all their songs in proverbs. The proverb is a special figure of speech which contains or combines similes, metaphors, alliteration, onomatopoeia, puns, allusions, and even short anecdotes. Minstrels may use narration or witty or interesting tales in simple direct or indirect prose. Our popular minstrels include 7–7, The Blackman Joseph, *Egwu ekpili*.

Music is related to the people who make and use it. Each group or tribe practises its own variant music. That is why we have Igbo music, Yoruba music, Hausa music, Ibibio music, etc., because the culture of the people vary to some degree; therefore, the music is reflective of culture.

Music and Words

While it is possible that the Hausas may have absolute music, non-Islamic cultured people do not seem to have. All non-Islamic music is first conceived at the back of the mind before the drum or other instrument plays. In other words, music has a close connection with words that express one's mood or situation. Most activities are performed musically and rhythmically such as co-operative work, work rhythm, etc. During wars, traditional music bands are attached to fighting units to play for amusement, announce war situations with their musical language, or work up fury in their fighting warriors. With songs of jeer, they demoralise their opponents, have the opportunity to lord it over them e.g. when people sing, "Ole ndi nwe ndia? Anyi nwe ndia".

All non-Islamic music which is referred to in this discussion as has something in common; the language of the music makers is tonal and, therefore, their music follows the rise and fall of the words which dictates the melody. A case of where music has not followed the words is where Christians began to sing their native songs translated from English tunes but since these languages are tonal, and the imported Christian tunes do not fit the words, the meaning of the printed text is sometimes at variance with the meaning of the sung text. For instance, there is a case where Igbo words, "Chineke nwere nuku ike", "God is omnipotent", ended up by meaning "God has large buttocks" because the music did not fit the words.

Qualities of Traditional Music

Traditional music prior to colonialization, then, had these qualities;

(a) it was characterized mainly by folk songs which were used on different occasions and festivities;
(b) the music was mostly functional;
(c) it was unadulterated by Western influence;
(d) it was handed orally from generation to generation;
(e) it was communicative because it fused both the performer and the participant into one indivisible unit, thereby promoting a corporate feeling in the society. In short, people understood the language of their music;
(f) it was a collective art, that is, everybody took part in it.

Traditional Music is Functional

In the memorable past, music to a Nigerian as well as any other African, served primarily a traditional purpose and function. It was a motivatory medium which accomplished itself as a visible sign of an invisible mechanism in a Nigerian. Its psychological aspects culminated in the stimulating effects on certain activities of the people. Music not only accompanied Nigerian life, it was part of life. Every stage of life, from cradle to death, was connected with one type of music or the other. In this sense life has a melodic and rhythmic orientation.

On the waters and seas, sea-farers and fishermen paddled their canoes more spiritedly against the waves with songs such as, "Nyabugbo, ekwe miri basi n'ugbo" which means, "paddle the canoe, don't allow water to enter the canoe." In the forests, hunters scared animals from their hiding places to their deaths with hunting songs. They equally used some of these songs to ward off fear in the bush or to praise the popular animal of their game, e.g. the Yoruba hunter's song called, *Ijala*.

Music constituted part of such traditional ceremonies as weddings, initiation of boys into adulthood, feasts of gods or ancestral heads, and festivities like new yams in Igbo. In these celebrations, music and dance assume prominence. For weddings, such dances as "Ranan 'yar mata asha" are performed in Hausa land (Kwari, Niger State), while in the same area they perform *Gebwari* (Kano) for initiation of boys into manhood. In Igbo areas, masqueraders constitute cults and secret societies and are ultimately used for only the esoteric. They are used as administrative machinery to detect evil doers, murders, thieves, by some mysterious powers and without fear or favour carry out the decisions of the council of elders on such culprits. They were regarded with awe as spiritual beings and so helped to maintain peace and order within and without the vicinity.

Minstrelsy links with eulogies and songs put together to recount and reflect striking historical events in chronological order. In traditional religion, the average Nigerian knows that through the medium of music, the native doctor can evoke and handle psychic forces of tremendous potential which his will can then direct as it suits his purpose.

Sacred or religious music plays vital roles in initiation rites and religious acts where it constitutes parts of the worship or acts as accompaniment to such acts. The extemporised songs culminate in incantations rendered by the traditional juju priests, and heighten the religious sentiments as the people intermingle with the swell of the music and the rhythmic movements of the songs and dance. The juju priests accompany these songs with musical instruments believed to possess divine properties. Such instruments are tortoise-shell, metal bell (*ogene*), and *sekere* (a sacred gourd used by Yoruba juju priests).

Instruments

Great importance is placed on the instruments to accompanied music. Various types of instruments exist and they have not been standardised.

Wind instruments. There are two types of these instruments. The first is used by titled men and kings (e.g. *kakaki* which is a long pipe blown for Emirs and Obas in their courts), hence the saying in Yoruba, "Ole ti o ja ti o gbe kakaki, Nibo ni yio ti fon" (If a thief steals a kakaki, where will he blow it?). This instrument got its name from the sound it makes when it is blown. The other is *odu* horn, which is produced from elephant tusks and are of varying sizes and are carried as part of a chief paraphanelia for transmitting signals by sounds of powerful blasts of dot and dashes.

Wind instruments played by commoners include the *Ekutu, Tioko, Iwo Etu, Oja, Opi.* They have limited ranges.

Stringed instruments. Stringed instruments are very common in the North and West. These include the *moho, dura, sibala sibolo.* The Igbo have *une, ubo akwala.* Apart from using stringed instruments in making music, *une* and *sibala sibolo* are used in games of hide and seek.

Instruments of inherently resonant materials. These include different types of clapper series, gong series, jungle series, sistrum series, rattles, hollow rattles, musical rasps and stamping tubes. There are also the single and double membrane drums such as *iya-ilu, ikoro, ogene, algaita,* all belonging to rhythm producing types. Complicated rhythms difficult for well-trained Western musicians to comprehend results when Nigerian music is played. Such rhythms include:

1. Systematic Modification of Rhythms. In Nigerian music, although most instruments for the accompaniment play ostinati, the master drum and or the vocalist modifies the musical lines after the theme has been announced, and follows it up with the inversion, retrograde, retrograde inversion, lengthening or shortening the value of notes in regular proportion, i.e. augmentation and diminution when appropriate. The master drummer does not always make use of the whole theme when he is using the device of augmentation and diminution. In making these modifications, the drummer not only has to devise these artistic ways of drumming; he has to make them fit certain words so that they become intelligible in the context.

2. Non-accentual rhythms. Usually the beat immediately after the bar line is stressed. To a lesser degree, the third beat in the bar of $\frac{4}{4}$ is also stressed. In non-accentual rhythms, bar-lines, when withdrawn, do not necessarily communicate authoritatively the location of the accent and when metric accents are not present notes which are lengthened, decorated, or approached by leap become points of attraction, and these assume the duty of metric stresses. These may fall anywhere in the measure and the result is often very effective. In Nigerian music again, this is brought about by the words.

FIG. 1.

3. Shifted accents. There are three kinds of accents: agogic, tonic (the highest or lowest extremity note in a phrase removed from its pitch area has the tendency to assume accentuation) and metrical accent (a regularly occurring pattern bar-line determines primary accentuation).

Now, when normally unaccented portions of the measure are accented, rhythmic modification is achieved, sometimes, it is done in such a way that a different metric time altogether is implied. In a vocal African line, this is usually dictated by the words.

4. Asymmetric meters. In asymmetric meters, instead of, say, the conventional $\frac{3}{4}$, you have $\frac{5}{4}$ in a measure. In Nigerian music, the accent may be only on the first beat, or the whole measure may be divided 3 & 2 or 2 & 3 and the accent may or may not be in the first of the subdivision. Listen to this sentence in Ibo, "Enwelum ya, bia k'ayi je". The whole of this is contained in two measures of $\frac{5}{4}$:

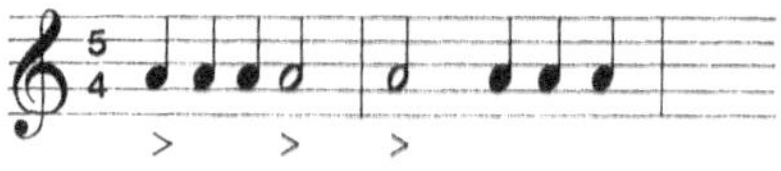

FIG. 2.

5. Asymmetric division. Another way in which the Nigerian speaks has given rise to yet another technique. These are what we may call asymmetric divisions. One can normally have $\frac{8}{8}$ in a bar, which means that the principal accent is on the first note and a very slight one on the fifth. But in certain melodies, the number of notes and accents may not follow the accepted pattern. One may have it thus expressed: (3 + 2 + 3)/8. If it were to be written, accents would fall on the 1st, 4th, and 6th notes. It is this kind of division more than anything else that baffles most foreigners who wish to write African folksongs down in note form. It is only when the person knows the language well that he can fully appreciate this type of division and be able to write it down. Compare the following:

FIG. 3.

The sentence means: "Do you hear that I am going to the market?"

Highly localized traditions are found within a single society. For instance, at Ibadan there is a family recognized as a family of drummers. The people of that family bear names with *Ayan* which means "drum" as either a prefix or a suffix. Examples of such names as *Alayande, Ayangbemi.*

Most cultures of the world have found it necessary to employ the drum for their music-making, but while some have used it merely as a secondary instrument, others have brought the playing of their various drums to the highest degree of performance and refinement. To the latter group belong the Nigerians.

The most important element in Nigerian music is its rhythm. The Nigerian loves rhythm, and, usually, whenever there is drumming there is also some dancing. Of all the Igbo musical instruments the drum assumes a position of greatest social importance. Any occasion whatsoever, be it funeral, marriage, or naming ceremony, is unimaginable without the drum. It is upon the drum that these social ceremonies are built. In contrast to European music which is built upon chords and which uses the drum to ornament the music played by other instruments, the Nigerian treats his drumming as music in its own right subordinate to no other instrument. The various rhythms and accents of the drums direct the movement of dancers and excite them to a frenzy.

The Nigerian has organized in a scientific way a rhythmic principle which the Western ear recognizes as being different from his own and which seems very complex, but which, upon analysis, is very simple. He achieves this by the interweaving of complex, contrasting rhythmic patterns on drums and other musical instruments. In most cases, the drum derives its rhythms from the rhythms of the words of the song; these rhythms are accentuated and varied by other drums and by the rest of the musical instruments. It does not matter which instruments are used to express the complicated rhythms; the result is always a conflict of rhythms in a highly organized rhythmic contrapuntal development. For example, a song which appears to have only one main rhythm will prove, upon examination, to have at least two rhythms, one in the melody and one in the accompaniment. The oldest and simplest method of instrumental accompaniment is that of hand clapping.

A common rhythm which drummers of clappers employ is:

FIG. 4.

The duration of these eight notes is of absolutely equal value. The clappers on 1, 3, 5, 8, 10 on every measure. Judging by conventional European standards, the claps are in the most improbable and unacceptable places and it is not easy for Europeans to devise or form a conception of a clapping accompaniment to a melody whose strong beats are not in the general agreement with their fixed usages. If upon this accompaniment a melody in $\frac{3}{8}$ time is superimposed, this is the result:

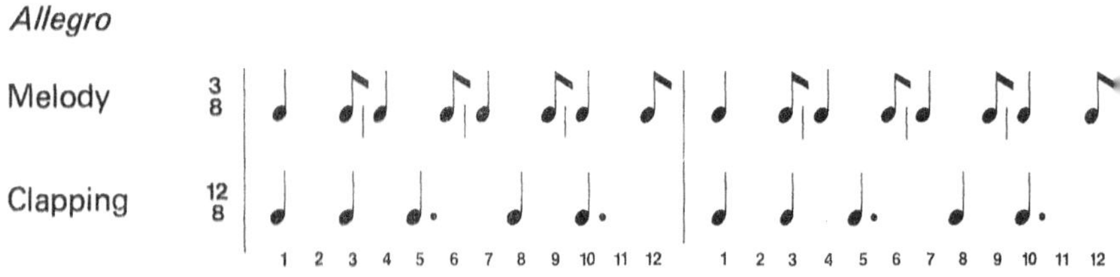

FIG. 5.

The above is the pattern when the melody is straightforward as in a European melody. When an exotic Igbo Melody is superimposed on the clap rhythm, the result is as follows:

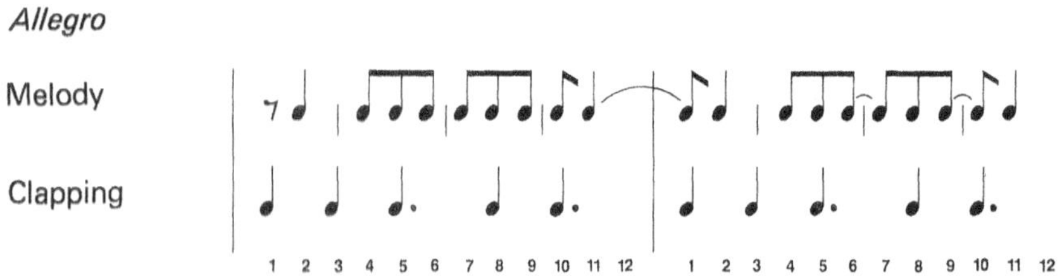

FIG. 6.

This latter melody is apparently controlled by the equally unseeming free rhythmic clapping. Once the clapping is established, the general pattern is maintained unless the music itself unmistakingly demands a change of the established rhythm.

Combined Clapping Patterns

There should be at least two people or groups, each group clapping either the first or the second beginning at the same time and maintaining the same regularity of time:

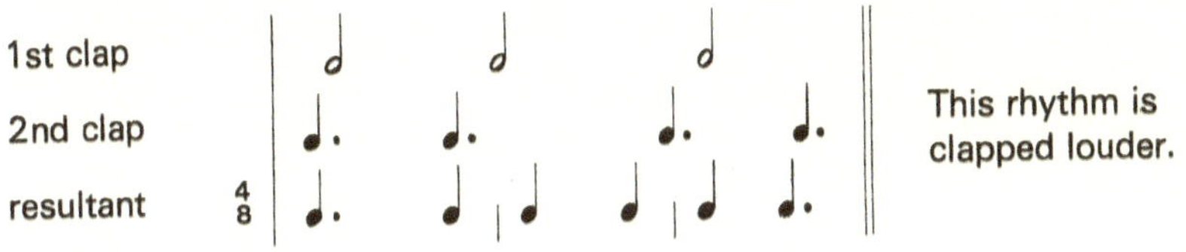

FIG. 7.

The resultant is duple time. See the 2nd measure of the 3rd line.

When clapping the same rhythms but this time reversing the line that is louder, this is the result:

FIG. 8.

The result is triple.

Here is another example:

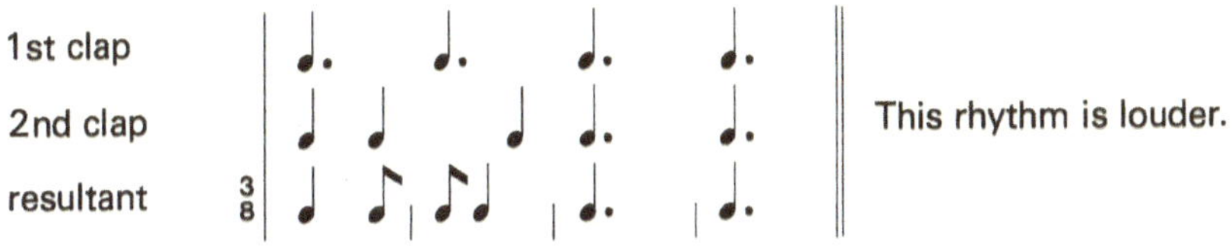

FIG. 9.

The first two examples demonstrate 4 against 4 and, according to which is made louder, the psychological resultant time is either duple or triple. Nigerians frequently employ these two methods of clapping. The clappings themselves are not different but when combined with a highly syncopated melody, the difficulty, of course, increases.

When another pattern of clapping is established, this is the result:

FIG. 10.

The first two sections are beating 3 against 2. That is simple enough but not so engaging the attention as the third. We have used the marks of emphasis on the third to show the lively, bouyant, springy motion which pervades the whole line, which is in $\frac{12}{8}$ rhythm. When the three patterns are combined, the resultant sound is an interesting $\frac{6}{8}$ rhythm. Combine this resultant rhythm with a Nigerian song with its syncopations, and the result is still very much more intricate. Most Nigerian youths will easily clap these rhythms at a tempo = 140. At this stage, it is unnecessary to remind the reader that the rhythm of the song closely follows the speech rhythms of the words which are tonal.

Here is another simple rhythm that two people can clap:

FIG. 11.

The reader should notice that at the beginning of each 12-beat measure, all the claps coincide. They may or may not coincide again until the beginning of the next measure.

Drumming Technique

Drums are to Nigerian music as strings are to classical compositions. It is in the drumming that all elements — melodic, harmonic and rhythmic —

are exhibited. All these elements are found in all the other media or Igbo music whether in singing, clapping, or in the medium of other instrumental displays, but were we to study Nigerian music without adequate reference to drums and drumming, we would be missing the most important element. It is true that occasionally one drum may be used to accompany a song, but usually, no fewer than two drums and more often three, four, and up to eight drums are used for all performances. Even this number does not rule out the use of other percussive instruments such as the xylophone, *udu*, *ogene*, and even clapping.

In Nigerian music the drums supply the melody and a harmony of free, uncalculated pitch relationships, as well as the timbre and a free rhythmic counterpoint. That is why there are usually more than two drums performing at the same time.

The art of drumming is organized in much the same way as the hand clapping which was discussed earlier, in that the rhythm is scientifically developed as in the hand clap but the interesting fact about drumming is that, in the first place, although as many or more rhythmic patterns are produced as in hand claps, the main beats in most cases often do not correspond exactly. Nigerians feel that the performers have no creative inventiveness if the beats always coincide. Let us see exactly how Nigerian drummers reason as they improvise their rhythmic counterpoint.

The master drummer first establishes his rhythm; the second drummer bears in mind where the original strong beats are and he then plays another rhythm which is both melodically and rhythmically as interesting but he avoids as much as possible having the main beats correspond with the original. We know that the melody that each drum produces is aurally satisfactory because each performer knows how to produce a good number of specific pitches on his instrument. In order to keep the main beats from falling together, the second drummer makes use of suspensions. Another means he uses to achieve the same effect is to have rests where normally a strong beat would occur.

A third device is that of a clapper who, after he has invented his rhythm, maintains it throughout unless there has been a very good reason why it should be changed, but the master drummer who is the leader of the thematic material frequently varies his rhythms because he has something specific to say. He does not begin from the beginning and say something at once. He says something and repeats it three or four times; he says something different, and repeats that three or four times and continues thus. All the other drums and percussive instruments continue with the rhythms that they have established. A close examination of the master drummer's devices include asymmetric meters, asymmetric divisions, non-accentual rhythms, shifting accents, and changing meters. When all these are superimposed on the fully organized harmonic contrapuntal rhythms of the other instruments; this becomes to most foreign ears a jumbled mixture of heterogeneous sounds.

A person brought up in a traditional way of musical rhythms would expect to see this:

FIG. 12.

A Nigerian would consider this arrangement unimaginative and dull. He would make use of the same two rhythmic patterns but arrange them differently:

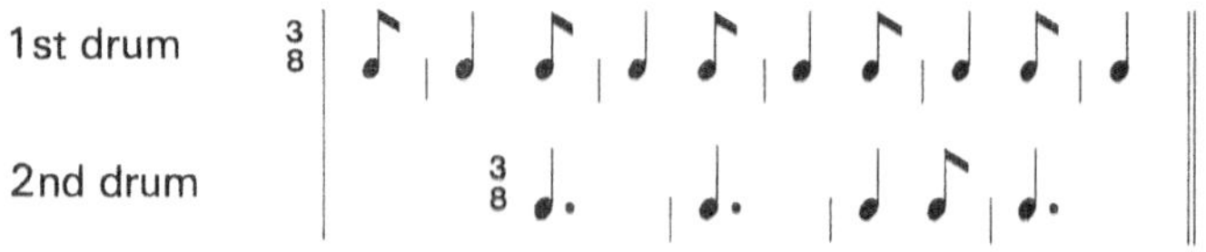

FIG. 13.

FIG. 14.

In Figure 13, the strong beat of the second drum happens to coincide with the third beat of the first drum. It would be a long time before such a coincidence would happen again but it would eventually happen. In Figure 14, the drums have started with no strong beats coinciding. The two drums would have to play long enough for them to coincide. So, the coincidence is only periodic and not always calculated. Because the strong beats of one do not coincide with the strong beats of the other, so-called "cross rhythms" or "cross beats" result.

In the last example, we have illustrated cross rhythms with two rhythms in triple time. Nigerians frequently have one rhythm going on in triple time and another in duple time, for example:

FIG. 15.

The resultant sound is not as monotonous as it looks on paper for the sounds of the first drum stand out in contrast with the sounds of the second drum. When the rhythms of the master drummer and all of the subordinate drummers are put together the combination is traditional and imaginative.

Melody

Aside from melody's rhythmic qualities discussed above, it also includes:

1. Polyphony. Formerly, Nigerian music was believed to consist of melody only. It was supposed to lack polyphony and harmony. Recent investigations have revealed that polyphony plays an important part in Nigerian music. As illustrated above, the beating of drums often becomes so elaborate in performance that it assumes the character of an "added part" rather than of a mere rhythmic accentuation. Polyphonic element is more noticeable where percussion instruments such as xylophones, having graded pitch, are used. Primitive polyphony also derives a great deal from drones, parallel fourths, antiphonal singing with overlapping of the two parts as in most fable songs, and even canonic imitation of short motives. Recent investigations have also found, in surprisingly large numbers, examples of singing in distinct parts.

2. Transposition and Sequence. In Nigerian music, although transposition in a vocal choir is not usual, in an ensemble, this is often done. The voice

might sing a phrase and an instrument may play the rhythm and tonality in its own register. This device helps to break up the monotony of the same key especially when the transposition is other than the octave, for then it suggests a new key centre. In vocal music, sequence is often used.

3. Shifted tonality. This resembles modulation in art music, but differs from regular modulation in two basic ways. Where regular modulations are most often prepared carefully with common pivotal material and move smoothly to the new key, in shifted tonality there is an abrupt change from one tonal centre to another remote centre. Shifted tonality involves an unexpected expulson of the old key centre by a new one. For a shifted tonality to be effective, the two centres must be very obviously sudden since the modulation is not prepared with common material, and, therefore, does not move smoothly to the new key.

4. Direct Imitation. Voices and instruments imitate themselves. There is no question of the treatment of dissonances because they do not exist except in as much as the lines themselves happen to introduce any dissonances while repeating the theme as it is.

5. Polytonality. When different instruments play together or combine with the voice, it should be remembered that these instruments are tuned to different specific keys and when played together, we have a good example of polytonality.

6. Ostinato. When a melodic or rhythmic pattern is everlastingly repeated in a composition or passage, we call this ostinato. This plan, which is sometimes modified, is being used extensively in twentieth century art music. From time immemorial, Nigerians have used their drums and other instruments in an ostinato style. Each instrument begins a fragment of rhythm and continues it, perhaps until the music stops.

Talking Drums

Talking drums are extensively used to warn the villagers of an impending danger such as neighbouring town's invasion. The British would never have defeated many Nigerian towns, in fact, the reverse would have been the case if they had not learned about the "talking drum". In each case, the British Soldiers made sure that the source of the tum-pi-ti was first silenced. A village scout with his drum on top of an iroko tree drummed to the whole town, warning them of the approach of the British soldiers, the direction from which they were coming, and how the villagers should surround and attack them first.

An early example of the "talking drum" appeared in "The Expedition to the Niger, 1841", concerning Kru men who are alleged to have been descendants of the Ibos and Yorubas. The account States:

> The Kru pilot, Glasgow, was in Captain Allen's cabin one day, answering some queries relating to the river. Suddenly he became totally abstracted and remained for a while in an attitude of listening. On being taxed with inattention, he said: "You no hear my son speak?" As we had heard no voice he was asked how he knew it. He said, "Drum speak me, tell me come up on deck." This seemed very singular, so Captain Allen desired him to remain below and privately sent messages to the performer in the boat alongside, who executed them by a variety of taps on his wooden drum; and these Glasgow interpreted in a way that left no doubt of his having understood perfectly all that the "drum spoke." He also said that they could communicate by this means at very great distances by "the war drum" which is kept in every village to give a repeat of these signals.[1]

Again, the talking drum is used to tell the villagers that such a man is dead, that he belongs to such an age group, that he is a titled man, and that his death has caused great sorrow to the whole town. Within a short time, people assemble to do the last honor to the deceased.

A long time ago when there was not much education in the Igbo country, when there was only one hospital, Iyi-Enu hospital at Ogidi, when Christianity was new to the people, and, when the power of the medicine man was great, the medicine men used his stock in trade and the drum to heal people both physically and psychologically, or to instill fear in the minds of people while taking advantage of their ignorance. His stock in trade included *Okpokoro mbe* (tortoise shell), *ikenga* (household god), *alusi* (a consecrated god), *ego ayolo* (cowries), *Okpukpu azu* (certain types of fish bones), *okwe* (epidermis of certain type of nuts of a certain tree), *nzu* (white lime), *edo* (a yellowish substance), *agwi isi* (god of magic), *oyo* (rattle), *ogene* (a type of gong), and a drum, all arranged in a certain order. It is interesting to see that a patient under the influence of a medicine man may seem so physically weak and in a critical condition, yet lying in this condition he may turn his head rhythmically at the gentle suggestive rhythms of the medicine man's drum.

Effects of Modern Trends·

From about 1914, Nigerian Music witnessed a turning point. The most primary purposes, functions, and elements discussed above were overtaken

[1] G. T. Basden, *Niger Ibos* (London: Seeley, Service & Co., 1921), p. 364.

by modern trends. The factors that appeat to have influenced the main lines of change in musical organization in Nigeria were migration or social interaction through trade or matrimonial affiliations, political considerations, acculturation through importation and exportation of ideas, and the desire to change with fashion and time.

The advent of Christianity contributed in no small measure to dampening the performing enthusiasm since the native clergy of most denominations objected to converts and the school children participating in local or traditional singing and dancing on tribal platforms as such were regarded as immoral and idolatrous acts.

In order to remedy this, churches are no more satisfied in singing translated words of European hymns. Choirmasters and other Christians compose original words which are sung to original tunes. Traditional singing and dancing are encouraged. Competitions and various festivals are staged. Music and arts councils are established on state and national levels. Nigerian church musicians compose new hymns and anthems whose melodies are in agreement with the inherent tonal patterns of the texts. Moreover, these new hymns employed a rhythmic style which is closer to that of traditional music. Traditional instruments and sometimes, dance, provide further links with traditional culture in some of Nigeria's indigenous church music especially that of the spiritual churches, for example apostolic, and cherubim and seraphin churches which have from the beginning used orchestral accompaniments by mainly local instruments to their vernacular hymns. Different organizations such as the Mother's Union, Youth Fellowship and praying bands compose words and melodies which they sing when they meet at church harvest festivals and at mothering Sundays. With the retention of native rhythms have almost completely indigenised their sacred music. They have approached society in an intimate manner through successfully incorporating some traditional native songs and musical instruments into the music of their churches. Harcourt Whyte, Wilberforce Echezona, Fela Sowande, Rev. Olude, Gibole, Dedeke and Lazarus Ekwueme have done the same for the Anglican Churches.

In contemporary Nigerian compositions, some use is made of folktales with little change in their melodies but with a folk-like treatment different from the original. Some works also use proverbs in order to achieve public acceptability especially in works like those of Felix Nwuba, David Okongwu, Sam Ojukwu, and Okeke. Some of the compositions today are based on commercial purposes. The creative urge of members of new communities formed in Nigeria found outlet in new compositions other than the traditional forms mentioned previously. One of these types of composition is the "popular music" which appears in different forms as:

1. Juju music in Yorubaland. Today, Juju music appears to be somewhat more popular than the other forms of popular music. Its rhythms are more indigenous and it conveys its message in the language of the land. The music of Ik. Dairo, Dele Ojo, Sunny Ade, Ebenezar Obey and Dele Obiodun are examples of this type of music. The Juju musicians use traditional musical instruments along with foreign instruments such as the guitar. They sing traditional songs at times and they also use traditional tunes for their compositions.

2. Highlife music is a popular music which originated from Ghana. The text is derived from functional situations rearranged for commercial entertainment and enjoyment for all ages. The language may be indigenous or foreign. Usually it is in $\frac{4}{4}$ time. Highlife music is played all over the country. Some of the musicians of this type include Roy Chicago, Victor Olaniga, Stephen Budele, Victor Uwaifo, and the late Rex Lawson.

3. Other new types such as that of Fela Anikulepo Kuti and his Afro Republic Band and that of Sunny Okose from Enugu are all examples of new types of music formed. Kuti plays Afro-rock, his different version of highlife music that makes use of heavy African drums and native language in most cases. Example of an artist and disciple of Kuti is Osibisa, a London-based band. Kuti also plays jazz-rock.

Venue, costume, time, and duration of performance are now influenced by the present context and media. Radio and television programmes, for example, cause adjustments in costume, duration of performance, and, of course, the studio does not offer a natural habitat or platform for traditional performance.

Since notation still poses a great problem, one way of preservation of this music in its original versions offers itself through electronic devices such as tapes and records. Most traditional music has lost its original purpose and ritualistic phases especially those that required human blood in sacrifices or those sacred membrane drums that were made from human skin and played at rituals in parts of Nigeria. Civilization with its educational values stopped such arts and lifted, to a certain extent, taboos imposed on the use of certain instruments; for instance, at Nsukka Local Government Area women could not see the xylophone played, now they even play it at the University.

War music such as *Iriaha* in the Igbo areas or *Kajan tawan* in the Hausa areas are now played at occasions for entertainment or at burial ceremonies of deceased valiant men. During such performances, men of valour come out to dance and with gestures demonstrate how bravely they fought and cut many heads. Wrestling music is no more played for wrestling but played now as lighthearted entertainment or as a tribute to a deceased full-fledged male, or as recreation for folks on moonlight nights. The Yoruba *Ijala*, originally composed and sung in praise of Ogun "god of Iron", is now sung by hunters in praise of popular animals they hunt or as a tribute at the funerals of fellow comrades who are skilled in the art of hunting.

Exportation and importation, and rapid emancipation from traditional patterns pose serious problems to African music. There is the inability to inculcate a serious awareness in the indigenes with which to develop a real understanding for their traditional music, rather than casting it aside in favour of dancing highlife and rock jazz in nightclubs. Acquisition of Western techniques should be to develop certain aspects of our music but should not be had at the expense of our traditional musical elements. There is undue emphasis on science at the expense of art and performance. Consequently, the heavy importation of electronic equipment such as stereo systems, micriphones, speakers and expensive instruments such as accordions, electric guitars, congos, drum sets, may be so intense that in the future, it is possible that all the instruments of our traditional music such as Juju Music may be superceded and improperly displaced by these Western instruments and styles.

In contemporary Nigerian music, group experiences and expression of sentiments exist but not much importance is attached to them as it was in the past. In short, it is not often functional. Although Nigerian music still includes dances of various types, compositions, texts, instruments, costumes, and the sophisticated performance of the people, and songs of different types. Composers are very careful about the words they set, these are more refined.

Nigerian dances offer abundant examples of highly original forms created from stored-up resources in the tradition for every community. These are at least eleven major families of Nigeria dances. These include masquerade, ritual, maiden, war, acrobatic, puppet theatre, occasional elders, creative, social-entertainment and ceremonial dances.

The general impressions of the dances are of picturesque social events full of vitality, colour, movement, music, song, and thought-provoking poetry. War dances are pantomimic in structure, naturalistic in costume, and motivated by a single and simple desire for victory or by heroic sense of male prowess. The war dance has a fairly straight-forward expression as a vocational dance which illustrates in rhythmic actions and movements significant activities of the given occupation.

Conclusion and Recommendations

It is to be observed that Nigerian traditional music, in spite of Western civilization, has today changed little from what it was before the advent of the Europeans. Apart from the fact that it is today played with less frequency, being played only on special occasions such as cultural festivals and during local festivals, the installation or death of a chief, or the death of a very important person in the community. There is not much adulteration as far as construction of melodies and rhythms are concerned. Indigenous instruments are frequently being discarded in favour of foreign instruments and recently, electronic instruments are being preferred to non-electronic.

Because of radio and TV demands, the natural venues are abandoned and therefore, the times of performances are curtailed as even the warming up time in the natural habitats take up the whole time alloted by radio and TV space. Functional music is performed out of context like when night masquerade music is heard in the middle of a day; not enough space is made available in the TV studio for full demonstrations of a performance; the producers continually put off performers by their incessant directions, and because there is not much space for performances, many little points of great importance are forgotten or deliberately dropped. TV screens help to destroy some traditions of a society as when a lady producer was trying to explain the mysteries of a masquerader. She did not know when to stop because in the village, she is not allowed to demonstrate any knowledge of a masquerader.

Because of the times, natural costumes are being abandoned for gorgeous ones. There is a great difference between costumes of certain masqueraders and those of the same type of masqueraders of the present day. Dancers, nowadays, dress in the best available materials as compared with those of the past. Instruments are used indiscriminately out of context in accompanying native music as when talking drums of Yoruba are used in accompanying Igbo wrestling music. These are only a few changes observed in the performance of Nigerian music now.

Nigerian classical traditional music and dance give a wide field for research and study and it is most urgent to do this now that there are still old drummers and other artists to help. Otherwise, it will be too late and the future Nigerian generation will not know whether there was, at anytime, in the history of the nation, any indigenous music and dance.

Most Nigerian tonal languages being musical, give a great advantage to Nigerian vocal music as it can be put into staff notation to give the words chanted the desired effective intonations. Fortunately, most southern music can be noted. This should be done in time. Many poems have been collected. The words are there. Merely reciting them will not be as effective as when they are chanted. This is a challenge to our musicologists.

Folklore songs are enjoyed by both young and old. Many of these songs are lost. Some have been collected and many variants exist; therefore, they need to be put into staff notation so that they may be standardised and used in schools. This is another challenge to our musicologists.

Finally, in collecting Nigerian music, in conducting research into Nigerian music, dance and drama, in writing down melodies and rhythms, and in composing Nigerian music, the means is unimportant; correctness means nothing itself; the effect is everything and the composer and performer try to make their piece very beautiful so that their art may be effective. Yet there are certain qualities which all musicians would agree are fundamental to a successful composition and rendition of Nigerian music: a sense of movement or flow and balanced formal structure; a balance of unity and variety; and a homogeneity of style resulting in a proper Nigerian idiomatic expression.

Bibliography

1. Ajibola, J. O., *Orin Yoruba: Yoruba Songs*. University of Ife Press, 1974.
2. Basden, G. T., *Niger Ibos*. London: Seeley, Service and Co., 1921.
3. Echezona, W. W. C., "*Ibo Musical Instruments in Ibo Culture*", Ph.D Thesis, Ann Arbor, Michigan University Microfilm, 1963.
4. Hornbostel, E. M. Von, "Ethnology of African Sound Instruments," from *Africa*. VI London: Royal African Music Society, 1933.
5. Merrian, Alan, "The Use of Music in the Study of a Problem of Acculteration," *American Anthropologist*, LVII/1 (February, 1955).
6. Nketia, J. H. K., *The Music of Africa*. New York: W. W. Norton, 1974. 1965, 1966, 1975, 1976 and 1977 —*Nigeria Magazine*.
7. Wachsmann, Klavs P., ed., *Essays on Music and History in Africa*. Evanston, Illinois: Northwestern University Press, 1971.
8. Wangemann, T., *Ein Zweites Reisejhar in Sud-Afrika*. Berlin: Wohlgemuth, 1868.

CHAPTER SEVENTEEN

Towards an African Philosophy

Rev. Dr. Innocent Onyewuenyi
Department of Philosophy,
University of Nigeria, Nsukka

The title of this chapter is such as would require us to focus directly on African philosophy, namely, is there an African philosophy as such, a discussion which has engaged African academic philosophers for the past two decades.[1] If there is, what is the content of this philosophy? who are African philosophers or exponents of African philosophy?

It would, however, be doing injustice to the discipline of philosophy if we were to begin this discussion on African philosophy without first introducing the discipline as a whole. It would be like treating the specific before the general. Therefore this lecture has been divided into two parts. Part I consists of the discussion of the fundamentals of philosophy as a discipline. Part II discusses specifically African philosophy.

Part One: What is Philosophy

Philosophy is generally regarded as perhaps the most abstruse and abstract of all subjects, far removed from the affairs of ordinary life. The unfortunate story about Thales of Miletus, the first Greek philosopher, who, while gazing at the stars, fell into a ditch and was told by a servant girl that because he was so eager to know what was in the sky, he could not see what was there at his feet, has given the picture of philosophers as people who are not interested

[1] John O'Donohue, "African Philosophy: The Problem of Definition," a paper read at the Nigerian Philosophical Association Conference 1975, University of Ife, Nigeria; Gordon Hunnings "Logic Language and Culture," a paper read at the N. P. A. Conference (as above); Innocent Onyewuenyi, "Is There An African Philosophy?" *Journal of African Studies*, III/4 (Winter, 1976), pp. 513–528; Theophilus Okere, "The Relation Between Culture and Philosophy," *UCHE: Journal of the Department of Philosophy U. N. N.* 2 (1976), pp. 4–11; Paulin Hountondji, "African Philosophy, Myth and Reality," *Thought and Practice* I/2 (1974), pp. 1–16.

in the practical questions of their day. There is a tendency to think of philosophy as some extremely complex intellectual activity.

While this picture has been created of the philosopher and what he is trying to do, there is also another image. This is that the philosopher is one who is ultimately responsible for the general outlook and the ideals of certain societies and cultures. Thinkers such as Karl Marx and Friedrich Engels, are ones who have created the point of view of the Communist Ideology John Locke and John Stuart Mill have largely developed the theories which prevail in democratic societies. St Augustine and St. Thomas Aquinas exerted their influence in the official interpretation of certain church teachings.

Contrary to the view that the philosopher's activities are remote from the immediate concerns of the human race, the fact remains that he is engaged in considering problems that are of importance to us all either directly or indirectly. Through careful critical examination, he has tried to evaluate the information and beliefs we have about the universe at large, and the world of human affairs.

The Old Testament book of Job reveals the defects of the traditionally held view about the nature of the world. Rather than rest content with inconsistent theories, the philosophical writer of the book of Job could only pose a question. The people who lived "the unexamined life" tried their best to avoid facing the problem, but the philosopher, because of his need for intellectually satisfactory beliefs, had to examine it. Even if he could not find a better theory than the traditional one, at least he would not accept a view that he knew was inadequate.

Philosophy is a combination of two greek words: *philein* — to love; *sophia* — wisdom. A philosopher is a lover of wisdom. Originally, it meant the rational explanation of anything. Mark the word *rational*, as distinct from common-sense, empirical explanation, or what we might call scientific explanation. Philosophy tries to understand the real nature of any given thing, fact, or event; it understands the object in itself.

Hence the objectives of the department of philosophy are: (1) to inculcate habits of clear, exact, logical and critical thinking, in other words, to think rationally; (2) to avoid blind emotional indoctrination; and (3) to develop the habit of examining critically and solving decisively life's problem in the light of rational principles.

Alfred North Whitehead, one of the greatest and most respected thinkers of modern times, describes philosophy as insight and foresight, and a sense of the worth of life. For Whitehead the importance of philosophy is based on the fact that it is an attempt to clarify those fundamental beliefs which finally determine the emphasis of attention that lies at the basis of character.

Philip Wheelwright defines philosophy or the philosophical attitude as "a persistent attempt to see life critically, appreciatively, and whole".[2] His definition agrees with these three more or less standard definitions of philosophy: philosophy is analysis; philosophy is synthesis; and philosophy is the quest for meaning in life.

Let us analyse these definitions:

1. To practice philosophy is to think critically or analytically. Philosophy is an unusually persistent criticism and analysis of beliefs, concepts, and statement. What we refer to as common-sense and ordinary language are rich sources of philosophic problems. They contain such beliefs and statements as "The paper on my desk is white", "This table is rectangular". When we analyse these statements we find they are unclear and questionable. What does white mean? (a) It could mean that it appears white now; (b) John said that it is white; (c) past experience shows that the paper has a disposition to look white whenever white light is cast on it; (d) the pigment molecules of the paper reflect or tend to reflect certain electromagnetic waves to which the nervous system is sensitive so as to give the experience of *white patch*; (e) the paper is white in an *absolute* sense, under all circumstances, whether white, red, blue, or green light is cast on it; whether it is seen or not, even when it is in total darkness.

The concept of "myself", "justice", "courage", "goodness", "love", "death", existence of the "world", involve grave questions of meaning and reality. Philosophy is concerned with meaning and clarification of these and other concepts.

2. To practice philosophy is to think *integrally* or to synthesize, i.e., the attempt to co-ordinate all experience and knowledge into one vision. This is what Hegel calls self-consciousness. This is the area of metaphysics, the product of man's need to have an all-encompassing vision of existence. The philosophic mind seeks wholeness or cosmos or the guiding idea, in the context of which particular happenings become more intelligible.

3. Philosophy can also be defined as a search for meaning in life. All men are philosophers to the degree that they make decisions about the good life. What is life's goal? What must one do in order to lead a life worth living? The existentialist approach represents perhaps the most significant contemporary philosophic examination of man's problem of finding meaning in life.

Albert Camus (1913–1960) says that life has no meaning; life is absurd. Jean-Paul Sartre feels that since for him God does not exist, man must create

[2] Philip Wheelwright, *The Way of Philosophy* (New York: The Odyssey Press 1960), p. 5.

through his choices a meaning for himself. Martin Buber (1878–1966) emphasizes the value and quality of friendship.

The three basic philosophic themes, around which all other philosophic problems are clustered are *Reality*, *Value* and *Knowledge*. The fields of philosophy exploring these areas are respectively *Metaphysics*, *Axiology* and *Epistemology*.

FIELDS OF PHILOSOPHY

METAPHYSICS (REALITY)	AXIOLOGY (VALUE)	EPISTEMOLOGY (KNOWLEDGE)
Ontology	Ethics	Theory of Knowledge
Cosmology	Aesthetics	Logic
	Social & Political Philosophy	Philosophy of Language
Philosophy of Religion	Value Theory	Philosophy of Science
Philosophy of History	Philosophy of Law	
Rational Psychology	Philosophy of Education	

Metaphysics: The science of being as such, to be distinguished from the study of being under some particular aspect.

Ontology: (from the greek onta – existence; logos – discourse), is the study of the meaning and nature of being. Whereas all things differ from one another in some respect or other, the most disparate items in the universe share one elusive property; being or existence. What is that property? Ontology deals with that.

Cosmology (Greek: Kosmos – world; logos – discourse) is that structure and development of the universe seen in its totality. The main topics of cosmology are the contingency, necessity, eternity, laws, and limitations of the world, the freedom of man and the origin of evil.

Rational Psychology is the study of the mind, self or soul of man. This is different from scientific experimental psychology. Here the question arises as to whether the self is a thing, or substance, or whether it is a name for certain types of passing states. Rational psychology is also an analysis of the structure and nature of consciousness.

Philosophy of Religion or *Natural theology* (to be distinguished from revealed religion) examines the nature of religion in general and it also deals with the typically metaphysical issues of the existence of God, the destiny of the universe and the immortality of the soul.

The Philosophy of History searches for the laws governing historical development and progression. It deals not with the external considerations of the narrative or story or history of philosophy. The central point of interest is the essential connection existing between what is apparently past and the present — the inner character of this connection.

Axiology: (Greek axios — worthy; and logos — discourse) is the study of values in general. It concerns itself with things that are thought to be good in themselves, such as the good life or intrinsic values and with values leading to the good life or instrumental values.

Ethics (Greek: ethos — custom or character), or moral philosophy, deals traditionally with the problems of values as these concern human conduct. It examines and seeks to answer questions involving right conduct, good character and fulfillment of life.

Aesthetics is, in part, the philosophic investigation of the beautiful. Aesthetics examines the nature of art in human experience, and sets the standard on the basis of which art may be judged.

Social and Political Philosophy is an extension of ethics. It concerns itself with questions about the nature and justification of social structures and political systems, that is, it examines theories of the state and the source of social obligations.

Philosophy of Law, examines questions such as what makes a law obligatory and what the connection is between law and natural rights, law and justice, law and social order, law and human nature, and law and the universal order.

Epistemology is the branch of philosophy which investigates the origin, structure, methods, and validity of knowledge.

Theory of Knowledge is the study of knowledge proper. Included are theories of perception, theories of concept formation, the question of universal's and views on the limits of knowledge.

Logic includes the examinations and definitions of truth and validity, as well as the vast fields of Aristotelean and symbolic logic, inductive and deductive reasoning, and that of the philosophy of language.

Part Two: African Philosophy

Philosophizing: A universal experience

Philip Wheelwright in his book *The Way of Philosophy* said: "To philosophize is to submit one's thought to the idea of a cosmos. Just what sort of cosmos is accepted as the guiding idea will depend partly on the individual philosopher's temperament and intellectual loyalties, partly on the climate of opinion in which he lives and has been reared. Materialists construct their cosmic idea on the analogy of bits of matter moving about in space. Idealists construct theirs on the analogy of rational minds. Whichever construction is preferred . . . they are at any rate alike in this: *that each of them finds particular happinings more intelligible when they are seen in the context of some large guiding idea to which its devotees give the honorific name 'reality'*."[3]

Note the phrases "individual philosopher's temperament and intellectual loyalties", "climate of opinion in which he lives and has been reared", "in the context of some large guiding idea to which its devotees give the name 'reality' ". These show that there are individual and cultural approaches or attitudes to philosophizing. Granted that various phenomena of the surrounding world things, events, facts, an intelligible world, an ethical world, and a metaphysical world — are the same in all cultures and dealt with in philosophy, yet how each culture traces the unity of these themes, synthesizes or organizes them into a totality is based on each culture's concept of life. Hence it is that the order or unity the people of a culture establish is their own order, relative to their own conception of life in which everything around them become meaningful. No culture has *the* order or *the* last word. Hence the establishment of various truths of a spontaneous logical, ethical, aesthetical, and metaphysical nature not one of them being of absolute or universal validity.

This is the basis for calling a philosophy European, Asian, Indian, or American. If what we have said is true, we can and should talk of African philosophy, because the African culture has its own way of establishing order; it has its own view of life. "Life" according to Dilthey, is the starting point

[3] *Ibid.*, p. 6.

of philosophy. George Misch, summarizes him thus:

> Dilthey regarded "life" as the starting-point of philosophy; life as actually lived and embodied or "objectified" in the spiritual world we live in. Life, according to Dilthey, is a subject for scientific investigation in so far as history and moral philosophy or the human sciences deal with it; but our knowledge of life is, above all, contained in certain cultural or personal views of the world — which plays a prominent part in philosophy as well as in religion and poetry.[4]

Hegel underscores the cultural and relative aspect of philosophy when he said:

> But men do not at certain epochs merely philosophize in general. For there is a definite philosophy which arises among a people and the definite character which permeates all the other historical sides of the Spirit of the people, which is most intimately related to them, and which constitutes their foundation. The particular form of philosophy is thus contemporaneous with a particular constitution of the people amongst whom it makes its appearance, with their institutions and forms of government, their morality, their social life and their capabilities, customs and enjoyments of the same.[5]

The notion of philosophy itself for Hegel, as can be deduced from his words, is a factor in the life history of the human experience of the individual mind, and is subject to the conditions of race, culture, and civilization. A further support to the issue of philosophical relativity was given by Victor Uchendu in his monograph *The Igbo of Southeast Nigeria*. He said,

> To know how a people view the world around them is to understand how they evaluate life, and a people's evaluation of life, both temporal and non-temporal, provides them with a "charter" of action, a guide of behaviour.[6]

The African has an unwritten timeless code of behaviour and attitudes which have persisted for centuries. The condition for the possibility of this, its explanation, lies in the presence of a corpus of co-ordinated mental or intellectual concepts. Placide Tempel sees behaviour as being neither universal nor permanent unless it is based upon a concatenation of ideas, a logical system of thought, a complete positive philosophy of the universe, of man and of the things which surround him, of existence, life, death and the life beyond.[7]

[4] Georg Misch, *The Dawn of Philosophy* (London, 1950), p. 49.

[5] G. W. F. Hegel, *Lectures on the History of Philosophy* (London, 1968), p. 53.

[6] Victor Uchendu, *The Igbo of Southeast Nigeria* (New York, 1965), p. 12.

[7] Placide Tempels, *Bantu Philosophy* (Paris: Presence Africaine: 1969), p. 19.

Having shown the possibility of its existence as well as its actual existence, the discussion now turns to the content of this African philosophy.

African metaphysics or ontology

Henry Alpern in his *March of Philosophy* said: "Metaphysics by the very definition that it is a study of reality, of that which does not appear to our senses, of truth in the absolute sense, is the groundwork of any theory concerning all phases of human behaviour."[8] In further support of this, he quotes the materialist philosopher David Hume as saying that "metaphysics is necessary for art, morality, religion, economics, sociology, for the abstract sciences, as well as for every branch of human endeavour considered from the practical angle. It is the foundation upon which one builds one's career consciously and unconsciously; it is the guide; the author of the human interests; upon its truth or falsity depends what type of man you may develop into".[9]

This quotation explains adequately the singular and unique importance of African ontology in the overall treatment and understanding of African philosophy. In recent decades, studies that were made of the scientific, religious, and practical human endeavours of Africans have accepted their foundation as consisting in ancestor worship, animism, totemism, and magic. These are only vague ideas because no well-founded definitions of animism, totemism, and magic have been laid down, and the roots of these conceptions have not been explored. The root is in the fundamental concept of African ontology. When we understand this ontology, the concepts of magic, ancestor worship, totemism, and sorcery, as ethnologists apply them to Africa, become ridiculous if not foolish.

Ontology is the science of "being as such", "the reality that is". The metaphysics of western philosophy has generally been based upon a static conception of being. In the African philosophical thought, being is dynamic. *Existence-in-relation* sums up the African conception of life and reality. The African does not separate being from force as its attribute. Rather "the Africans speak, act, live, as if for them beings were forces . . . Force, for them, is the nature of being, force is being, being is force".[10] When Western philosophy says that beings are differentiated by their essences or nature; Africans say that forces differ in their essences or nature. There is the divine force,

[8] Henry Alpern, *The March of Philosophy* (New York, 1934) p. 99.

[9] *Ibid.*, p. 99.

[10] Temples, pp. 51—52.

terrestrial, or celestial forces, human forces, and vegetable and even mineral forces. When western metaphysics define "being" as "that which is" or "the thing insofar as it is", the African definition reads: "that which is force," or "an existent force." God of course is the Great Force. There is a hierarchy of forces starting from God spirits, founding fathers, the dead according to the order of primogeniture, then the living according to their rank in terms of seniority. After living man come animals, vegetables, and minerals, which are, in turn, categorized by their relative importance in their own classes.

The concept of separate beings, of substances, to use a scholastic term, which exist side by side independent one of another, is foreign to African thought.[11] African thought holds that created beings preserve a bond one with another, an intimate ontological relationship. There is interaction of being with being, that is to say, of force with force. This is more so among rational beings known as *Muntu*, a term which includes the living and the dead, *Orishas*, and God.

Muntu is a force endowed with intelligence, a force which has control over irrational creatures known as *bintu*. Because of this ontological relationship among beings, the African knows and feels himself to be in intimate and personal relationships with other forces acting above or below him in the hierarchy of forces. "The human being, apart from the ontological hierarchy and interaction of forces, has no existence in the conception of the Bantu."[12]

African epistemology or theory of knowledge

Theory of knowledge follows closely upon ontology. The view adopted by African theory of knowledge is consistent with their metaphisics. Knowledge or wisdom to the African consists in how deeply he understands the nature of forces and their interaction. "True wiedom," Tempels tells us, "lies in ontological knowledge; it is the intelligence of forces, of their hierarchy, their cohesion and their interaction."[13] We said earlier that God is Force; God is also wisdom in that He knows all forces, their ordering, their dependence, their potential, and their mutual interaction. A person is said to know or have wisdom inasmuch as he approaches divine wisdom. One approaches divine

[11] *Ibid.*, p. 58.
[12] *Ibid.*, p. 104.
[13] *Ibid.*, p. 73.

wisdom when "one's flesh becomes less fleshly", to use Leopold Senghor's expression. This means that the older a person gets, the more wisdom he has. The same note of hierarchy comes into play here. The ancestors have more wisdom, followed by the elders, dead, or living.

Distinction must be made here of the two levels of human intelligence. Intelligence can be either practical or habitual. Practical intelligence is cleverness, slyness in dealing with the contingent aspects of forces. Habitual intelligence is active knowledge of the nature of forces and, their relationship. This knowledge includes how man, the being with intelligence, makes use of things and activates the forces asleep in them. This kind of wisdom is different from book knowledge which is not regarded as wisdom in the strict traditional sense.

> Study and personal search for knowledge does not give wisdom. One can learn to read, to write; but all that has nothing in common with "wisdom". It gives no ontological knowledge of the nature of beings. There are many talents and clever skills that remain far short of wisdom.[14]

Having a college degree does not qualify an African as a wise person in a community. This, in part, explains why there has been confusion in Africa since the colonial era, because the colonial administrators regarded the educated as the wise people, and, consequently, arbitrarily appointed them legislators and leaders in the community, contrary to Africa political philosophy which took the eldest of the community to be, by divine law, the repository of wisdom and the link between God, the ancestors, and the living. He alone is "divine". Swailem Sidhem in his article "The Theological Estimate of Man" laments the present state of affairs when he said:

> Power is conceived by the African as something pertaining to the divine. Hence it cannot be placed into unexercised hands. But the hands are rarely exercised nowadays. Scheduled education has replaced experience and has toppled the accepted standards. Seniority of age does not mean much anymore, and a father may now be instructed by the child of his bowels. Nevertheless, power is dangerous and it kills. Like a live coal from upon the very altar of God, it can only be cared for by those who have been graduated into maturity.[15]

This despair is understandable if one grasps the African's conception of existence and his philosophy of vital forces.

[14] *Ibid.*, p. 74.

[15] Swailem Sidhom, "The Theological Estimate of Man," in Kwasi Dickson, ed., *Biblical Revelation and African Beliefs* (London, 1969), p. 115.

African ethical theory

Some foreign observers of the African scene have declared that the African has no sense of sin. An example is Edwin Smith, who said in his *African Ideas of God*: "It would seem that in general Africans are not conscious of any direct relation between their theism and their ethic of dynamism".[16] Others maintain that Africans have but a vague idea of the Supreme Being, that he always keeps his distance and does not associate himself with the daily lives of men. These and others are mere prejudices. The Nigerian writer, E. Adeolu Adegbola, said about African morality:

> Everywhere African morality is hinged on many sanctions. But the most fundamental sanction is the fact that God's all-seeing eyes scan the total area of human behaviour and personal relationships. God is spoken of as having eyes all over like a sieve.[17]

Placide Tempels, who questioned Africans closely on this point, informs us that "the influence of God in the daily life of man is recognized in many African proverbs and sayings . . ."[18] He says that such authors, as mentioned above, are speaking under the influence of western moral theory, according to which the social order is mere conformity with conventionalized behaviour. On the contrary, African morality and moral law are filled with fixed beliefs, unshakable principles held from convinction. They surely know the distinction between good and evil. They refer to moral evil as "stinking"; they feel it deeply in their spirit.

The norms of good and evil are objective and of universal validity; no room exists for subjectivism or solipsism and situational ethics. African ethical truths are not relative. Except for cases of ignorance, there are few if any mitigating circumstance.

The root of their knowledge of good and evil is bound up with their philosophy. The African sees a relationship between morality and the ontological order. Everything is associated and co-ordinated under the all-embracing unity of "vital force". In his judgement of his conduct the African takes into consideration the fact that he is not alone, that he is a cog in a wheel of interacting forces. He knows that the most important thing in his action is not how it affects him personally, but how it affects the world order, the

[16] Edwin Smith, *African Ideas of God* (London, 1950), p. 22.

[17] Kwesi Dickson, p. 116.

[18] Tempels, p. 117.

spiritual republic, outside of which he does not exist as a *muntu*, outside of which he is a planet off its orbit, meaningless and nonexisting. His life is not his own in a selfish manner; it belongs to God. The strengthening of this life and its preservation are in the hands of his ancestors and elders. In the life of the community each person has his place and each has his right to well-being and happiness. Therefore, what to do and what to avoid in order to preserve, increase, and strengthen the vital force within himself and others of his clan constitute morality. "Objective morality to the Bantu is ontological, immanent and intrinsic morality. Bantu moral standards depend essentially on things ontologically understood."[19]

It follows that an act will be accounted ethically good if it can be judged ontologically good and, by deduction, be assessed as juridically just. The same idea is introduced by Plato in the *Republic*. The individual Greek citizen is to interpret an action good or evil, not in reference to selfish interests, but in reference to the community of which he is a part. The African ethical theory could be called metaphysical ethics in one sense and ethical communialism in another sense, where an individual takes into consideration the community of vital forces in deciding the goodness or evil of his proper actions.

Human positive or customary laws are made in reference to the growth of preservation of *Muntu's* vital force; otherwise they are meaningless. All customary law that is worthy of the name is inspired, animated, and justified from the African's point of view by the philosophy of living forces, of growth, of influence, and of the vital hierarchy. The validity and strength of the customary law of indigenous peoples reside in its foundation in their philosophy. This is it is said in African ethical theory that an act which is characterized as ontologically good "will therefore be accounted ethically good; and at length, be assessed as juridically just".[20] "In contrast to the European sense of justice, which measures liability by material damage, it is according to Afıican philosophy the loss in force, in joy of life, that is evaluated, independently of material considerations."[21]

Conclusion

The rediscovery of African philosophy has influenced African scholars in writing about African personality or what the French-speaking Africans call

[19] *Ibid.*, p. 121.
[20] *Ibid.*, p. 121.
[21] Jahneinz Jahn, *Muntu: An Outline of the New African Culture* (New York, 1961), p. 117.

Negritude. Kwame Nkrumah, Julius Nyerere, Leopold Senghor, Aime Cesaire, Nnamdi Azikiwe, and Chinua Achebe have written prose and verses to celebrate this philosophy, a philosophy of unity and complete encounter of all things and beings, which by reason of the dynamic character of African ontology, has surfaced on the communal structure of our society based on the division of labour and rights in which man attains growth and recognition by how well he fulfills a function for the overall well-being of the community. We Africans have not yet yielded to the subtlety (and I pray we shall never) which would allow our traditional law-makers and judges to design customary laws divorced from our philosophy, from the nature of beings, as we understand them, and from our view of the world.

CHAPTER EIGHTEEN

Traditional African Languages as a Medium for Scientific Creativity and Innovation

Prof. S. Ejikeme Okoye
Professor of Physics and Director,
Division of General Studies,
University of Nigeria, Nsukka

"We dissect nature along lines laid down by our native languages."

Benjamin Lee Whorf.

Virtually all African countries are today classed among the developing countries of the world. The word "developing" is, of course, a euphemism for "underdeveloped", a comparative and essentially negative concept conveying the impression of an impoverished pre-industrial society.[1] In this context, development, which can be viewed as the processes leading from the pre-industrial to the industrial stage, inevitably becomes a natural preoccupation of the leaders of a developing country, the conventional wisdom being that the pursuit of economic and industrial development is greatly facilitated by the agencies of science and technology.

Although a number of treaties have been written on the problem of development and remedies of the present technological gap between the technologically underdeveloped and the wealthy industrial countries, especially of the West, it does not appear that enough basic questions are being asked about why the technological gap should exist in the first place. Since science and technology are now accepted as an integral part of the culture of the Western World, it seems legitimate to examine what possible role language and culture could have played (and could still play) in ordering nations into a technological peck order. In particular, it should be of interest to inquire whether African languages *per se* as a medium of intellectual activity have proved a hinderance to serious intellectual activity especially in the area of

[1] H. M. Philips, "Factors Contributing Towards Modernization and Socio-Economic Performance, Science and Technology," in Peter Langyel, ed., *Approaches to the Science of Socio-Economic Development* (Paris: UNESCO, 1971), p. 11.

scientific creativity and innovation. A natural extension of this line of thought is the age-old question of a possible correlation between race and intelligence. Although such a topic does violence to the African ego and his social dignity, the tantalizing fact of the present world economic order is that development and underdevelopment appear to follow fairly well defined racial lines. The question arises as to whether this development is accidental or not.

This paper is, therefore, committed not merely to understanding or revolving the different issues raised above, but more importantly, it is the hope that through this study one can gain a better insight into the meaning of culture and of scientific creativity, their possible connection, interaction, and role in the developmental process in general.

The Nature of Human Intelligence and Creativity

Let us begin with the writings of the Spanish physician, Juan Huarte, who, in the late sixteenth century, published a widely translated study on the nature of human intelligence.[2] In the course of his investigations, Huarte questioned the fact that the Spanish word, for intelligence, *ingenio*, seems to have the same Latin root as various words connoting "engender" or "generate". From this relationship he drew conclusions as to the nature of the human mind stating that "One may discern two generative powers in man, one common with the beasts and the plants, and the other participating of spiritual substance. Wit (Ingenio) is a generative power. The understanding is a generative faculty."

Huarte goes on to distinguish between three levels of intelligence. At the lowest level is the "docile wit" which satisfies the principle that there is nothing in the mind that is not transmitted to it by the senses. The next level, known as "normal intelligence", goes well beyond the "docile wit" in that it is able to "engender within itself, by its own power, the principles on which knowledge rests". Thus, normal human minds are such that "assisted by the subject alone, without the help of any body, they will produce a thousand conceits they never heard spoke of . . . inventing and saying such things as they never heard from their masters, nor any mouth".[3] In other words, normal human intelligence is capable of generating and acquiring knowledge through its own internal resources which are often data supplied by the

[2] Quoted in Noam Chomsky, *Language and Mind* (New York: Harcourt, Brace, Jovanovick, Inc. 1968), p. 9.

[3] *Ibid.*, p. 9.

senses, but nevertheless it is able to construct a cognitive system in terms of concepts and principles that are developed on independent grounds. Further, it is capable of generating new thoughts and finding appropriate and novel ways of expressing them in a manner that training or experience could not have made possible.

Huarte postulates a third kind of wit "by means of which some, without art or study, speak such subtle and surprising things, yet true, that were never before seen, heard, or written, no, nor ever so much as thought of".[4] This third kind refers to true creativity, an exercise of the creative imagination in ways that go beyond normal intelligence that may, according to Huarte, involve "a mixture of madness". Huarte maintains that the distinction between docile wit, involving stimuliresponse, and normal intelligence with its full generative capacities, is the distinction between beast and man. In this conclusion Huarte had the support of Descartes who argued that there is a basic element lacking in animals, as it is lacking in even the most complex automaton that develops its "intellectual structures" completely in terms of conditioning and association, namely Huarte's second type of wit, the generative ability that is revealed in the human use of language as a free instrument of thought. It follows that should another organism exhibit evidence of the normal, creative use of language, we must conclude that, like us, it has a mind and that its mental activity transcends any mechanical or other type of stimulus within the framework of stimulus-response psychology.

The above considerations lead to the condition that language is an index of human intelligence, that it distinguishes man from animals. In this connection, it must be pointed out that animals do not lack appropriate organs of communication, nor are they simply lower along some scale of "general intelligence". In fact, as Descartes quite rightly observed, language is a species-specific human possession, and, even at low levels of intelligence such as pathological levels, for example, we find a command of language that is totally unattainable by an ape that may in other respects, surpass a human imbecile in problem-solving ability and other adaptive behaviour. However, it has been argued that "if beasts reasoned, they would be capable of fine speech with its infinite variety".[5] However, in the Cartesian view even animal behaviour is potentially infinite in its variety, in the special sense in which the readings of a clock can be said, with an obvious idealization, to be

[4] *Ibid.*, p. 9.

[5] *Ibid.*, p. 12.

potentially infinite in variety. That is, if animal behaviour is controlled by external stimuli or internal states, then as the stimuli vary over an indefinite range, so also may the behaviour of the animal. But the normal use of language is not only innovative and potentially infinite in scope, but also free from the control of detectable stimuli, either external or internal. *It is because of this freedom from stimulus control that language can serve as an instrument of thought and self-expression* as it does, not only for the exceptionally gifted and talented, but also, in fact, for every normal human.

It is particularly important to emphasize that the normal use of language is innovative, in the sense that much of what we say in the course of normal language is entirely new, not a repetition of anything that we have heard before nor even similar in pattern to sentences or discourse that we have heard in the past. This may further be appreciated by the fact that the number of sentences in one's native language that one will immediately understand with no feeling of difficulty or strangeness is astronomical. Similarly, the number of patterns underlying our normal use of language and corresponding to meaningful and easily comprehensible sentences in our language is a greater magnitude than the number of seconds in a life time. It is, therefore, in this sense that the normal use of language is innovative.

The issue of human intelligence on the other hand is one of the most controversial and sensitive questions in the sphere of social relations. At issue is the central question as to whether there are significant differences of "innate intelligence" between different races of mankind. The difficulty of giving an objective quantitative answer is apparent when it is remembered that the concept of "race" is anything but precise. In fact, up to the 19th century there was a genuine scientific interest in the biological differences between human groups. The discipline of "physical anthropology" was devoted not only to the characterization of various groups according to the colour of their skin but also to the differentiation of the very mixed-up inhabitants of Europe according to such refined indices as the shape of the skull. The classification schemes worked out then, like those for many genera of plants and animals, did not always agree in detail, but at least the questions that were being asked were capable of falsification by direct observation. *The trouble was that the social and cultural characteristics of each racial group were also regarded, without proof, as outward manifestation of innate, biologically heritable traits*. In particular the economic and technological dominance of the white races were attributed to genetic superiority of the intellect, character, etc. This view was apparently involved with the attempt to justify political domination, as in the case of American slavery and European colonialism. The modern controversy concerning race and intelligence is an intellectual relic of this old bogey. The attempt is made to prove, by statistical analysis of batteries of intelligence tests, that the old conjectured differences really exist. John Ziman has summed up the situation most rationally in the following words:

> With "intelligence" itself being very far from a culturally neutral concept, what would one be saying if one simply pointed out that blacks, on the average, score ten points less than whites on a given set of puzzles? In any case, the range of variation amongst individuals in each group is so large that one could never make this piece of "scientific knowledge" the basis of an educational policy.
>
> So formidable are these obstacles to "scientific" study of the relations between race and intelligence that one must begin to question the motives of those honest seekers after truth or do they have political, ideological ends which they are attempting to justify by an appeal to scientific authority?[6]

One is led to suspect by the foregoing that every member of the human species possesses the same innate potential for normal human intelligence and creativity. The degree to which that potential is tapped by any individual may be conditioned by circumstances such as social needs, pressures, or the environment, physical, emotional and intellectual. In other words the degree and domain of man's intellectual activity must be culturally bound.

Language as Vehicle for Intellectual Activity

It is appropriate to begin this discussion with evidence for a connection between language and thought and to open with a consideration of the relationship between vocabulary and perception. It does not require much study to observe that languages differ notoriously in vocabulary, and this difference is generally correlated with differences in environment. Thus Whorf notices that Eskimo languages have a variety of words for different kinds of snow, as opposed to one in English. On the other hand, the language of the Aztecs is even poorer than English in this respect, since it uses the same word stem for cold, ice, and snow.[7] Sapir gives detailed evidence over a broader field in claiming that the vocabulary of a language clearly reflects the

[6] John Ziman, *The Force of Knowledge: The Scientific Discussions of Society* (Cambridge: Cambridge University Press, 1976), pp. 288–289.

[7] See Paul Henley, ed., *Language, Thought and Culture* (Ann Arbor: University of Michigan Press, 1965), pp. 5–6.

physical and social environment of a people. According to him, the complete vocabulary of a language would be "a complex inventory of all the ideas, interests, and occupations that take up the attention of the community . . ."[8] Sapir points out that what holds for the physical environment, holds even more clearly for the social status systems in various cultures, however complex, and differentiations due to occupations are all mirrowed in languages.

Therefore, vocabulary reflects the environment of a people. Similarly culture is largely dependent on the environment especially in those places where technology is relatively underdeveloped. Thus we are led to a dialectical position suggesting at least that vocabulary and general human behaviour are effects of a common cause; in other words one may be an index to the other.

All that has been stated above still says nothing about perception and would have little to do with it, if perception were merely a matter of recording what is presented. This is certainly not the case as there is abundant evidence to show that perception is influenced by the mind. Such effects have been reported by the psychologists, Brunner and Goodman in the following classic words:

> . . . subjects can be conditioned to see and hear things in much the same way as they can be conditioned to perform such overt acts as knee jerking, eye blinking or salivating. Pair a sound and a faint image, and the subject sees it anyway when the sound is presented. Any student of suggestion, whether or not he has pursued Bird's exhaustive bibliography of the literature on the subject, know that. Not perception? Why not? The subject sees what he reports as vividly as he sees the phi-phenomenon.[9]

In addition, Brunner and Goodman point out, reward and punishment, experience, and social factors may all be of influence. Furthermore, their own research shows that children overestimate the size of coins and that the amount of overestimation is, in general, dependent upon the value of the coin, that the error is greater with coins than with cardboard discs of the same size. Clearly, as the two authors observed, it will not do to consider a perceiver as a passive recording instrument of rather complex design.

This brings us immediately to the connection between language and thought, a subject studied in some depth by the eminent American linguisticist, Benjamin Whorf. Whorf made two cardinal hypothesis in this regard:

[8] *Ibid.*, p. 6.

[9] See Paul Henley, ed., p. 6.

(a) that all higher levels of thinking are dependent on language, (b) that the structure of the language one habitually uses influences the manner in which one understands his environment. *The picture of the Universe shifts from tongue to tongue.*[10] Language, Whorf observes, is the best show man puts on. Other creatures have developed communication systems but no true language. Language is cardinal in rearing human young, in organizing human communities, in handing down the culture from generation to generation. On the other hand the power to reason constitutes the "uniqueness of man" to philosophers as well as biologists. Unprotected by claws, teeth, thick hide, fleetness of foot, or sheer strength, the *homo sapien* has to think his way out of tight corners. His reason has been his chief weapon for survival.

According to natural logic, talking is merely an incidental process concerned strictly with communication, not with formulation of ideas. Talking, or the use of language, is supposed only to "express" what is essentially already formulated nonlinguistically. *Formulation is an independent process, called thought or thinking, and is supposed to be largely indifferent to the nature of particular languages.*

Languages have grammars, which are assumed to be merely norms of conventional and social correctness, but the use of language is supposed to be guided not so much by these norms as by correct, rational or intelligent thinking. Thought, therefore, does not depend on grammar but on *laws of logic or reason which are supposed to be the same for all observers of the universe*, to represent a rationale in the universe that can be "found" independently by all intelligent observers whether they speak Chinese or Ijaw.

With the foregoing as background we can now consider the connection between the restricted form of science, originally termed natural philosophy (or the study of natural objects and phenomena) with language and thought. We start by noting the familiar saying that the exception proves the rule. However, from the standpoint of formal logic it became an absurdity, as soon as "prove" no longer means "put on trial". What the saying might well suggest to us today is that if a rule has absolutely no exceptions, it is not recognized as a rule or as anything else; it is then part of the background experience of which we tend to remain unaware. Thus, never having experienced anything in contrast to it, we cannot isolate it and formulate it as a rule until we so enlarge our experience and expand our base of reference, that we encounter an interruption of its regularity. For instance, if a race of

[10] Stuart Chase in John B. Carroll, ed., *Language, Thought and Reality: Selected Writings of Benjamin Lee Whorf*, (Mass: Massachusetts Institute of Technology Press, 1967), p. vi.

people had the physiological defect of being able to see only the colour blue, they would hardly be able to formulate the rule that they saw only blue. The term blue would convey no meaning to them and their language will lack colour terms. The phenomenon of gravitation forms a rule without exceptions; needless to say, the untutored person is utterly unaware of any law of gravitation, for it would never occur to him to conceive of a universe in which bodies behaved otherwise than they do on the earth's surface. In fact, the law could not be formulated until bodies that always fell were seen in terms of a wider astronomical world in which bodies moved in orbits or went this way or that. What the above illustrations point to is the fact "that the background linguistic system (in other words, grammar) of each language is not merely a reproducing instrument for voicing ideas but rather is itself the shape of ideas, the programme and guide for the individuals mental activities, for his analysis of impressions, for his synthesis of his mental stock in trade. Formulation of ideas is not an independent process, strictly rational in the old sense, but is part of a particular grammar, and differs from slightly to greatly, between different grammars".[11]

Thus we tend to dissect nature along lines laid down by our native language. Not only that, we cut nature up, organize it into concepts, and ascribe significant features largely because we are parties to an agreement to organize it this way, an agreement that holds throughout our speech community and is codified in the pattern of our language.[12] This realization is indeed very significant for modern science, for it means that no individual is free to describe nature with absolute impartiality but is constrained to certain modes of interpretation even while he thinks himself most free. The person most nearly free in such respects would be a linguist familiar with very many widely different linguistic systems. As yet no such privileged linguist exists. According to Whorf we are led to a new principle of relativity, which postulates that "*all observers are not led by the same physical evidence to the same picture of the universe, unless their linguistic backgrounds are similar, or in some way can be calibrated*".[13] This rather revolutionary principle is not so apparent if only modern European languages are compared. Among these tongues there is a unanimity of a major pattern which at first seems to bear out natural logic. But this unanimity exists only because these tongues are all

[11] *Ibid.*, p. 206.
[12] *Ibid.*, p. 206.
[13] *Ibid.*, p. 207.

Indo-European dialects designed from the same basic plan, being historically transmitted from what was long ago one speech community.[14] On the other hand if modern Chinese, Nigerian, or Turkish scientists describe the world in the same terms as western scientists, this can only mean that they have taken over bodily the entire western system of rationalizations, not that they have corroborated that system from their native posts of observation.

It should be apparent that intellectual activity as we know it would be impossible without language as a tool and vehicle. This however, should not be construed as an argument for an "intellectual monism". As we have seen, the concept of intellectual activity is necessarily not only relative but also culturally bound. It is probably for this reason that the superiority of a particular culture confers an apparent intellectual superiority. Thus in a world culture dominated and ruled by science and technology, the western intellectual pattern of thought appears supreme and dominant but, of course, this is only an artifact of modern human history.

Traditional African Languages as a Medium for Scientific Creativity and Innovation

It has been said that language is the means through which culture finds expression.[14] On the other hand, man communicates through and lives by culture.[15] The basic question which these definitions raise is whether science can take root and thrive in the western form within the context of African cultures. Although the above discussion would appear to supply a ready answer in the negative, yet an answer cannot come in such a straight-forward manner. In the first place, no culture is static, and one of the effects of the phenomenal improvements in the speed and quality of communication and intercourse between various peoples at various corners of the globe is that culture as a concept is now not so precise. It is as if the trend is towards a "cultural monism". Nevertheless, the hard reality is that the relatively few languages of the dominant cultures which have emerged in the present era of world civilization threaten to overspread the globe and to push to the obscure background hundreds of diverse linguistic species belonging to the so-called developing countries. But it is foolish to assume that the presently dominant

[14] Private correspondence from Dr. Phil. Nwachukwu, Dept. of English, University of Nigeria, Nsukka.

[15] Paul Bohannan, *Social Anthropology* (Oxford: Oxford University Press, 1963), p. 3.

languages represent any superiority of type. On the contrary, it takes but little scientific study of pre-literate languages, especially those of native America, to show how much more precise and finely elaborated is the system of relationships in such tongues than in the European ones.[16] According to Whorf, "by comparison with many native American languages, the formal systematization of ideas in English, German, French or Italian seems poor and jejune".[17]

There is also a historical perspective supplied by religious wars of persecution, slavery, and colonialism which have shaped the present African polities as we know them. As Joshua Fishman has noted,[18] one of the most serious problems confronting new nations, be they African or not, is that "their political boundaries correspond rather imperfectly to any pre-existing ethnic-cultural unity. Thus in the absence of a common, nation-wide, ethnic and cultural identity new nations proceeded to plan and create such an identity through national symbols that can lead to common mobilization and involvement above, beyond, and at the expense of pre-existing ethnic-cultural particularities. It is at this point that a national language is frequently involved (along with a national flag, a national ruler, etc.) as a unifying symbol".[19] We thus see language in a new role, "as a symbol of supralocal ethnic cultural identification at the nationality level".[20]

Another problem facing political leaders of emergent nations is that of language policy. In the new nations of Africa, diglossia is extremely widespread. Thus, instead of trying to cope with hundreds of local languages and dialects as instruments of government, education, industrialization, etc., most African nations have decided to assign all of them equally to their respective home, family, and neighbourhood domains, and to utilize a single, major European language (usually English or French) for all more formal occasions. The uniformizing requirements and consequences of science and technology are such that for many years to come even the monolingual nations in control of "old languages", such as Japan, will need to resort to diglossian compromises (if this has not been done) in various technological

[16] Stuart Case, *op. cit*., p. 85.

[17] *Ibid.*, p. 85.

[18] J. A. Fishman, "Sociolinguistics and the Language Problems of the Developing Countries," in Joshua A. Fishman, *et al.* eds., *Language Problems of Developing Nations* (New York: J. Wiley & Sons, 1968), p. 6.

[19] *Ibid.*, p. 231.

[20] *Ibid.*, p. 231.

and education domains. According to Das Gupta, "this trend should be much stronger than the countertrend, namely, the abandonment of diglossia on behalf of new national standard languages with undisputed hegemony in all domains of national expression".[21]

The emergence of the diglossian situation in which a single society recognizes two or more languages as its own, with each having its own functionally exclusive domain need not be lamented. After all, "language makes it possible for human beings to think together, to feel together, and to act together. For those who know a language, words may establish similar preferences, and words may be the cue to similar behaviour. To know a language is to have a common ground upon which to meet others".[22]

To return to the main theme of this lecture, one may say that the question of whether traditional African languages provide an effective medium for scientific creativity and innovation would appear to be irrelevant if we accept science and technology as potent forces of acculturation, and if we accept the prevalent diglossian situation in all African countries emanating from their colonial history. A more relevant question is whether Africans brought up in western traditions and culture can be equally creative and innovative in science and technology compared with scientists indigenous to the Western World. At this point in time, it is not easy to give an unbiased answer. However, juding from their brief encounter with western culture, most African countries have produced impressive results. The experience of India, a Third World country with a much longer scientific tradition than African countries shows that both the potential and possibilities for African scientists are there. Although India has produced two Nobel prize winners and seventeen fellows of the Royal Society of London, it must be remembered that India joined the scientific arena when the horizons of scientific knowledge were tractable and certainly long before the geopolitical structures of Africa were determined at the infamous Berlin Conference of 1884.

What seems clear, however, is that in the diglossian situation of African countries, an indigenous scientist, if he is truly talented may be able to take over *en mass*, the entire western system of thought and can thus perform extremely well in it, though at a cost to his cultural equilibrium. The ploddlers, of course, may find the projection of an elaborate imported language upon a

[21] Jyotirindra Das Gupta, "Language Diversity and National Development," in J. A. Fishman, *et al.*, p. 47.

[22] Bess Sondel, *The Humanity of Words: A Primer of Semantus* (New York: The World Publishing Co., 1958), p. 21.

limited tradition-based cultural experience inadequate for exemplary performance. Furthermore, it must be appreciated that in modern times, the growth and spread of science is evidently a complex process, with very different characteristics in different countries. The mere fact of industrial development is not a sufficient explanation for this growth; general cultural, economic and political forces are also significant.

As John Ziman has observed, although India has produced first class scientists, these scientists are burdened with masses of students and they are employed in universities poor in staff, buildings and equipment, often disrupted by strikes and demoralized by the high level of graduate unemployment. According to him, if these talented people were exposed to a somewhat broader view of their scientific specialities, and given the material resources of their European counterparts, India would quickly become a major power in basic science; it is the poverty of the nation as a whole that confines their creative abilities.[23] In short, science has developed so rapidly that it is becoming "industrialized" as a human activity. It is, therefore, only the wealthy and/or industrialized nations that can afford the kind of research facilities that enable a scientist to be really creative at least in the international context. Of course, there are levels of creativity which the poor and developing African countries are certainly not debarred from by contributing their widow's mite at the lower levels, and neither their stamina nor intellectual vigour can be doubted in the circumstance.

Conclusion

We have seen in the course of the present discourse that the vocabulary of a given language reflects the environment of its users. In this connection, language is not merely a vehicle for voicing thought, i.e., non-linguistic formulation of ideas, but actually shapes not only ideas but the form of mental activity. This leads to the conclusion that intellectual activity must be culturally bound. Whorf has stated this elegantly in his principle of relativity according to which all observers are not led by the same physical evidence to the same picture of the universe, unless their linguistic backgrounds are similar. In other words, we dissect nature along lines laid down by our native languages, so that the physical picture of the universe shifts from tongue to tongue.

[23] John Ziman, *The Force of Knowledge* (Cambridge: Cambridge University Press, 1976), p. 275.

It is important to bear in mind, finally, that although thought is said to be a non-linguistic formulation of ideas, it is nevertheless guided by laws of logic, which being the rationale of the universe can be discovered independently by any individual of any tongue. Furthermore, western science is essentially a system of thought and activity based entirely on logic. Given the above facts, the pressing question which remains is why traditional African cultures were *ab initio* unable to develop or sustain the scientific method, considering the enormous contribution of the Egyptians (particularly Euclid) to the science of geometry in early history. Furthermore, what is the prime cause of the ordering of the nations of the world in the present technological peck order? Or put differently, why does the technological gap between the developed and developing nations exist?

Intellectual activity is culturally bound, that is to say that it is conditioned by the social and physical environment in which the culture is based. In the first place, the industrial revolution of the eighteenth century seems to be more of a social phenomenon than a development triggered by science. In fact, science in that era was yet in its infancy and only came of age at the turn of the last century; it is only in our modern times that developments in science are impacting on the rate of technological growth. The technological gap, to a large extent, has a historical origin not unconnected with the enterprising spirit of the inhabitants of the temperate zones and their quest for survival through the exploration of foreign lands in search of material goods.

Traditional African science no doubt existed in some form, but the social customs of most traditional African cultures were such that knowledge was largely treated as a valuable commodity which should be hoarded and therefore guarded jealously in much the same manner as material possessions. This is evident in the restricted way in which the science or secrets of native medicine is transmitted from generation to generation. In western culture on the other hand, the growth of science has depended tremendously on the improvements in scientific communication and intercourse between scientists and "laymen" many of whom made significant scientific discoveries. Further, western science represents a cumulative effort in which each scientist builds on the work of his predecessors. The closed system of the initiated of African societies predictably led to a stale stock of scientific knowledge, often obscured from public view by contrived mysticism. The open western system meanwhile thrived.

History shows that any progressive society cannot barricade itself against cultural change especially in the modern era of science and technology. The dilemma remaining is what kind of balance a nation should strike between the competing cultures of modernization if national pride is to be maintained. Since change itself is difficult to envisage in a rigid culture, whatever balance is struck must take place in the context of a sufficiently laxed culture.

CHAPTER NINETEEN

Doubts and Directions in Cultural Revival

Prof. E. Obiechina
Department of English,
University of Nigeria, Nsukka

Introduction

Large-scale festivals, whether of arts, culture or sports, are not new in the world. From very remote antiquity, peoples of the world with a common sense of identity, history, race, civilization, nationality or religion, have made a point of coming together, periodically, to express their sense of communion through those things which have given them their feeling of unity, those things which not only defined their unique relatedness but also distinguished them from all other peoples.

A few examples would illustrate the matter. The Greeks of old knew themselves as one people who shared a destiny different and distinct from the destiny of the rest of mankind. They gave expression to this feeling of their distinctness by staging periodic games, sports and cultural activities. At such times, Greeks of the homeland (the Greek Mainland), as well as those of the Greek archipelagos and others scattered over the numerous islands of the Ionian and Aeolian seas and those inhabiting the Orient and Eastern Mediterranean, as far south as the Alexandria and northern Egypt, converged at certain centres to celebrate the Greek cult of physical fitness and the love for the arts and culture. The four major Pan-Hellenic Games (Olympic, Delphic, Nemean and Corinthian) named after the places of celebrations brought together great sportsmen, the great playwrights and actors, the great poets who wrote praise-poems in honour of the successful competitors. The atmosphere was often of a great festivity in which sporting, religious, literary and musical events combined to give the people an integrated sense of enjoyment which no other event was capable of conferring on them.

The world has since borrowed the sporting aspect of the Pan-Hellenic games from the Greeks by staging every four years the well-known Olympic Games. The Greeks enacted their first Olympiad, according to their historians, in 776 BC. It is necessary to observe, however, that what was borrowed from them was the most mechanical aspect of the event, the mere husk of the real thing, the sports. The humanistic interests which derived from the cultural activities, the great tragic and comic dramas, the panegyric odes, and so on, could not be borrowed as well. Thus, contemporary Olympic Games have become savage affairs in which rivalry and cut-throat competition have tended to overtake everything else and the obsession with victory has overridden every other consideration.

Peoples other than the Greeks also appreciated the virtue of periodic festivals that conferred a sense of communion and solidarity. The Jews, during their long chequered history, managed to remain an identifiable people by clinging to an indestructible sense of their destiny through the festival of incorporation, during which all Jews at home and in dispersion, converged in Jerusalem, their holy city, to participate in the Feast of the Passover. Even after the Jewish race had been scattered by the Romans and Jerusalem had been wiped away in 70 A.D. the Jews, in their two thousand years of journeyings and precariousness, kept the Festival, often under the cover of secrecy in hostile times and places.

An important fact however remained that the Festival which appeared essentially as a religious and ritual communion always had a very strong cultural and artistic aspect to it. The eating of a special source and cakes and the drinking of a special wine, the sacrifice of the paschal lamb and the other rituals, were always followed by special poetical recitations and the singing of special psalms. Even long after the paschal sacrifice had been played out, the poetical recitations and the psalmody survive, as well as the cultural narrative of the Exodus transmitted to the children from generation to genaration.

More recently, the Arabs harrassed, paradoxically, by the overpowering presence of Israel have responded strongly by drawing upon those areas of their history and traditions which give them a strong sense of unity and solidarity. They have drawn upon their common religious heritage, as well as upon their culture and arts. They have staged Pan-Arabic cultural and artistic festivals during which their literature, their arts and crafts, their cinematographic and theatrical achievements, their songs and dances have been amply displayed. They have also at other times staged Pan-Arabic Games and Sports.

The point being made here is that those peoples of the world who have strong, compelling reasons to dramatize their unity of interest and collective solidarity have inevitably stressed those aspects of their experiences which offer them maximum scope for underlining this unity and solidarity. The more those around them threaten their sense of security, the more tenaciously they cling to those things which enhance their unity and solidarity.

A second point worthy of note is that culture and the arts, because they form a solid basis for mobilizing and channelling human emotions, also provide one of the strongest forces for consolidating a people's response when they are threatened or are oppressed as a collectivity. Culture and the arts become those people's ready-to-hand weapon for fighting back and answering the challenge of the oppressors. In other words culture and the arts become a dialectal instrument for dramatizing the sense of a people's injury no less than such a people's counter-blast to the oppressor's strike.

Thirdly, given the dialectal nature of human oppression, in which the battlelines are often well and firmly drawn, culture and the arts lend themselves maximally to group responses. A festival becomes a structure of optimal mobilization; for, it is only when the isolated and incipient emotional responses of single individuals are pooled and directed through a structured festival that the sum-total of a people's emotive energy assumes a significance far and above its original inspiration.

In introducing the WORLD BLACK AND AFRICAN FESTIVAL OF ARTS AND CULTURE, it should be borne in mind that just as the Greeks, the Jews and the Arabs, in their encounter with non-Greeks, non-Jews and non-Arabs (an encounter that sometimes brought their survival into serious jeopardy) found their Pan-Hellenic, Zionist and Arabic Festivals (reinforced by their arts and cultures) important means of preserving their essential unity and identity in the face of a world that was determined to undermine their feeling of security, so Black Peoples of the world and the Continent of Africa, have found that their culture and arts organized in a festival of solidarity would become a powerful weapon for opposing themselves to a world that has helmed them in with hostilities and the threat of emasculation.

It should also be stated that of all the peoples of the world, with the possible exception of the Jews, the Black and African Peoples of the world have suffered greater oppression and been treated with greater contempt and ignominy than any others. They are for that very reason in greater need for unity and solidarity. As communities and groups of individuals, African and Black Peoples of the world require constantly to celebrate those things that unite and give them strength; for, their impotence which has for long made them victims of exploitation by more powerful and aggressive peoples is transformed into strength when they band themselves meaningfully together to outface their oppressors. Their culture and arts draw them together at favourable points of contact and by so doing integrate their emotional and psychological impulses and steel their will to freedom and positive assertiveness.

FESTAC was a great historic event, necessary almost to a point of inevitability at a time when the African and Black Peoples of the world stood at the crossroads, threatened with total obscurity and renewed emasculation on the one hand and faced with immense opportunities for recovering lost dignity, humanity and freedom on the other. They needed to gather together their emotional and psychological energies for the coming stuggle. FESTAC provided a rallying point for those energies. The sponsoring of the Festival by Nigeria, the largest and potentially greatest Black African country, seemed almost inevitable also.

It must be said, however, that serious mistakes were made which reduced the effectiveness of the Festival and made it a mixed affair, even to the very fair-minded and well informed. Its weaknesses and strengths will be looked at in this short discussion.

Necessity for Festac

Ever since the British naval commander and pirate, Sir John Hawkins (1532—1595), carried his first cargo of Black people from West Africa to the West Indies and America in 1562 to be sold as plantation slaves, the image and fortunes of African and Black Peoples have suffered systematic deterioration for four hundred years. The Continent of Africa was laid waste by the European adventurers and their collaborators. Millions of Africans perished on the Continent under raids, ambushes and inter-territorial wars stimulated by the slave traders. Millions more died on transportation across the Atlantic Ocean under the most inhuman and primitive conditions, during what historians have called "the horrors of the Middle Passage". For four hundred years, Black and African Peoples lost their dignity as human beings, lost their human rights and basic freedoms and became mere chattels to those who had overpowered and enslaved them. As recently as 1856—1857, Dred Scott, a Black slave who had managed to live free for several years but was later enchained again tried to obtain legal support by testing his case in court. The court ruled against him. The slave was defined as "three-fifths" of a man with hardly any rights.

While the slaves lived under varying degrees of inhumanity and were prevented from speaking their languages, from beating their beloved drums and expressing themselves in a way they knew how; in other words, while they were culturally being dehumanized and "castrated" in the plantations of the Americas and the Carribeans, their relatives who remained behind faced one disaster after another; those who had transported their distant cousins into ignominy inflicted on them one disaster after another.

The African in his Continent sank deeper and deeper. The very people who built and ran universities while Europe was still chained to the barbarism of the Dark and Middle Ages were soon reduced to a state of barbarity and incivility, the like of which the world had hardly experienced before. The old empires disintegrated under the virulence and systematic military pressures of European imperialists. Towns and villages were destroyed in the name of pacification and the erstwhile avid slave traders began to pose as pacifiers and restorers of peaceful trade, which yielded raw materials to the new industrial establishments of Europe.

In a characteristic act of cynical contempt, the imperialist powers met in the German city of Berlin in 1885 and shared the Continent among themselves. From then, the tragedy was complete. No African was autonomous thereafter; he became the colonial ward of Great Britain, France, Germany, Belgium, Spain, Portugal, or Italy, Ethiopia escaped this fate for a while by beating Italy in battle and preserving her ancient empire. But Italy used treachery and subterfuge to come back later to snuff out the single candlelight of freedom. Liberia was founded for manumitted Black slaves from America, but its independence was only nominal. To all intents and purposes and in spite of all its paraphernalia of the presidential system, it remained an American satellite and a near parody of an independent state.

In spite of all these vicissitudes, "the Soul of the Black Folk", as DuBois has called it, remained awake everywhere African and Black Peoples found themselves, on the African Continent or in diaspora. The attempts to destroy the humanity and self-respect of Africans and Blacks all over the world in order to render them permanently servile and exploitable failed woefully. The spirit of rebellion lay within them, sometimes dormant, sometimes active, like a vulcano. Their basic African humanity survived in spite of all odds. They found ways of perserving their cultures and their arts which their oppressors were trying to stamp out. By all manner of disguises, including transferring African cultural elements into what appeared to be Euro-American cultural contexts, the Blacks and people of African origins preserved their essential Africanness and ancestral authenticity.

African music found outlet through jazz, the blues and the Spirituals; African dance flourished in the tcha-tcha-tcha, the bolero, the rhumba, the rock-'n-roll, etc., African folklore flourished all over the land, transmitted from generation to generation through the matriarchal Black mothers and by such routes as the lullaby; African religion infiltrated white christianity and produced the great phenomenon of syncretic sects. In a sense, African culture and the arts found renewal and constant growth in expatriation. This is the greatest paradox of them all.

On the Continent itself, attempts were made by the colonialists to undermine the cultural and artistic confidence of the African Peoples. The method varied, as well as the styles. The British were surreptitious and pragmatic about it; the French, the Belgians and the Germans were brutal and open; the Portuguese were the most unenlightened and barbarous in trying to stamp out what they had nothing of real worth to replace with. The words "assimilado", "deraciné", "evolué" crept into the language of cultural description in Africa and the African Peoples suffered an ignominy, perhaps more devastating than the slave trade, because it struck at the very heart and soul of the peoples' way of life, their self-respect and their self-confidence as human beings.

More seriously still, the essential unity of Africans was undermined and a tiny fraction of the people absorbed the lifeways, cultural and artistic values of the colonizers. They became virtual hostages to the imperialists and the spiritual children of those who have done so much to rob them of their manhood. Luckily, however, the process of alienating the African of the Continent is never successful because of the very nature of the African environment itself and the network of communal ties which bind the individuals tightly to the community. In spite of attempts to Westernize and assimilate a small elite class of black collaborators, the colonialists have not won real victories. As in the Americas, the Caribbeans and elsewhere, the Western colonizers of the African Continent have suffered considerable defeat on the cultural and artistic question. The products of their schools of emasculation still retain their cultural and artistic contact with their African cultural and artistic base. Only very few, and I have not seen any example myself, may have been so culturally Westernized that they have become those whom Frantz Fanon calls "Black Skins, White Masks", blacks whose souls are whiter than snow.

Here, therefore, is the centre of our argument. If it is true that Africans and the Black People of the African Continent and the Peoples of African descent dispersed all over the world and separated from their African Continental cousins by four hundred years, if it is true that, in spite of the treacherous efforts of their oppressors and exploiters to rob them of their culture and their arts, they (the Africans and Blacks of Africa and the diaspora) still retain the essential core and elements of their African artistic and cultural traditions, then any effort to demonstrate this survival of essential cultural and artistic unity is a "religious" obligation. And which country is best qualified to meet this obligation than the largest and potentially greatest Black African country in the world, Nigeria?

The re-unification of the African and Black Peoples of the Continent and in those in diaspora, if not literally, then metaphorically, emotionally and psychologically, has been the dream of the greatest sons of the people. Not surprisingly, the dream began in the diaspora at first and found fertile ground to germinate in the ancestral homeland. Names like Marcus Garvey, DuBois, George Padmore, Frantz Fanon, Delaney, Garnet, Silver Williams, Edward Wilmot Blyden and Malcolm X come readily to mind. From the mid-nineteenth century to the mid-twentieth, these inspired sons of Africa in diaspora nursed and tended this dream, and worked assiduously to see it come to fruition.

On the African Continent itself, the dream matured in the hearts and will of Africa's illustrious sons. Nkrumah, Nyerere, Azikiwe, Lumumba, Cabral, Toure, Nasser, Bella, Neto, Sedar Senghor, among others, are names to conjure with, ardent Pan-Africanists who saw the destiny of the Africans of the Continent woven inextricably into the destiny of their cousins in diaspora. FESTAC for them and the people of the Continent was a realization of this dream that at some stage seemed too distant and too difficult to be practicable.

Nor did FESTAC just happen without earlier efforts and without antecedents. The attempts to give the African and the Black Peoples a voice and a philosophical-cum-political-cum-cultural forum on which to articulate their deepest aspirations gave rise to Garvism (return to Africa movement in the Americas and the West Indies), Pan-Africanism, Negritude, the African Personality, the Black Power Movement, and so on. Each was some attempt to create an awareness and a matching possibility to give the Black and African Peoples of the Continent and/or in dispersion a human voice and a role befitting the human being. FESTAC crystallized and sublimated these aspirations. It made the apparently impossible become possible, transformed a delightful dream into a delicious reality.

Cultural and artistic congresses had been held before, in the very bosom of imperialist Europe, first in Paris (1956) and next in Rome (1959). More promisingly, one was held in Algeria (1962) and Senegal (1966), but in scope, inspiration and emotional and psychological commitment, there was nothing to match the Nigerian Festival. To compare any of the others with the Nigerian example would be as ridiculous as comparing a solo-flutist's performance with a magnificent musical orchestrar, embodying all known instruments and in which all great virtuosi perform. The other congresses and festivals might, at best, be seen as mere rehearsals for the great, real thing.

The Gains of Festac

From 15 January to 12 February, 1977, participants converged in the Nigerian Capital of Lagos and there staged the most spectacular and varied cultural and artistic festival of its kind in recent world history, probably in all world history.

From places as far away as South America, the Caribbeans, North America, the United Kingdom and Ireland, Europe and Australasia Black Peoples and Peoples of African descent, in their scores and hundreds, brought their cultural achievements to swell the immensity of cultural styles and traits assembled at the Festival. From Haiti to Ivory Coast, from Guinea to Guayana, from Morocco to Malagasy Republic, from Senegal to Jamaica, from Swaziland to Papua New Guinea, from Botswana to Brazil, from Mozambique to Mauritania, African and Black Peoples poured into Lagos, bringing with them their songs and dances, their dramatic arts and music, their plastic arts and their crafts, their films and folklore, their costumes and decorative styles, their literatures and intellectual exhibits, to celebrate, even if only for a mere fitting moment in the vast eternity of time, their sense of historical unity and shared cultural heritage.

The Colloquium which was part of the Festival arrayed the largest assembly of Black and African intellectuals who devoted their intellectual resources towards the exploration of the numerous educational-cum-cultural problems of the Black and African Peoples, especially the critical problems of exorcising the evils of colonialism and laying the ghost of its even more invidious cousin, neo-colonialism. They attempted to grasp the nettle of the ways in which independent African and Black States in African and in diaspora could strengthen African cultural values and use them to fight the subversive values of Western education planted firmly in the soul of the colonized elites. The problems were seen as critical since the elites of Africa and new Black States are everywhere "in power" and have so far failed to cut the intellectual umbilical cord tying them to the socio-political systems of their imperialist mentors.

The achievements or, rather, the possible gains of FESTAC can now be summarized under a number of headings based largely on what I have sought to establish in the Introduction as the possible limits and possibilities of a cultural and artistic movement. They should include the following:

(i) Solidarity: FESTAC created the psychological and emotional atmosphere for the experiencing of a sense of solidarity among Black Peoples of the World and Peoples of African origin. That a desire for this solidarity exists I will illustrate by quoting from one of Africa's greatest sons in the diaspora, Marcus Garvey, a West Indian who lived for the greater part in U.S.A. Here is how he emphasizes the need for collective action and solidarity:

> Black men, you were once great; you shall be great again. Lose not courage, lose not faith, go forward. The thing to do is to get organized; keep separated and you will be exploited, you will be robbed, you will be killed. Get organized, and you will compel the world to respect you. If the world fails to give you consideration, because you are black men, because you are Negroes, four hundred million of you shall, through organization, shake the pillars of the universe and bring down creation, even as Samson brought down the temple upon his head and upon the heads of the Philistines. (Ronald Segal, *America's Receding Future*, Penguin, p. 211).

This is powerful and purposeful rhetoric. Garvey strained very hard to create Black Awareness and the need for the Blacks of the Americas to make common cause with their ancestral Continent and to go back there and help to build a viable civilization that could effectively challenge White racial arrogance and dogged, exploitative tendencies. In FESTAC 77, part of Garvey's call was answered and Blacks came "home" together to participate in a communion of solidarity, to celebrate their sense of unity and common belongingness.

Significantly, the White Press, always eager to discuss Black and African affairs with the endemic intent of putting down African efforts tried feebly at first to pooh-pooh the Black and African Resurgence and finding that catcalls and cynical laughter made no difference to the determination of those on the march of history, fell into sulking silence. That was a sign that the movement held something for the Blacks and Africans in and outside Africa. The bloodhounds were sensitive enough to sense defeat. FESTAC, from the point of view of Black and African Solidarity, must be scored a high achievement. Even if what it did was to sharpen the interest in the plight of Black and African Peoples fighting for their freedom in southern Africa and elsewhere and to engender a spiritual solidarity with their cause, something useful would have been gained. The Black and African Peoples are on the march at last. That is a certainty.

(ii) Sense of pride in the black heritage: Those who have suffered most from the Western attacks on the humanity and integrity of Black and African Peoples have been their sons and daughters in diaspora. Because the Whites found it profitable to exploit the labours of the Blacks in the Americas, the Caribbeans and elsewhere, they evolved the psychological necessity of undermining the sense of human worth of those Blacks and of pressuring them into accepting the status of inferiority. All conceivable and inconceivably cruel means were adopted to undermine the Blacks, to "castrate" them culturally and emotionally by making them believe that of all the vagrants who flooded the vast American mainland and outlying territories, only the Blacks had a heritage of shame about which they must be for ever defensive and apologetic. White Americans who in Europe were regarded as "niggers" of a sort, themselves and their country, made a studied and deliberate policy of systematically destroying the confidence of the Blacks among them by perennially painting the apocryphal image of Africa, as a brutish, irredeemable jungle with no rational people, no rational way of life and nothing that could be remotely called a civilization.

Blacks and Africans in diaspora therefore stood in the greatest need of something like FESTAC that could restore to them a rational homeland, a cultured heritage, something precious to hold on to and with which to fight back against those who over the centuries had done nothing better than to push them into the womb of chaos and despondency from which they could never eke out any positive thing of historical significance to give them human pride.

Out of the depth of their despair, the perceptive Blacks ultimately began to see a distant light to which they ran breathlessly as the last and only hope to resurrect their buried sense of their own human worth and pride. That light was the Continent of Africa itself and the truth that far from being a place of primeval barabarism it was in reality the cradle of human civilization. Let me refer here to a brief statement by the late Malcolm X, one of Africa's and, perhaps, the world's most sensitive minds:

> Our history and our culture were completely destroyed when we were forcibly brought to America in chains. And now it is important for us to know that our history did not begin with slavery's scars. We come from Africa, a great continent and a proud and varied people, a land which is the new world and was the cradle of civilization. Our culture and history are as old as man himself and yet we know almost nothing of it. We must recapture our heritage and our identity if we are ever to liberate ourselves from the bond of white supremacy. We must launch a cultural revolution to unbrainwash an entire people . . .

> Armed with the knowledge of the past, we can with confidence chart a course for our future. Culture is an indispensable weapon in the freedom stuggle. We must take hold of it and forge the future with the past.

Malcolm X was right, as he had always been. Those young American boys and girls from Harlem who on alighting from the aeroplane, ran to the sideline, took handfuls of the African soil and poured them on their beautifully done-up heads might to the undiscerning appear theatrical, but to the understanding, such a gesture was moving and came straight out of the depths of the human soul. Those from whom salvation had been wickedly veiled had torn off the veil and seen the "beatific" vision. The raptures were like a martyr's vision of heaven.

(iii) Revolutionary impact: For the People of Africa itself, FESTAC represented a revolutionary advance in the direct line of progress, represented by a synthesis of old and new and the will of the Africans to adopt culture as an instrument for the enrichment of human consciousness. President Sekou Toure of Guinea reflects this view when he spoke thus of cultural development of the entire African People:

> Culture is an accumulated experience which modifies man in a linear progressive and quantitative manner, but with additional qualitative phases of mutation. The result is a new man, a new society, more skilful and more apt, integrating to an ever-increasing extent the means and the ends of action, and perfecting to an ever greater extent technology and means of action.

This view hardly requires a comment. It is something which progressive mankind has known from time immemorial. Those who see culture as a static thing, or as a means whereby the peasants and the proletariat entertain the ruling class cannot enjoy the rich qualitative development which culture brings to bear on the human consciousness. Culture is something which unites the best aspirations of a people, prepares them to participate in corporate action and sharpens their will to move forward, confidently, holding hands together, in a common endeavour to build a lasting human heritage about which all will be proud. Culture prepares a people emotionally and psychologically for the great leap forward. The ultimate test of the success or failure of FESTAC 77 is yet to come. If it does not create the emotional and psychological atmosphere for the emergence of a just, humane and harmonious society which has eluded Africans and African Peoples and their countries up till now, then history, distanced and objectified, would not pronounce the Festival a success.

Conclusion

FESTAC happened just a year and a half ago, too recently for a proper assessment of its lasting effects to be made. A number of criticisms were raised against it in the Nigerian Press. Some of the criticisms were serious; others almost frivolous. For a conclusion of the discussion, some of these criticisms would now be looked at in some detail.

By far the most serious and recurrent criticism of FESTAC 77 was that it was planned on too elaborate scale and therefore took away too large a portion of the resources that could have been expended on development and in raising the living standards of the Nigerian people.

The first response to this criticism is that it is completely logical if it affords to ignore the international dimension to the FESTAC Festival. Of course, Nigerians have every good reason to complain that the precious money which ought of right to have been spent on them had been "squandered away on foreigners" coming from all over the world.

This is a point of view which I personally cannot share. It is too narrowly based and too dangerously parochial to meet the need of the wider solidarities of African and Black Peoples for whom the only real hope of success in the attempt to shake off the yoke that has held them down for centuries is in collective action. Those who have considerable advantages, like the Nigerian People, must make real sacrifice to pull others up. Nigerians may prosper, but if the other Black and African Peoples on the Continent and in diaspora do not improve their chances of freedom and psychological emancipation, then Nigerian prosperity would be a sham. If our brothers and sisters in the Americas and elsewhere continue to be daily buried under the age-old psychological burden of "the Dark Continent" and we do not do anything to raise their morale and to restore the confidence so cruelly withheld from them by the other racial groups, then we may, everyone of us, become as rich as the fabled Croesus of Asia Minor, but our wealth and "success" would be a curse instead of a blessing.

Recently, a Federal Government Official bulletin put the cost of FESTAC at a little above 141 million naira. It explained also that some of the money went into the building of permanent structures and purchase of vehicles which had outlasted the Festival. In spite of these explanations, views continued to be expressed strongly that the contractors and middlemen who handled utility purchases made unreasonably wide marginal gains and that, for this reason, a sizeable proportion of the FESTAC funds disappeared into private pockets.

Now, that must be deprecated in very strong terms. The opportunistic middle class will, if allowed, cash in on anything; it would even cash in on a national emergency because all idealism perishes at its door. The "busy" go-betweens, the dubious "contractors" and their collaborative principals, the spivs and hangers-around-the-corridors-of-power probably saw FESTAC as an opportunity to make quick, easy money behind the scenes and then disappear as surreptitiously as if they never existed.

Part of the consequence of Africa's underdevelopment is that these miscreants and thieves and their principal backers could operate and not be found out in contexts in which they would never have escaped detection and retribution in better organized countries. Such wreckers of the people's aspirations are absolute philistines who care nothing at all for or about culture and the arts. They would be seen nowhere near real cultural activities. Their sole allegiance is to their bellies. Some of the resources of FESTAC may well have been lost through the activities of these sharks. But FESTAC and its usefulness can, and should be seen, independently of the sharks.

Other allegations, such as that every morning "hot-breakfast" had to be flown in from London for the benefit of the participants, took many people by surprise. If this particular case was so, then it was an act of consummate folly, for it not only led to unnecessary expenditure but undermined the spirit of the thing. T. S. Eliot, the English poet and sage, once said that a people's level of civilization could be determined by how carefully they attended to their cuisine. If we must have to go to a temperate country (and an imperialist country for that matter) to obtain "hot breakfast" for our guests, then nothing could have determined our inadequacy and lack of preparedness to host the Festival better than that. Not having personally investigated these allegations, the best and the fairest position to take would be to keep an open mind until one can discover the evidence for oneself one way or another.

Finally, the general view that 141 million naira was far too heavy for a cultural and artistic festival, especially in the context of our underdevelopment could be well taken. It might well be so, but I hold a different view. I regard culture and the arts as very important matters. I do not regard money spent on them as money thrown away. I regard such expenditure as worthy investment from which the people, especially generations yet to come, might gain invaluable and incalculable benefits. Culture and the arts are important enough matters for resources to be expended on them. More money had and is still being expended on less deserving projects!

FESTAC has come and gone but the verdict on it is yet to come. I do not prtened to be in a position to pronounce that verdict, which belongs strictly to the future. What I have attempted here is to put it in perspective and to give one man's tentative assessement of its achievements and potentialities. I would, for example, regard it as sad and tragic if anyone were to affirm unequivocally that FESTAC alone would answer the African and Black Peoples' problems, whether in the immediate present or in the very remote future. We must maintain a proper sense of balance between what is realizable and what must be realized.

www.ingramcontent.com/pod-product-compliance
Lightning Source LLC
Chambersburg PA
CBHW031321230926
51848CB00001B/40
9789781560286